SABBATH AND SYNAGOGUE

RELIGIONS IN THE GRAECO-ROMAN WORLD

FORMERLY

ÉTUDES PRÉLIMINAIRES
AUX RELIGIONS ORIENTALES
DANS L'EMPIRE ROMAIN

EDITORS

R. VAN DEN BROEK   H.J.W. DRIJVERS
H.S. VERSNEL

VOLUME 122

SABBATH AND SYNAGOGUE

The Question of Sabbath Worship in Ancient Judaism

BY

HEATHER A. McKAY

E.J. BRILL

LEIDEN · NEW YORK · KÖLN

1994

This series Religions in the Graeco-Roman World presents a forum for studies in the social and cultural function of religions in the Greek and the Roman world, dealing with pagan religions both in their own right and in their interaction with and influence on Christianity and Judaism during a lengthy period of fundamental change. Special attention will be given to the religious history of regions and cities which illustrate the practical workings of these processes.

Enquiries regarding the submission of works for publication in the series may be directed to Professor H.J.W. Drijvers, Faculty of Letters, University of Groningen, 9712 EK Groningen, The Netherlands.

The paper in this book meets the guidelines for permanence and durability of the Committee on Production Guidelines for Book Longevity of the Council on Library Resources.

Library of Congress Cataloging-in-Publication Data

McKay, Heather A.
    Sabbath and synagogue : the question of sabbath worship in ancient Judaism
/ by Heather A. McKay
      p.   cm. — (Religions in the Graeco-Roman world, ISSN
0927-7633; v. 122)
    Includes bibliographical references and indexes.
    ISBN 9004100601
    1. Sabbath—Biblical teaching.   2. Sabbath in rabbinical
literature.   3. Judaism—History—Post-exilic period, 586 B.C.-210
A.D.—Sources.   I. Title II. Series.
BS1199.S18M35   1994
296.4'1'09015—dc20
                                                94-22552
                                                 CIP

Die Deutsche Bibliothek – CIP-Einheitsaufnahme

MacKay, Heather A.:
Sabbath and synagogue : the question of sabbath worship in ancient
judaism / by Heather A. Mckay. – Leiden ; New York ; Köln :
Brill, 1994
   (Religions in the Graeco-Roman world ; Vol. 122)
   ISBN 90-04-10060-1
NE: GT

ISSN   0927-7633
ISBN   90 04 10060 1

PRINTED IN THE NETHERLANDS

In loving memory of my father

Robert Houston Ayre

and to all those who keep his memory alive for me

CONTENTS

ACKNOWLEDGEMENTS

I wish to express my thanks to friends in The Society for Old Testament Study and in the Society of Biblical Literature for their encouragement since I began this project in 1987, and for all their stimulation of my research by their varied questions and by their attitudes ranging from intrigued curiosity to outright disbelief.

In particular I would like to thank Robert P. Carroll for his sustained interest in my work, and David J.A. Clines, Loveday C.A. Alexander, Lester L. Grabbe and A. Graeme Auld for the benefit of in-depth discussion on the possibilities and pitfalls of working within such a wide-ranging subject area. Without their encouragement and genuine interest, my interest would not have maintained its steady level throughout. I wish to give special thanks to David Clines for freely giving of his technical expertise in the preparation of the final text.

Members of my family have provided a more uncritical support, but that has nonetheless been of inestimable value to me, and I would like to state my gratitude to them also.

It is relevant to state at this point that some of the ideas and explanations which have been fully worked through in this book have been published by me in shorter form in articles in collections of essays. These are:

McKay, H.A., 'New Moon or Sabbath?', in *The Sabbath in Jewish and Christian Tradition* (ed. T.C. Eskenazi, D.J. Harrington and W.H. Shea; New York: Crossroad, 1991), pp. 13-27.

McKay, H.A. 'From Evidence to Edifice: Four Fallacies about the Sabbath', in *Text as Pretext: Essays in Honour of Robert Davidson* (ed. R.P. Carroll; JSOT Supplement Series, 138; Sheffield: JSOT Press, 1992), pp. 179-99.

I acknowledge my gratitude to The Crossroad Publishing Company, as publisher, and to The University of Denver (Colorado Seminary), as copyright holder, for permission to make use of material from *The Sabbath in Jewish and Christian Traditions* and to Sheffield Academic Press for permission to use material from *Text as Pretext: Essays in Honour of Robert Davidson*.

My thanks are also due to the Pontificio Istituto di Archeologia Cristiana for permission to use the numbering system, the texts and translations of inscriptions published by them in

Frey, J.-B., *Corpus inscriptionum judaicarum*. I. *Europe* (rev. B. Lifshitz, ed.; New York: Ktav, 1975), and
Frey, J.-B., *Corpus inscriptionum judaicarum*. II. *Asie–Afrique* (Città del Vaticano, Rome: Pontificio Istituto di Archeologia Cristiana, 1952).

And finally I wish to express my gratitude to Harvard University Press for their permission to reprint texts and translations from the Loeb Classical Library Series, and also for the use of epigraphic material published by them.

Texts and translations from the works of classical authors are reprinted by permission of the publishers and the Loeb Classical Library from:

Apuleius, *Metamorphoses* (tr. J.A. Hanson; Cambridge, MA: Harvard University Press, 1989).
Augustine, *The City of God against the Pagans*, II (tr. W.H. Green; Cambridge, MA: Harvard University Press, 1963).
Cicero, *Pro Flacco*, in *Cicero*, X (tr. C. MacDonald; Cambridge, MA: Harvard University Press, 1977).
Epictetus, *Discourses*, preserved by Arrianus, in *The Discourses of Epictetus* (tr. W.A. Oldfather; Cambridge, MA: Harvard University Press, 1980).
Frontinus, *Stratagems*, in *The Stratagems and the Aqueducts of Rome* (tr. C.E. Bennett, rev. M.B. McElwain; Cambridge, MA: Harvard University Press, 1980).
Horace, *Satires*, in *Satires, Epistles and Ars Poetica* (tr. H.R. Fairclough; Cambridge, MA: Harvard University Press, 1970).
Josephus, *The Life*, in *Josephus*, I (tr. H.St.J. Thackeray; Cambridge, MA: Harvard University Press, 1926).
——*Against Apion*, in *Josephus*, I (tr. H.St.J. Thackeray; Cambridge, MA: Harvard University Press, 1926).
——*Jewish War*, Books I-III, in *Josephus*, II (tr. H.St.J. Thackeray; Cambridge, MA: Harvard University Press, 1976).
Juvenal, *Satires*, in *Juvenal and Persius* (tr. G.G. Ramsay; Cambridge, MA: Harvard University Press, 1940).
Martial, *Epigrams* (tr. W.C.A. Ker; Cambridge, MA: Harvard University Press, 1919; rev. edn, 1968).
Meleager, *The Greek Anthology*, I (tr. W.R. Paton; Cambridge, MA: Harvard University Press, 1916).
Ovid, *The Art of Love*, in *Ovid*, II (tr. J.H. Mozley, rev. G.P. Goold; Cambridge, MA: Harvard University Press, 1979).
Persius, *Satires*, in *Juvenal and Persius* (tr. G.G. Ramsay; Cambridge, MA: Harvard University Press, 1940).
Petronius, *The Satyricon*, in *Petronius* (tr. M. Heseltine; Cambridge, MA: Harvard University Press, 1975).

Philo, *On Dreams*, in *Philo*, V (tr. F.H. Colson and G.L. Whitaker; Cambridge, MA: Harvard University Press, 1949).
——*Every Good Man is Free*, in *Philo*, IX (tr. F.H. Colson; Cambridge, MA: Harvard University Press, 1960).
——*On the Contemplative Life*, in *Philo*, IX (tr. F.H. Colson; Cambridge, MA: Harvard University Press, 1960).
——*Flaccus*, in *Philo*, IX (tr. F.H. Colson; Cambridge, MA: Harvard University Press, 1960).
——*The Embassy to Gaius*, in *Philo*, X (tr. F.H. Colson; Cambridge, MA: Harvard University Press, 1962).
Plutarch, *De superstitione* in *Plutarch's Moralia*, II (tr. F.C. Babbitt; Cambridge, MA: Harvard University Press, 1928).
Seneca, *Ad Lucilium epistulae morales* (tr. R.M. Gummere; Cambridge, MA: Harvard University Press, 1925).
Suetonius, *The Lives of the Caesars*, II in *Suetonius*, I (tr. J.C. Rolfe; Cambridge, MA: Harvard University Press, 1914).
Tacitus, *Histories*, in *Tacitus in Five Volumes*, III (tr. C.H. Moore and J. Jackson; Cambridge, MA: Harvard University Press, 1969).

Texts and translations of inscriptions and papyri are reprinted by permission of the publishers from:

Tcherikover, V.A., and A. Fuks, *Corpus papyrorum judaicarum*, I (Cambridge, MA: Harvard University Press, 1957).
Tcherikover, V.A., and A. Fuks, *Corpus papyrorum judaicarum*, II (Cambridge, MA: Harvard University Press, 1960).
Tcherikover, V.A., A. Fuks AND M. Stern, with an Epigraphical Contribution by D.M. Lewis, *Corpus papyrorum judaicarum*, III (Cambridge, MA: Harvard University Press, 1964).

ABBREVIATIONS

AJSL   *American Journal of Semitic Languages*
ANRW   *Aufstieg und Niedergang der römischen Welt*
ATD   Das Alte Testament Deutsch
AUSS   *Andrews University Seminary Studies*
BK   Biblischer Kommentar
CBC   The Cambridge Bible Commentary
CUP   Cambridge University Press
DJD   Discoveries in the Judaean Desert
EKK   Evangelisch-Katholischer Kommentar zum Neuen
          Testament
ICC   The International Critical Commentary
JBL   *Journal of Biblical Literature*
JJS   *Journal of Jewish Studies*
JTS   *Journal of Theological Studies*
KAT   Kommentar zum Alten Testament
LCL   Loeb Classical Library
LXX   Septuagint
MT   Masoretic Text
NRSV   The New Revised Standard Version of the Bible
NTS   *New Testament Studies*
OTL   Old Testament Library
OUP   Oxford University Press
PAAJR   *Proceedings of the American Academy of Jewish Research*
RB   *Revue biblique*
SBLDS   Society of Biblical Literature Dissertation Series
SNTS   Society for New Testament Studies
WBC   Word Biblical Commentary

INTRODUCTION

This book aims to set before the reader the evidence of what may be known, *with certainty*, about the sabbath activities of Jews in the cities and towns of the central and eastern Mediterranean, through the period prior to 200 CE.[1]

Increasingly within that time Jews were active in the civic and commercial life of the Roman Empire, particularly in the provinces along the eastern Mediterranean seaboard, from Italy to Cyrenaica. Evidence of Jewish communal life remains in inscriptions and papyri from those communities as well as in Greek and Latin literary texts and in religious texts, both Jewish and Christian.

Scholars of the past have many times amassed the available evidence for Jewish organisation and praxis but have generally pooled findings from different sources, harmonising them into a large picture and thereby smoothing away the distinctiveness of the contributions from each source. I, on the contrary, have looked at each body of evidence in its own right and drawn from it the particular conclusions relevant to that source, whether they agree with those from other sources or not. In my opinion an overall picture can be formed only if the agreements and disagreements of the different sources are used as a means of *controlling* the data. By indicating the disparity possible in the evidence, and by refining and modulating the conclusions that can be drawn, divergent findings restrict any tendency to over-simplification and unwarranted normalisation.

Inferences and conclusions from the evidence are made, but separately for each set of data, and cautiously, avoiding—where possible—the making, or perpetuating, of hidden assumptions such as the common view that Christian Sunday worship grew out of Jewish sabbath worship. Throughout the book the validity of this and other

---

[1] By Jew I mean a member of the Jewish community, in Palestine or in the Diaspora towns and cities, born into a Jewish household, and following the beliefs and practices of that faith, current at the time. Males, females and children can be included in this grouping, but the texts more usually mention, or imply, adult males.

constructions made of the evidence are open to scrutiny by the reader. Conclusions and inferences made by other scholars are evaluated and categorised against the perspective adopted here, which some would call minimalist.

Most books dealing with either Jewish or Christian worship use as a key source of evidence the Hebrew Bible and I have also begun my study there. But that does not mean that this source is given privileged status in any way other than the priority due to its antiquity.

The Hebrew Bible texts make it clear that priests carried out, or were expected to carry out, sabbath acts of worship in the Jerusalem Temple in the times when the cult was operative. But that practice ceased after 70 CE when the Temple was destroyed. Nothing, as I shall argue, is said about the sabbath activities of other Jews, since the few prophetic texts that mention sabbath give only idealised pictures of perfect future behaviour and worship whose connection with real weekly practice is problematic.

The possibilities of activities for non-priestly Jews are limited, but can be envisaged and evaluated: perhaps they carried out particular acts of worship on sabbath in communal buildings, or met together on sabbath for activities that included worship, or met together for purposes other than worship on sabbath, or met together for worship on sabbath as they did on every other day, or perhaps they had no sabbath worship activities, as such, reserving sabbath as a day of rest and inactivity, and worshipping on weekdays or festal days.

I re-examine the evidence that could show whether sabbath was a day with special worship practices for non-priestly Jews, and discover, if possible, what Jews actually did on sabbath, and discuss whether these actions may be evaluated as worship or not.

Although it is frequently assumed that the Jewish attitude to the sabbath and the behaviour of Jews on the sabbath were unchanging over hundreds of years, I resist that assumption and present evidence that points to the occurrence of changes in the importance of the sabbath to the different Jewish communities whose views have been preserved in texts. One unified understanding of sabbath activities for all Jews in the ancient world cannot satisfy a scrupulous enquirer.

A fundamental distinction that needs to be drawn is that sabbath observance and sabbath worship are not synonymous, the former denoting mainly inactivity on the sabbath, the sabbath rest and cessation of work and trading that are plainly and frequently enjoined throughout the biblical and associated literature and the latter indicating a purposive, communal activity which is directed towards the attention of a specific deity with the intention of worship. Many scholars writing on the topic of sabbath, or on the development of Sunday as the Christian day of worship, make no distinction between sabbath observance and sabbath worship. But, for this study, progress can be made, and the arguments followed, only if this distinction is kept in mind at all times.

Worship has been defined as, for example, 'Religious acts ... directed to a deity who is recognised to be infinitely higher than man, to be righteous and faithful, and to be compassionate towards men' and as including recitation of the mighty works of God, sacrifice and offering, offering of praise, and attendance at feasts as renewed dedication of the people of God,[2] and as 'the attitude and acts of reverence to a deity'.[3]

For the purposes of this study I define worship more specifically as rites and rituals which pay homage, with adoration and awe, to a particular god or gods.[4] Worship could include sacrificing plants and animals, dancing, playing music, singing hymns or psalms, reading or reciting sacred texts, prayers and blessings. Instructions for, or descriptions of, these types of activity in the texts are regarded by me as evidences of worship either expected of, or carried out by, the religious community.

Prayer to the deity and singing of psalms to or about the deity, exhortations to follow the commands of the deity as understood by the believing community—all these count for me as worship. Community business, discipline sessions and political arguments do not. Reading, studying and explaining sacred texts I do not necessarily regard as worship, *unless* given a place in a planned session of worship. Otherwise I regard these activities as educational, or as serving the purpose of preserving and strengthening group identity,

---

[2] *Concise Dictionary of the Bible* (ed. S. Neill, J. Goodwin, A. Dowle; London: Lutterworth, 1967), pp. 331-32; I would prefer to see the use of inclusive language in all such definitions.

[3] S. Rattray, 'Worship', in *Harper's Bible Dictionary* (ed. P.J. Achtemeier; San Francisco: Harper & Row, 1985), pp. 1143-47.

[4] See also Introduction; Rattray, 'Worship'; and the section 'Worship' in *Concise Dictionary of the Bible*, pp. 331-32.

and not *necessarily* implying worship; the group's understanding of the god as *addressee* of the worship is vital in my definition.

Another important distinction is that between *daily* worship, which is also carried out on the sabbath in its role as the seventh day in a sequence of days, and *sabbath* worship, which is carried out, only and particularly, on the seventh day precisely because it is the seventh day—precisely because it is the sabbath. As worship in the form of prayers took place on weekdays, even if the same prayers were to be performed on sabbath that would not, in my view, necessarily represent sabbath worship. And while individual prayer is undoubtedly worship, only prayer that is organised, communal and taking place on the sabbath is considered here to be an indication of communal sabbath worship. A specific, intended relationship of the communal prayer activity to the community, the deity and to the seventh day would be necessary before prayer on the sabbath can be properly described as sabbath worship.

Similarly, a description of any other particular worship activity specific to the sabbath, for example, the singing of a particular psalm on the sabbath day, or the offering of a particular sabbath sacrifice, would indicate an intended worship event peculiar to the sabbath, although if it applied only to priests and not to the common people it would not be directly germane to this study, except in so far as it would indicate the people's commitment to providing sacrificial animals for each sabbath.

Admittedly, lack of descriptions of sabbath worship cannot be regarded as definite evidence that sabbath worship did not happen. But even more so, the lack of evidence, which lack I intend to highlight, *cannot* support a definite conclusion that worship *did* take place.

In addition to the technique of close reading, I have found the scientific concept of 'controls' to be useful in working with the various texts.[5] That means that wherever possible I have studied parallel institutions within one source or a particular institution in parallel sources. The different answers allow comparison of the ways key

---

[5] The sources I have used are, in the main, literary works: the Hebrew Bible, the Apocryphal and Deutero-Canonical works, the Dead Sea Scrolls, the works of Philo and Josephus, the New Testament, the Mishnah and also Graeco-Roman sources from both secular and Christian backgrounds.

concepts and issues are perceived and expressed from the perspectives of the sources. Through this process of comparison the reader is able to notice, and make allowance for, the bias of the sources and to make a more balanced appreciation of the data collected. Thus when trying to assess whether sabbath is presented as a day of worship in the Hebrew Bible, I carry out a parallel investigation on new moon, the most similar holy day in the Hebrew Bible, and one that is fourteen times coupled with sabbath in the texts.

In a similar way, when trying to discover the origins and locations of meeting-houses for Jews, and when trying to find out what happened in them on sabbath, I put the same questions to the texts from different groups of authors who provide different estimates of the same institutions. And because Jewish authors, gospel writers, Roman literary figures and later Christian authors, representing benevolent, argumentative, satirical and hostile perspectives respectively, give four different descriptions and evaluations of the same Jewish institutions, the comments of each group can be used to modulate the views of the others and facilitate an appreciation of the effects their respective biasses have had on their accounts. If the pictures from all four perspectives are essentially the same, though coloured by their authors' viewpoints, then I have more confidence that the mental pictures deduced, for example, of prayer-houses or of synagogues—whether groups or buildings—and of the meetings that took place in them, that these *constructs* have a good basis in historical reality.

This point leads on to a third important distinction, namely, the distinction between the two meanings of the word 'synagogue'. What appears to be the basic meaning of the word is the group of people—the adult, and usually the male, Jews of the community—who met together to discuss matters of concern to them and who made community decisions and carried them out. That meaning of 'synagogue' can be found, for example, in the catacomb inscriptions of Rome and in the gospels. The secondary meaning seems to have been that of a building in which Jews met for prayer, for reading Torah and for carrying out community business,[6] a meaning which may be found much more rarely—with certainty in one inscription

---

[6] A building is always subsequent to the thought and plans of the people who build it.

and three times in the writings of Josephus, and in some places in the New Testament. The modern-day view of synagogues as buildings where God is worshipped is not necessarily evidenced in the texts of the ancient world, though it has often been inferred from statements which prove on close scrutiny to be ambiguous. Part of the purpose of this study is to lay bare such ambiguities.

In Chapter 1, the evidence of the Hebrew Bible is assessed to see whether it presents the sabbath as a day on which private or communal worship activities were compulsory, or appropriate, or even permitted or possible, by making a detailed comparative study of the texts that mention, explain or discuss sabbath and new moon. Both these are regularly recurring days with religious connotations, and by comparing what happens on them, and how they are spoken of in the texts, the biblical writers' expectations of what constitutes a day of worship are made apparent.

So, groupings of festivals, such as linkings of names of festivals in word pairs, or in lists of three or four, are studied to find out whether they give a consistent indication of how the sabbath was perceived by the community, and the cultic calendars that list the sacrifices specified for the several sorts of holy day are compared to discover whether there is a unified portrayal of the place of the sabbath in religious behaviour—as pictured in the texts.

In Chapter 2, early Jewish writings are studied. By comparing the views held, or details given, about sabbath in the Apocryphal and Deutero-Canonical texts we can assess whether the sabbath had a similar role and status in the perceptions of the authors of these texts. Comparisons of the degree of interest each text reveals about the sabbath, and of how each text regards sabbath compared with other holy days, highlight differences in the importance of the various days, and allow exploration of changes in the status of the sabbath with the passage of time.

Because the Dead Sea Scrolls have a similar date to the Apocryphal and Deutero-Canonical works, but come from a community that concentrated its life on the religious sphere, they are a good place to look for an expansion of interest in all holy days, and in particular, sabbath. The ramifications of their rules for behaviour on the sabbath are studied.[7]

Chapter 3 draws information from the works of Philo of Alexandria and Flavius Josephus who, living in the secular world of the eastern Mediterranean, spanned in their writing lives most of the first century CE. These two authors give descriptions of Judaism at the time of Jesus, Paul, and the early church. Because both were prolific writers, much helpful material about the meetings of the Jews can be gleaned from their writings. What they disclose increases our knowledge of sabbath activities of Jews, for they describe a variety of types of meetings of Jews on the sabbath.

And because the developed form of Jewish sabbath worship that has continued until today takes place in buildings called synagogues, and because Philo and Josephus paint the fullest and most direct pictures that we have of the meeting-houses of the Jews, the details they give about προσευχαί and synagogues—for example, information on their structures and contents—are also dealt with in Chapter 3.

Chapter 3, then, provides a picture of the Jewish religious scene contemporary to the narrative time of the New Testament texts studied in Chapter 5. This background material is valuable, because the New Testament texts can rarely be dated accurately, either for the time of their composition, or for the time of their final editing, or for any of the hypothetical stages in between. So the pictures of Jewish religious life supplied by Philo and Josephus, both Jewish men of letters, involved in public life and living in a similar cultural ambience, but at slightly different dates in the first century, form a more secure basis for our knowledge of what was common and familiar in the Jewish communities of the central and eastern Mediterranean provinces.

Following the study of Jewish texts and before studying the New Testament texts in Chapter 5, I have also surveyed secular source material from the Graeco-Roman world in order to provide a wider background, and one with dates that can be more closely determined than those of the New Testament material. These secular texts provide an alternative picture of the religious world of the Jews.

So, in Chapter 4, I have surveyed the writings of Seneca, Persius,

---

[7] I realise that this section of the work may well be proved incomplete when more Qumrân material is published.

Juvenal and others,[8] which have well-attested dates across the first century CE and into the second. These writings provide a useful range of control materials against which to read the religious texts, because the perspectives of those authors on the Jews, and their reasons for writing, are quite different from those of the writers of the New Testament texts.

These secular writers did not have a confessional stance; they wrote to provoke interest in, amusement at, and sale of, their work. Any descriptions or comments they have in common with those of the religious sources are of the highest importance, especially if the same hard facts are expressed in language that is coloured by their different agenda. It is also of importance that these works were written within a short time span and for a certain purpose or occasion and therefore reflect the mind of the author at that particular time—so recording what each author observed from one single perspective. This unity of purpose creates a definite contrast with the frequently edited texts of, for example, the gospels, for which the idea of one unedited author is hardly applicable. So, Latin and Greek literary works dating from the second century BCE to the second century CE are a valuable alternative source for information about the Jewish sabbath, and about the meeting-houses of Jews, as these were perceived by the Graeco-Roman *literati*.

Because Jesus and Paul were Jews and are portrayed in the Gospels, Acts and Epistles as attending synagogues, Chapter 5 gathers what evidence the New Testament can provide about the sabbath practice of Jews and any relationship that evidence bears to 'synagogues'—whether people or buildings—and prayer-houses. Appreciating the complexity of the material recorded in these texts involves having an awareness of at least two time zones clearly discernible in the gospels and Acts: the time avowedly being described, the time of Jesus or Paul, and the time of the gospel writers, which time and cultural environment have informed all their thinking and forms of expression. The differences among the four gospel accounts of Jesus' relations with the synagogue on the one hand, and the difference between the lack of any references to synagogues in Paul's letters and Luke's Paul working frequently in synagogues on

---

[8] All of them writers from the second century BCE to the second century CE.

the other, are noted. Any conclusions subsequently drawn about 'synagogues' in the first century and the activities that took place in them must take account of these differences.

The concentration of attention on activities prohibited on the sabbath in the gospel texts is also surveyed to see how it bears upon the issue of sabbath worship activities. The New Testament's increased interest in sabbath as a day with many prohibitions shown is comparable with the strict view of sabbath revealed in the Dead Sea Scrolls and *Jubilees*.

Chapter 6 discusses the further useful control material provided by the writings of some early Christian authors: Ignatius, Barnabas, Justin, Hippolytus and Tertullian. Here the datings within the second century CE are relatively reliable and, here, as with the secular writers of the same time, the works were composed without the layers of editing familiar to readers of biblical texts.

Many of the Christian works of that time have what is often termed an anti-Jewish flavour and frequently present the Jews and Christians as a matched pair of opposites who originally sprang from the same stock. The understandings the writers have of regular worship in the two communities and their expectations for the observance of one special, and different, day in seven in each community provide an indication of the behaviours and beliefs that are attributed to Jews by these Christian writers.

Chapter 7 deals with the evidence for sabbath behaviour and worship in the Mishnah, great care being taken to separate what is relevant to the sabbath from material about daily or festal worship. Instructions for sabbath observance and instructions for sabbath worship in the Mishnah will be collated to see whether the sabbath gathering includes worship practices as well as study and reading of Torah.

In Chapter 8, archaeological and epigraphic material is presented to complement the information obtained from literary works. This evidence acts as another control on the literary material, so it is important to discover whether both types of evidence present essentially the same picture of Jewish religious life. Due to the wider geographical range of inscriptions any such common picture found underwrites greater confidence about matters of common practice and language throughout the widespread Jewish communities.

On a more general note, the need for undertaking this study can be seen by consulting either articles in Bible dictionaries on the sabbath, or on synagogues or on worship, or similar sections in introductions to the Bible and related topics. The conflation, and concomitant confusion, of many of the points that this study has determined to distinguish can quickly be seen, and also the unexamined assumption of an unchanging and uniform pattern of sabbath behaviour and worship over many centuries.

The resultant misconstruing of all types of evidence creates an overall picture that is quite false. Each error or looseness of argument or description, not crucial on its own, combines into an imprecise, and on some occasions, inaccurate picture of the religious life of the Jews in the eastern Mediterranean area during the time span of this study.

So, I have felt it necessary to reassess what firm evidence may be found, unconditioned by the conclusions and interpretations based on that evidence by other scholars. Since many others have looked at the evidence before me, but have construed it differently, I have taken care to deal with each piece of evidence, as far as possible, on its own and to add insights from explanations and interpretations afterwards to illumine the sparse picture the evidence affords. But I have also been concerned to make clear what can be known with clarity and certainty, before I have collated what may be known as probabilities or possibilities.

CHAPTER ONE

SABBATH AND NEW MOON: THE HEBREW BIBLE

The Approach to be Taken in this Chapter

This chapter will survey all the Hebrew Bible references to sabbath
as a day with religious meaning and attempt to analyse:
—whether the texts present sabbath as a day of worship or rest,
—whether worship practices are described for the sabbath,
—whether such practices are carried out only by priests, and
—whether any observance of sabbath—other than inactivity—is
expected of the ordinary Israelite populace.

To set this study of sabbath in a context that will make our appreciation of the answers to the above questions more focussed, I will
also look at the new moon since it is a festal day in many ways similar to the sabbath.

Introduction

It is a commonplace in biblical studies that the sabbath in ancient
Israel was a day of rest and a day of worship. Typical comments are:

> The centre of their religious life was the synagogue, where they held
> services without sacrifices on the Sabbath.[1]

> Since the exile (and partly even beforehand) *worship* had formed an
> essential part of the image of the sabbath.[2]

---

[1] B. Otzen, *Judaism in Antiquity: Political Development and Religious Currents
from Alexander to Hadrian* (The Biblical Seminar, 7; Sheffield: JSOT Press, 1990),
pp. 56-57, speaking of Diaspora Jews.

[2] W. Rordorf, *Sunday: The History of the Day of Rest and Worship in the Earliest
Centuries of the Christian Church* (London: SCM Press, 1968), pp. 53-54; cf. the views
of R.E. Clements, in *God and Temple* (Oxford: Blackwell, 1965), p. 130; N.-E.A.
Andreasen, *The Old Testament Sabbath: A Tradition-Historical Investigation* (SBLDS,
7; Missoula: SBL, 1972), pp. 251-54; M. Greenberg, 'Sabbath', in *Encyclopaedia
Judaica*, XIV (Jerusalem: Keter Publishing House, 1972), pp. 558-62; E. Ferguson,
Backgrounds of Early Christianity (Grand Rapids: Eerdmans, 1987), p. 441; 'Sabbath'

The Sabbath was a joyous day, much like the festivals.[3]

[I]t became a day of positive worship of the Deity, characterized not only by complete abstention from all ordinary occupations and activities but also by assemblage in temple or synagogue and sacrifice or prayer and ritual observance there.[4]

God instituted the Sabbath for His people ... [to be]....celebrated as a day of joyful assembling before God ...[on which] ... their devotions, praises and thanksgivings ... flow from grateful and appreciative hearts.[5]

But these comments embody unexamined assumptions, and beg various questions. They imply that Jews had special sabbath activities distinct from observing a sabbath rest. They assume that 'ancient Israel' provided a uniform religious experience for all Jews living in the land. They assume a knowledge of who was actually worshipping, and of what their worship might consist.

Because these and similar assertions have been made without adequate consideration of what the texts actually say, this chapter will take a closer look at the textual evidence about the function of the sabbath and other holy days in the life of the Israelite community.[6]

Background to the Study of Israelite Worship

In order to make a study of specific religious practices in the Israelite community, distinctions must be made between texts that speak of

---

in *Concise Dictionary of the Bible*, p. 273, but note the opposite conclusion on p. 332.

[3] D.A. Glatt and J.H. Tigay, 'Sabbath', in *Harper's Bible Dictionary* (ed. P.J. Achtemeier; San Francisco: Harper & Row, 1985), pp. 888-89 (888).

[4] J. Morgenstern, 'Sabbath', in *The Interpreter's Dictionary of the Bible*, IV (New York: Abingdon Press, 1962), pp. 135-41 (135).

[5] H.H.P. Dressler, 'The Sabbath in the Old Testament', in *From Sabbath to Lord's Day: A Biblical, Historical and Theological Investigation* (ed. D.A. Carson; Grand Rapids: Zondervan, 1982), pp. 21-41 (23, 35). For the purposes of this study, I have accepted that the sabbath is a day which recurs hebdomadally throughout the year, with no breaks in that rhythm (cf. Philo, *Decalogue* 96). Therefore, I have not included any discussion of the origin of the sabbath, or of the origins of its name. These matters have been amply dealt with elsewhere; see, for example: R. North, 'Sabbath', in *New Catholic Encyclopedia*, XII (Washington, DC: McGraw-Hill, 1967), pp. 778-82 (780); Andreasen, *Sabbath*, pp. 93-121; Dressler, 'Sabbath', pp. 22-24.

[6] All texts that refer to the sabbath have been surveyed and from them texts that describe sabbath praxis, and texts that show the importance of sabbath in relation to other holy days have been utilised. Texts that refer to the sabbaths of the land, or sabbatical years, have not been included, nor texts that merely use sabbath as a dating reference.

observing the sabbath and those that speak of worship on festal days, between texts that describe private devotions and those that refer to Temple worship, and between texts that detail the religious life of Temple personnel and those narrating the religious life of ordinary people.

Sabbath observance means the cessation of work and trading, as is repeatedly required in the Hebrew Bible.[7] There is no lack of clarity about the command to do no work on the sabbath, although what counted as work is not entirely clear—nor whose work counted.[8] The biblical sabbath was a weekly day of rest, apparently observed by Jewish communities at least from the post-exilic period.[9] The Hebrew Bible describes a sabbath of rest for the ordinary people, but for the functionaries of the Jerusalem Temple it was a day among other days, on which they carried out religious duties.

On the other hand, it is never made clear in the texts that there was sabbath worship by ordinary members of the community. So, many scholars fill that lacuna from the detail of what is required for priests, rulers and populace on a variety of religious occasions. Thus, it is often stated in commentaries and works of reference that psalm singing was a part of the people's worship and that—following the first assumption with a second assumption—it took place on the sabbath day. There are, however, no texts that refer to, or imply, such psalm singing.

Another common form of worship, prayer, is similarly not referred to at all as part of worship on sabbath, but is, mostly, a personal activity that can take place anywhere, not excluding a holy site, for example, the prayer of childless Hannah at the shrine in Shiloh,[10] during the time spent there with her husband Elkanah on their annual visit to offer worship and sacrifice. But this text too tells us nothing about activities on the sabbath.

Sacrifice is depicted a worship activity throughout the Hebrew Bible—for example, in the narrative about the request of Moses to Pharaoh to let the Hebrews go into the wilderness to sacrifice to

---

[7] Exod. 20.10; 31.14, 15; 35.2; Lev. 16.29, 31; 23.3; Deut. 5.13, 14; Jer. 17.22, 24.

[8] It is notable, in both versions of the ten commandments, that among all those told to rest on the sabbath, wives are not mentioned (Exod. 20.10; Deut. 5.14).

[9] Andreasen, *Sabbath*, pp. 235-36.

[10] 1 Sam. 1–2.

God.[11] Similarly, in the book of Job,[12] there is an indication that Job could carry out sacrifices to cleanse his whole family in the sight of the Lord. And Elijah puts the prophets of Ba'al to shame when he totally eclipses their efforts towards sacrificing a bull.[13] In all these stories sacrifice is presented as a usual and acceptable way to worship God.

But none of the stories gives details about the nature and execution of the sacrifices, or about whether they were to be offered on a particular day—such as the sabbath. And these sacrificial actions of local religious activists seem, in later times, to have been replaced by centralised worship in the Temple cult, with priests taking over the role of leader acting on behalf of the people. So we find, among the instructions given to priests in the Hebrew Bible, cultic calendars which provide details about the Temple sacrifices to be offered by them on special days.

By worship, I understand a planned activity, in which people of similar beliefs carry out similar rites and rituals with the intention of paying homage to a specific deity or deities.[14] Worship may be carried out individually or in groups, silently or aloud, with singing, dancing, music, reading or reciting of sacred texts, hymns, prayers and blessings, or by sacrificing plants and animals. Only such instructions and descriptions can be regarded as evidence of worship either expected of, or carried out by, the Jewish community.

To help the reader see more clearly whether the sabbath is presented as a day of worship or as a day of rest and to make the distinctions between what would count as evidence for either conclusion more obvious, I have carried out similar studies on the texts about new moon. When the same questions are posed about the two special days and when the answers to these questions are evaluated, then any misprision prompted by hindsight becomes recognisable, and any reading back of beliefs about the sabbath from more recent times into the time of the Hebrew Bible can be seen for what it is. If we can treat the evidence about the two days in a parallel way we can be more certain that we are seeing what the texts actually contain

---

[11] Exod. 3.18; 5.3.
[12] Job 1.5.
[13] 1 Kgs 18.
[14] See also the discussion of definitions of worship in the Introduction.

rather than what we expect them to contain.

Texts about the Sabbath

The small amount of textual material that describes sabbath activities will now be summarised, showing that the holy day sabbath appears in only fifteen books of the Hebrew Bible.[15]

In the Pentateuch, the sabbath is referred to in Exodus fourteen times about the cessation of work; there is nothing about worship. The picture is similar in Leviticus with eight references to appropriate sabbath observance. The sabbath is also mentioned in the cultic calendar in Leviticus 23 but without any directions for worship or sacrifice on the sabbath, though there are detailed prescriptions for festal days. The book of Numbers has one reference to the sabbath regarding an infringement of sabbath laws, and in Numbers 28–29 there is another cultic calendar, where the sabbath sacrifice is described as a doubling of the daily offering.[16] Then, in the book of Deuteronomy the sabbath is spoken of three times in the motive clause of the fourth commandment.

The next book to refer to the sabbath is 2 Kings where there is the question, framed by the Shunammite's husband, which indicates that the sabbath is a day worth visiting a shrine in search of a holy man— a day when he would be there.[17] There are also four references to guard rotas at the king's house and their change-over on the sabbath.[18] And later in the same book there is one sabbath reference which is almost totally cryptic:[19]

> The covered portal for use on the sabbath that had been built inside the palace, and the outer entrance for the king he [Ahaz] removed from the house of the Lord. He did this because of the king of Assyria (2 Kgs 16.18, NRSV).

Because of difficulties with the Hebrew, commentators provide less than coherent translations, for example:

---

[15] Exod., Lev., Num., Deut., 2 Kgs, 1 & 2 Chr., Neh., Pss, Isa., Jer., Lam., Ezek., Hos., Amos. Sabbath is not mentioned at all in twenty-four books of the Hebrew Bible.

[16] This material will be discussed in more detail later in this chapter.

[17] 2 Kgs 4.23.

[18] 2 Kgs 11.5-8.

[19] R.D. Nelson, *First and Second Kings* (Atlanta: John Knox Press, 1987), p. 227.

> And the covered-way of the Sabbath that he built in the house (i.e. the Temple), and the king's entry outwards he turned about in/to the house of YHWH.[20]

> The Sabbath structure which they had built in the house (temple? palace?) and the royal entrance to the outside he reorientated in regard to the house of the Lord because of the king of Assyria.[21]

> And the barrier of the sabbath which they had built in the Temple and the king's entrance into the court he removed from the Temple of Yahweh because of the king of Assyria.[22]

This reference may indicate a barrier or grille into the Temple which would admit the king on special occasions similar to that described for the prince in Ezekiel's vision of the restored Temple (Ezek. 46), but it is possible that some sort of exterior sabbath shelter is intended, perhaps for the guard, possibly for use during the change-over. However, no matter which interpretation we adopt, this text supplies no unambiguous information about sabbath worship practice either for king or commoner.[23]

1 Chronicles mentions the sabbath twice in connection with preparation of showbread on sabbath by the Kohathites, and once in a list of days for burnt offerings. In 2 Chronicles we find three references to the guard duty on the sabbath—but none to any covered portal although this is a parallel text to the one discussed above. There are also three lists of days (including sabbath) suitable for burnt offerings, one of which implies that the king provided the sacrifices (31.3).

Nehemiah 9.14 speaks of the sabbath being made known to Israel by God, then twice in ch. 10 and ten times in ch. 13 we find the sabbath spoken of in terms of restrictions on business transactions, in rules promulgated to ensure sabbath observance by the community

---

[20] J.A. Montgomery, *A Critical and Exegetical Commentary on the Book of Kings* (ICC; Edinburgh: T. & T. Clark, 1951), p. 462.

[21] Nelson, *Kings*, p. 227.

[22] J. Gray, *I and II Kings: A Commentary* (OTL; 3rd edn; London: SCM Press, 1977), p. 635.

[23] It could possibly be taken to mean that the entrance for the king was an entrance specially for use on the sabbath, rather than on other days, but it seems more likely that the king would use the same entrance whatever day he visited the Temple. The syntax of the first part of the verse implies a structure specially for the sabbath—which the entrance could not be. A shelter for the guard as they waited to change over could have been used only on the sabbath. The king's entrance could be quite a different structure altogether, and included in the same text only because the text lists those structures removed from the building by Ahaz.

and co-operation by outsiders who otherwise would have wished to trade on that day as on other days.

In the book of Psalms only Psalm 92 is described in its title as 'a song for the Sabbath Day' and there are no other references to the sabbath in the psalms. Such a title, however, whatever its provenance, gives no clue as to who might be either singing the psalm or listening to it.

In the prophetic books, the book of Isaiah has several references to sabbath. There is a text (1.13-14) at the beginning of the collection, which includes sabbath in a list of occasions when God is displeased by what goes on, probably, though not certainly—or perhaps exclusively—in the Temple. This text will be discussed in detail later in this chapter, along with related texts, as it seems at first sight to offer information about the sabbath activities of ordinary people.

In Isaiah 56 there are three references to avoiding profanation of the sabbath and in Isa. 58.13 two about proper enjoyment of the sabbath, although these do not include any specific references to worship, demanding only that Israelites refrain from pursuing their own interests or affairs (NRSV) on the sabbath. And at the end of the Isaianic collection there is one text which does imply that worship (שחה hithpal.) before Yahweh by all flesh on the sabbath will be part of the delights of the New Age (66.23).

In the book of Jeremiah, the discourse on carrying burdens on the sabbath in ch. 17 contains all six references to the sabbath in that book, and Lam. 2.6 has one retrospective and mournful comment on the loss of the sabbath and appointed feasts, but the writer does not make clear what it is exactly that has been lost.

Ezekiel 20–23 has nine references to 'my sabbaths' with respect to their profanation, the phrase 'my sabbaths' appearing rhythmically and punctuating the text like a refrain. Chapter 46 has two references to the sabbath, one about the people of the land worshipping (שחה hithpal.) Yahweh at the gate of the inner court of the future, restored temple, the other listing the burnt offerings to be made by the prince on that day. There are also four references to the sabbath in association with other holy days (44.24; 45.17; 46.1, 3).

In Hosea the sabbath appears once (2.13; EVV 11) in a list of holy days that are going to be obliterated by Yahweh, and Amos has one reference to sabbath in connection with the suspending of trading on these days (8.5).

In summary, most of the references to the sabbath in the Hebrew Bible are about avoiding working on the sabbath. There is indeed the enigmatic reference to the use on the sabbath of a special entrance to the Temple from the palace. But the only places where the word 'sabbath' is used in the Hebrew Bible in reference to actual worship are in details of the sabbath sacrifice at Numbers 28.9-10 and in the title of Psalm 92, the former referring to actions of priests and the latter implying a group of singers, not, however, identified in the text. In Ezekiel 46, in a vision of a glorious and perfect temple cult at some time in the future, the burnt offerings to be made on the sabbath by the prince are detailed and the people of the land are directed to worship at one of the temple gates.

In the Ezekiel text, however, there is no indication of the forms of worship possible, or desirable, at a temple gate—presumably *outside* the temple gate is implied—nor of their frequency or availability to large or small numbers of 'the people of the land', whether all adult males or family groups. The phrase 'at a gate' does eliminate the possibility of a large static congregation of worshippers, although a moving stream of people could be envisaged.

Similarly obscure is the prophecy in Isa. 66.23 about all flesh coming to worship God at the end of time. In order to comprehend it—even as a promise or as a vision—the reader has to envisage all of a future humanity converging on Jerusalem, in some amicable and co-operative way, to give a concerted offering of worship to God. Unfortunately, these two references specifically about the sabbath worship of ordinary people in the whole Hebrew Bible are couched in the language of the prophetic vision and leave more issues unresolved than they clarify. These, and other important texts, will be discussed later in this Chapter.

So, apart from the allusions to future sabbath worship supplied by these two intriguing texts, there are no texts about regular sabbath worship for the ordinary worshipper in the Hebrew Bible.

Texts about Prayer

Although there are no specific references to general sabbath worship for non-priestly Jews in the Hebrew Bible, it is possible that particular worship activities, such as prayer, may be described or implied as typical or desirable sabbath practice.

However, none of the texts about prayer in the Hebrew Bible refers directly to prayer taking place on the sabbath. None describes communal prayer clearly, although when reading the texts of the book of Psalms one may imagine a scenario where a leader speaks a psalm and many listeners are incorporated into the sentiments of the psalm. But without any description in the text of this type of event such constructs must remain conjecture. All that is certain and clear are the words of the prayer and the necessity of a speaker. The type of group, its size, its composition by age, gender, or place of origin, its frequency of meeting, its location, the time of day—all these are left to the imagination of the reader.

One text (Isa. 1.15) refers to massed individual or communal prayer, and will be discussed below. Many texts refer to a king, prophet, patriarch or other leader, wise man or priest, praying to God. The anonymous voice of the Psalms, as also of Lamentations, refers to prayer.[24] And some texts describe ordinary people praying to God about matters important to them—such as childlessness.[25]

Of the kings, David; Solomon, Hezekiah and Manasseh pray.[26] The prophets Moses, Samuel, Elisha, Isaiah, Jeremiah, Jonah, and Habakkuk, all pray to God.[27] Among the leaders of the Israelites, Ezra and Nehemiah pray as leaders,[28] Abraham prays for Abimelech's healing,[29] and Isaac prays that Rebekah will conceive.[30] Job,[31] Daniel,[32] and the righteous of Proverbs[33] pray to God, as do

---

[24] Pss. 4.1; 5.2; 6.9; 17.heading, 1; 32.6; 35.3; etc.; Lam. 3.8, 44.

[25] Also two non-Israelite groups, Moabites and idol worshippers, are described as praying to beings—or idols—other than God (Isa. 16.12; 44.17; 45.20).

[26] 2 Sam. 7.27; 1 Kgs 8–9, and parallels (1 Chr. 17.25; 2 Chr. 6–7); 2 Kgs 19 and parallels (2 Chr. 32); 2 Chr. 30.18; 2 Chr. 33.

[27] *Moses*: Exod. 8.29; 32.32; 34.9; Num. 11.2; 14.17, 19; 21.7; Deut. 3.25; 9.20, 26; *Samuel*: 1 Sam. 7.5; 8.6; 12.19, 23; *Elisha*: 2 Kgs 4.33; 6.17, 18; *Isaiah*: 2 Kgs 19 and parallels (2 Chr. 32); 2 Chr. 30.18; 2 Chr. 33; *Jeremiah*: Jer. 7.16; 11.14; 14.11; 29.7, 12; 32.16; 37.2; 42.2, 4, 20; *Jonah*: Jon. 2.1, 7; 4.2; *Habakkuk*: Hab. 3.1.

[28] Ezra 10.1; Neh. 1.4, 6, 11; 2.4; 4.9.

[29] Gen. 20.7, 17.

[30] Gen. 25.21.

[31] Job 16.17; 21.15; 22.27; 24.12; etc.

[32] Dan. 6.10; 9.3, 4, 17, 20, 21.

[33] Prov. 15.8, 29; 28.9.

priests,[34] on their own, or accompanied by Levites,[35] or a single
Levite.[36] Two ordinary people are described as praying: they are
Abraham's servant,[37] and Hannah.[38]

The reference in Isa. 1.15 is apparently about prayer by the males
of the Israelite community. The text refers to those who 'stretch out
their hands' in God's courts. The inference that this means prayer in
the Temple arises because stretching out one's hands is a description
of prayer in Ps. 143.6, and because the phrase in Isa. 1.12, 'when you
appear before me', has verbal similarities with 'do not appear before
me empty-handed' in the instructions in Exod. 23.15 and 34.20 about
the required attendance of Israelite males at the three pilgrim festivals. This implied prayer could be communal prayer or it could be
simply the combined effect of massed individual prayers, perhaps
during the pilgrim festivals.

This text on prayer follows close on the heels of a list of religious
occasions: new moon, sabbath, convocation, solemn assemblies, new
moons, appointed festivals (Isa. 1.13-14), and seems to suggest that
male Israelites would be thronging the Temple courts and praying
aloud on all these occasions. But, in the passage immediately following this text, the deity's suggestions and instructions (Isa. 1.15-20)
give no clue about any congregation praying communally in the
Temple who require the goading of these words.[39]

So, in spite of the profusion of references to individuals praying,
those individual prayers are never described as taking place on the
sabbath, and, apart from the reference to male prayer in the Temple,
are never clearly described as prayer offered by a community of
Jews, and even that reference, as I shall argue below is no unequivocal evidence that communal prayer took place as part of an act of
celebration or worship on sabbath.

---

[34] Ezra 6.10.
[35] 2 Chr. 30.27.
[36] Neh. 11.17.
[37] Gen. 24.12.
[38] 1 Sam. 1–2.
[39] In any case, whatever the implication of this text, it would seem to be limited to
men and the commitment of women to prayer is unaddressed.

Discussion about Sabbath Worship and Prayer

The data that have been gathered from reading the Hebrew Bible make it very hard to follow such a view as that of Clements that the 'expatriated Jews in Babylon had learnt to worship as best they could in their own homes' and that 'the existence of regular sabbath worship, which was practised by the faithful nucleus of the exiles ... could not have left the people with the feeling that God had utterly deserted them'.[40]

Presenting the opposing position, Talmon rejects the claim that 'synagogue and communal prayer came to replace the Temple and animal sacrifice' because, as he says, the 'factual evidence adduced in support of this theory is pitifully slim; one might say that it is non-existent'.[41] Talmon pens a scathing exposé of those scholars who write about what they believe in, in spite of not finding evidence of it. In this instance, he refers to a belief in an ongoing tradition of prayer in the Jewish community in exile in Babylon. He concludes that scholars, having been unable to 'visualize a community, and a Jewish community at that, which existed for ... at least several generations, without any tangible form of institutionalized worship', have created for themselves the image of Diaspora Jews worshipping by means of prayer in synagogues. This is a helpful outline of the way suggestions or hypotheses become embedded in the scholarly consciousness as explanations and facts about Jewish worship—the outcome of commentators expressing their convictions about what must have been the case.

Talmon construes the worship offered by Israel as being primarily offered by priests, in the ambience of holy silence in the Temple, and as not including prayer.[42] Prayer, he claims, had no particular locus; anywhere, including the Temple, was a suitable place for prayer.[43] Thus, in his understanding—with which I concur—any sabbath prayers made by ordinary people would be *ad hoc* and individual,

---

[40] Clements, *God and Temple*, p. 130.

[41] S. Talmon, 'The Emergence of Institutionalized Prayer in Israel in the Light of the Qumrân Literature', in *Qumrân: Sa piété, sa théologie et son milieu* (Paris: Editions Duculot and Gembloux: Les Editions du Cerf, 1978), pp. 265-84 (270).

[42] Talmon, 'Institutionalized Prayer', pp. 267-68.

[43] Talmon, 'Institutionalized Prayer', pp. 268-69.

and not made in accordance with custom or tradition.[44]

A similar understanding of the general population's entitlement to, or involvement in, sabbath worship is provided by Haran,[45] who reads the sabbath texts with a seasoning of scepticism, and comes to the conclusion that the pattern of rites and observances (including the sabbath) reported by the P source 'cannot originate with the common people, but of necessity is an esoteric prerogative of the priestly family'. He implies that it is this priestly group who concern themselves with the preservation and recording of all religious rites, and supposes that priestly 'ritual takes place in the arcana of the house of God, unseen by the people as a whole'. By the very nature of the activity and the instincts of self-preservation of the group in charge, worship is kept apart and hidden from the common people.

But Haran also holds the seemingly contradictory belief that the populace visited the temple to 'prostrate themselves before the Lord there on all the holy days all year round'.[46] As evidence for this he adduces Isa. 1.12-15; Ezek. 36.38; Lam. 1.4; 2.7. I am not able to agree that these texts show the people worshipping or prostrating themselves before God in the temple on every possible holy day, but consider the writing to be more rhetorical and idealistic in intention. I believe Haran's reading depends on combining texts which independently refer to different things, for example, some to worship during the three pilgrim festivals and some to the role of the priests in Temple services, then adding to these what he 'knows' of sabbath observance.

Pious Jews would no doubt make the journey to the Temple for the three pilgrim feasts and possibly at other times, and prayers would be offered in conjunction with sacrifices in the Temple on sabbaths and other holy days.[47] But no details are given in our texts of who would say prayers, nor of the content of such prayers, nor of who could hear them or participate in them. Suggestions of content for these lacunae in our knowledge have no more status than guesses.

---

[44] Talmon, 'Institutionalized Prayer', pp. 270-73, argues extensively that there was actual opposition to insitutionalised prayer—including a ban on the writing of prayers that continued till rabbinic times.

[45] M. Haran, *Temples and Temple-Service in Ancient Israel* (Oxford: Clarendon Press, 1978), pp. 224, 291, 348.

[46] Haran, *Temples*, p. 292.

[47] Talmon, 'Institutionalized Prayer', p. 267.

Prayers could well be offered by the assembled males of the community who had come the Temple three times a year for the great festivals (Isa. 1.15), and by local Jews at the annual days such as new year and the day of atonement, but not necessarily in unison—or even about a common theme. And even if the Jerusalem population—within walking distance of the Temple—had the option of offering individual, and spontaneous, prayers there on the sabbath, there are no injunctions to do so extant in any of the biblical texts. It is my view that belief in the regular practice of communal sabbath prayers cannot be sustained from this one text from Isaiah.[48]

There is equally little evidence in the Hebrew Bible for the communal singing of sabbath psalms, only Psalm 92 having as its title 'A Psalm. A Song for the Sabbath Day', and no other Psalm referring to the sabbath at all. Also, even if psalm singing were a regular feature of worship on holy days (including the sabbath) it is not clear who was singing. There is evidence in Chronicles and Nehemiah that there were choirs of Temple singers,[49] but whether others could listen, or join in, is never made explicit in the biblical sources. All we can be certain of is that Temple officials sang psalms as part of worship, and possibly a particular psalm on the sabbath. Ordinary worshippers are not described as singing psalms on any occasion.

Other writers before me have gathered and analysed the sabbath material from the Hebrew Bible with a view to understanding the role of the sabbath in the religious life of Israel. But studies on the sabbath are usually written in such a way as to avoid being overly critical about an institution so respected by many people. The handling of the evidence is gentle and generous, often giving way to conscious or unconscious embargoes on what may finally be concluded. As a result of this respectful attitude, the distinctions pointed out above by me have rarely been observed and the vital sharpness of critical thinking has been blunted.

I refer to only a few standard studies of the sabbath, by way of example. Of these, Andreasen proceeds without making the all-important distinction between sabbath observance and sabbath worship,[50] and although he recognises that 'we have few and only sketchy

---

[48] See also further discussion below on Isa. 1.13-15.
[49] 1 Chr. 6.31-33; 9.33; Neh. 7.1, 44; 11.22.
[50] Andreasen, *Sabbath*, p. ix.

descriptions of Sabbath keeping in the Old Testament',[51] and that 'most references to the Sabbath are strangely monotonous and unimaginative',[52] he draws the unadventurous, and—even in terms of his own discussion—unwarranted, conclusion that the 'Sabbath material frequently antedates its literary formulation'.[53] Similarly, Andreasen repeatedly assumes that the sabbath involved both rest and festal activities, while admitting that such views are based on very meagre evidence.[54] He allows his belief that the sabbath was always a day of worship to override the evidence of his textual studies.

Presenting an opposing point of view, and displaying an open and unequivocal agnosticism as to the origins of, and practices relevant to sabbath, Herbert declares the origin of sabbath to be obscure, and finds that 'the infrequency with which it is mentioned and the lack of information about its manner of observation in the pre-exilic histories and prophets add to our difficulty'.[55] It does indeed.

Kraus also notes that there is a great lack of stipulation for worship of any kind on the sabbath, and concludes that 'Both the explanations are secondary, but they show how the Old Testament tradition attempted to anchor the sabbath day in the fundamental mighty acts of Yahweh'.[56] He claims that 'the sabbath was not really a feast' because 'there is no indication of a ritual that might have set the pattern for the day'; it was 'merely a day of rest'. I take him to say that there were no extra activities peculiar to the sabbath, there were simply regular everyday activities that were avoided on sabbath, and I completely concur with that view.

The texts give so very little information about the sabbath as a day of worship, that comments made on the subject must stress the lack of information, and resist any inclination to synthesise answers from other material.

---

[51] Andreasen, *Sabbath*, p. 10.

[52] Andreasen, *Sabbath*, p. 92.

[53] Andreasen, *Sabbath*, p. 92.

[54] Andreasen, *Sabbath*, pp. 140, 149, 150, 237, 239, 241.

[55] A.S. Herbert, *Worship in Ancient Israel* (Ecumenical Studies in Worship, 5; London: Lutterworth, 1959), p. 45.

[56] H.-J. Kraus, *Worship in Israel* (tr. G. Buswell; Oxford: Blackwell, 1966), pp. 76-88, especially pp. 79, 80, 86.

Texts about New Moon

Kraus realised that a useful comparison for sabbath material in biblical texts can be made with the texts relating to new moon. He contrasts the lack of detail for sabbath activities with the details given for new moon, which, in his view, was a monthly feast, held within the homes of the families of Israel.[57] Wildberger also remarks on the similarly of the two days, and the frequency with which they are linked together in the biblical texts;[58] for new moon is another holy day that occurs regularly throughout the year, rather than once only like the great pilgrim feasts.

The fact that sabbath and new moon are dealt with in like manner in the biblical texts allows the religious importance of the two days to become apparent, from details given of actions to be undertaken or avoided and of rituals or sacrifices carried out. These details can then be compared with what is required on the annual feasts so that the picture of worship within the community becomes clearer and any activities associated with sabbath can be evaluated. If there is plain evidence of expected worship behaviour on new moon or on the annual feasts, this will highlight any paucity of stipulations for worship behaviour on the sabbath.

Instructions for rituals to be employed at the beginnings of months are detailed at Num. 10.10, 28.11-15, 29.6. There trumpet blowing is prescribed as a feature of new moon celebrations as is also a sacrifice several times larger than that of the sabbath. Ps. 81.3 similarly indicates that trumpet blowing was traditional at the new moon. In Ezek. 46.6 the prince is told to make a burnt offering on both sabbath and new moon—the new moon sacrifice being increased by one bull compared with the sabbath offering—and the people of the land are expected to worship at the entrance of a gate (to the Temple) on the sabbaths and the new moons.

---

[57] Num. 10.10; 1 Sam. 20; Ezek. 46.6. Similar conclusions are noted by G.F. Hasel, 'The Sabbath in the Pentateuch', in *The Sabbath in Scripture and History* (ed. K.A. Strand; Washington, DC: Review and Herald Publishing Corporation, 1982), pp. 21-43, by W.G.C. Murdoch, 'The Sabbath in the Prophetic and Historical Literature of the Old Testament', in *The Sabbath in Scripture*, pp. 44-56 (45), and by S. Kubo, 'The Sabbath in the Intertestamental Period', in *The Sabbath in Scripture*, pp. 57-69 (57).

[58] H. Wildberger, *Jesaja*, I (BKAT, X/I: Neukirchen–Vluyn: Neukirchener Verlag, 1972), p. 42: 'Sie gehören zusammen, weil sie regelmässig im Jahresablauf wiederkehren'.

On a domestic level, new moon is described as a holy day to be celebrated in Saul's family home (1 Sam. 20.5-34) with a celebration meal to which Saul invites David.[59]

And in Hosea 5.7 there is an enigmatic reference to the new moon devouring [the people] with their fields.

There is another way to consider references to sabbath and new moon, which is, to look at places where sabbath and new moon occur in lists of sacred days, either together or linked with other named days. These texts will be studied in the next section of this Chapter.

Texts Giving Lists or Sequences of Holy Days

Further insight about whether or not we should consider the sabbath to be a sacred day with worship practices similar to new moon and the annual feasts can be gained from scrutinising lists and sequences of holy days in the Hebrew Bible, for such a study can give some indication of how the compilers viewed sabbath in relation to the other holy days.

Lists with three names of holy days

Isa. 1.13   new moon and sabbath ... solemn assemblies (מועד)[60]
Ezek. 45.17   feasts (חג), new moons, sabbaths, appointed feasts (מועד)
Hos. 2.13 (EVV 11)   feast, new moon, sabbath, appointed feasts

Also relevant for consideration at this point are:

1 Macc. 10.34   feasts, sabbaths, new moons, appointed feasts
Jub. 1.14   new moons, sabbaths, festivals, jubilees
Jub. 23.19   festivals and months and sabbaths and jubilees

The texts from Ezekiel and Hosea list holy days in order of frequency through the year and are alike even though the former

---

[59] New moons can, like the sabbaths, occur in the texts as holy days with religious observance, and as date markers, and here, as for the sabbath, the latter have been ignored.

[60] חג is the Hebrew for an annual pilgrim feast, such as passover, weeks and booths, and מועד for an appointed feast, which term can sometimes include the pilgrim feasts along with new year (first day of the seventh month) and the day of atonement, although the term 'appointed feasts' is usually present in lists as a summarising or general term.

describes the sacrifices that the prince will make in the future restored temple and the latter is a list of days that the Lord will eliminate. Sabbath is a member of both those lists.

Lists, or parallelisms, with two names of holy days

new moon, sabbath

2 Kgs 4.23	neither new moon nor sabbath
Isa. 66.23	from new moon to new moon ... from sabbath to sabbath
Amos 8.5	when will the new moon be over? ... And the sabbath ...

sabbath, new moon

1 Chr. 23.31	sabbath, new moons, appointed feasts
2 Chr. 2.4	sabbath, new moons, appointed feasts
2 Chr. 8.13	sabbath, new moons, appointed feasts
2 Chr. 31.3	sabbath, new moons, appointed feasts
Neh. 10.33	sabbath, new moons, appointed feasts
Ezek. 46.1	on the sabbath day ... on the day of the new moon
Ezek. 46.3	on the sabbaths and on the new moons

appointed feasts, sabbath

Lam. 2.6	appointed feasts and sabbath
Ezek. 44.24	They shall keep my laws and my statutes in all my appointed feasts, and they shall keep my sabbaths holy.

sabbath, feasts

1 Macc. 1.45	sabbaths and feast days
2 Macc. 6.6	to observe sabbaths or keep the traditional feasts

new moon, other feasts

Ezra 3.5	at the new moons and at all the appointed feasts
Isa. 1.14	your new moons and your appointed feasts
Psalm 81.3	new moon, full moon, feast day

Also relevant for consideration at this point are:

Jdt. 8.6	sabbaths, new moons, feasts
1 Esdr. 05.52	sabbaths, new moons, all holy feasts
Col. 2.16	feast, new moon, sabbath[61]
Jub. 2.9	sabbaths, months, feast days
War Scroll 2.4	appointed feasts, new moons, sabbaths
Justin[62]	sabbaths, feasts, new moons
Philo[63]	daily…7th day…new moons…fasts…3 festal seasons

The first important observation to be made from these texts is that new moon and sabbath are linked together on very many occasions throughout the Hebrew Bible and related literature. Secondly, that this means of grouping sabbath with the other sacred days implies that it was understood to be, in some way, a sacred day like them. However, as will become evident from discussions on the cultic calendars, there is no real consistency or clarity about the status of these days, about what should, or should not be done on them, where, and by whom. The days seem to be serious and important occasions, yet there are no consistent prescriptions for behaviour or rituals for the different days. If one were to read all the texts about feasts in the Hebrew Bible as if they were told by one narrator, the confusions that would occur would cause that narrator to be labelled completely unreliable. The only way to find the texts coherent is to assume different authors with very different understandings of the sacred days.

Discussion about New Moon

The picture of new moon gleaned from the Hebrew Bible is not as straightforward as one would have hoped—giving details of activities for both Temple staff and Israelite citizens. The depiction of new moon is incomplete and puzzling in a number of respects.

---

[61] This is a quotation of the LXX version of Hos. 2.13 (EVV 11), and Ezek. 45.17 (E. Schweizer, *The Letter to the Colossians: A Commentary* [tr. A. Chester; London: SPCK, 1982]).

[62] *Dialogue* 8.

[63] Philo, *The Special Laws*, 1.168-9, in *Philo*, VII (tr. F.H. Colson; LCL; Cambridge, MA: Harvard University Press, 1937); elsewhere in his writings, in *The Special Laws*, 2.140-44), in *Philo*, VII (tr. F.H. Colson; LCL; Cambridge, MA: Harvard University Press, 1937), Philo devotes a lengthy section to defending the value of the new moon day to the Jewish people.

First, in the Samuel narrative about Saul's family celebration, new moon is described as an important family religious occasion, from which absenting oneself was a serious matter, but, there is a total lack of interest in this domestic celebration of the new moon elsewhere in the narratives of the Hebrew Bible—as there is about the domestic celebration of the sabbath.

Secondly, the lack of information about new moon is odd when one realises that new moon is referred to in sixteen other places in the Hebrew Bible. This number of references implies that it was a reasonably well-known feast in Israelite society (cf. a mere five occurrences of the feast of weeks).

Thirdly, the text of Hos. 5.7 referring to the new moon devouring the people is enigmatic, the solutions proposed being quite varied and the emendations proposed being aptly described by Mays as 'creatures of need'.[64] He gives three possible readings of the verse: first the almost unintelligible MT reading that the new moon/month will devour them, second—following the Greek—that the locust or destroyer will devour them, or third, that in a month's time they will be devoured.

This text from Hosea seems to provide commentators with a focus for venting bias against the idea that new moon was a perfectly respectable Israelite holy day on which God was worshipped in the Temple, many scholars treating new moon as being nothing more than an alien and somewhat tainted festival. Thus Andersen and Freedman, while following up every other point with greatly detailed arguments and references, merely assert that 'New Moon festivals were important in Canaanite religion', and go on from there to say that 'it would be appropriate if some kind of disaster were to take place at that sacred time'.[65] They read this text as implying punishment for the fruits of harlotry, symbolic or otherwise. But it seems to me that one particular reading of the text is expatiated on while others remain only partially considered.[66]

---

[64] J.L. Mays, *Hosea: A Commentary* (OTL; London: SCM Press, 1969), pp. 84-85.

[65] F.I. Andersen and D.N. Freedman, *Hosea: A New Translation with Introduction and Commentary* (The Anchor Bible, 24; New York: Doubleday, 1980), pp. 396-97.

[66] See also C. Hauret, *Amos et Osée* (Paris: Beauchesne, 1969), p. 185; H.W. Wolff, *Hosea: A Commentary on the Book of the Prophet Hosea* (Hermeneia; tr. G. Stansell; Philadelphia: Fortress Press, 1965), p. 101.

So the new moon, perhaps because of the teasing insufficiency of detail about it in the Hebrew Bible, has attracted much unfavourable comment in the secondary literature, which seems to me to be out of harmony with the generally equanimous treatment of the festival in the biblical texts.

There seems to me to be similar biblical evidence about the character of, and possible activities on, both new moon and sabbath, and, therefore, no justification for regarding sabbath as a pure and holy day and regarding new moon as somewhat unsavoury. I believe it is important for our study to realise what very different constructions may be put upon the little textual evidence there is, and to reflect on the possibility that the image of the sabbath may also have suffered from similar [mis]reading of texts—though for very different reasons and with very different results.

Discussion on the Word Pair New Moon and Sabbath

Because new moon and sabbath occur together so often in the texts and because the two names are never separated in those lists where both occur, I regard them as, in some sense, a word pair, and the use of word pairs or the parallel use of two words means that the words are either *alike* in some way, or they are in some way being *opposed*.

In all the texts where these two days are linked, it is because they are alike. For example, on both days the holy man will be at the shrine (2 Kgs 4.23), on both days business will be suspended (Amos 8.5), and on both days the gate of the Temple court will be open and on both days the people of the land will bow down at that gate (Ezek. 46.1, 3). This assumption of similarity between the two days occurs in all the texts where both are named.

Also, when the number of texts where those two days occur are counted for the Hebrew Bible, the result shows that new moon occurs slightly more often than sabbath.[67] There is, therefore, no evidence for the common assumption that sabbath dominated the religious scene in the Hebrew Bible; its visibility—as a day of worship at the Temple—is similar to that of new moon.

---

[67] New moon occurs eighteen times and sabbath fifteen.

Discussion of Isa. 1.13-15 and Isa. 66.23

The occurrence of the phrase 'new moon and sabbath' at both the beginning and the end of the book of Isaiah is also worth some attention. The first occurrence in Isaiah 1 has a negative flavour and the oracle speaks against new moon and sabbath, but the other, in Isaiah 66, uses the combination of the two days as a symbol of new hope.

In Isa. 1.13-15, new moon and sabbath are spoken of between texts dealing with God's disgust over the narratees' sacrificial practice and with their prayers. The condemnation is non-specific and overwhelming, with the different feast days grouped together indiscriminately. The Lord seems to be blaming throngs of people for coming to celebrate feast days (although the particular word for the pilgrim feasts, חגים, is not included in the text). Yet that is apparently their understanding of what he, himself, requires of them.

However, I find it difficult to distinguish any worship practice peculiar to, or prescribed for, the sabbath from the text of this oracle. The voice of the speaker is combining every religious occasion together in a comprehensive condemnation of the cult. And the complaints seem rather to be aimed at the practices of *priests within the cult* than at the ordinary worshipper. For it is the giving of offerings and incense that are mentioned as examples of what is particularly irritating to the Almighty, and those would be delivered through the hands of the priests.

I agree with Kaiser who regards this oracle as coming from the period of the Second Temple, and as being a 'criticism of the cult', blaming the priests for 'the juxtaposition and combination of conduct which injures the community … with the festive assemblies'.[68] There is no criticism of the activities of, and therefore no reference to, the ordinary worshippers; the voice of the Lord is castigating those who have the power to change cultic and other practices.

Watts finds another nuance in the meaning of Isa. 1.13. He sees an opposition between the reference to new moon and sabbath here and the references to new moon and sabbath in Isa. 66.23, where the holy days are part of the joys to come in the future as part of the vision of

---

[68] O. Kaiser, *Isaiah 1–12: A Commentary* (English translation of 5th German edition; OTL; London: SCM Press, 1983), pp. 25, 31.

the New Jerusalem given there.[69] The contrast between the glorious age ahead and the harsh realities of the present is, in his view, the main force of the oracle. He believes that sacrificial worship, because unaccompanied by right living, is being rejected in Isa. 1.13, and that future worship—as described in Isaiah 66—will reflect a more sincere attitude of reverence on the part of 'all flesh' who come to worship God on new moon and sabbath.[70] The phrase 'new moon and sabbath' is used, therefore, in both oracles, as a catch-all phrase, to sum up the whole religious relationship between the cult and God. Nonetheless, it is the religion only of the priests that it sums up.[71]

Other writers, for example, Smart, see Isa. 66.23 as describing a glorification of worship at the Temple, with the climax of the new creation being represented by renewed sabbath worship.[72] He holds the view that because sabbath represents the summation of the first creation, it should be celebrated more enthusiastically in the new creation. So, in discussing this theme, Smart is able to include new moons along with the sabbaths as part of the 'consummation' in the form of 'the coming of all nations ... to participate in the Temple worship'. But although he gives the reason for the presence in the oracle of the sabbath, on which worship is 'the primary observance

---

[69] J.D.W. Watts, *Isaiah 1–33* (WBC, 24; Waco, TX: Word Books, 1972), p. 21.

[70] Another possibility is that the word 'sabbath' has become attached to 'new moon' secondarily in this oracle, and as its complement in the word pair. Certainly, in the interplay of terms in Isa. 1.13b-14a 'sabbath' is not repeated or paralleled by another term, as new moon and assembly/convocation are. That pattern of repeating and alternating names of holy days would flow more smoothly and poetically were the 'sabbath' reference to be removed. If this argument can be maintained, then the presence of the word 'sabbath' in Isa. 1.13 can be considered secondary, and the original acerbic condemnation would have been aimed at the annual and the monthly Israelite celebrations, with nothing at all being said about the sabbath as a day on which Israelites worshipped. Then, at a later date, sabbath was added to indicate the summing up of the totality of worship by means of the word pair, new moon and sabbath. Because of the frequency with which the two words occur together in the the Hebrew Bible texts, I incline to this explanation.

[71] Another interpretation of Isa. 66.23 (C.C. Torrey, *The Second Isaiah: A New Interpretation* [Edinburgh: T. & T. Clark, 1928], p. 475; and P. Volz, *Jesaia II: übersetzt und erklärt* [KAT, 9; Leipzig: A. Deichert, 1932], pp. 295, 299), claims that the phrase 'from new moon to new moon, and from sabbath to sabbath' implies nothing more than the lengthiness of the time scale in the mind of the prophet and the regular nature of the worship to be carried out, rather than specifying that it is on these days that the worship should take place. But this wrongly discounts the rhetorical freight of the phrase.

[72] J.D. Smart, *History and Theology in Second Isaiah: A Commentary on Isaiah 35, 40–66* (London: Epworth Press, 1967), pp. 291-92.

of a true Israelite', he gives no parallel argument for the new moon being singled out for mention as well.[73] It acquires the invisibility of an embarrassing gate-crasher. It looks as if Smart sees in the text something he expected to see, namely the supremacy of sabbath and sabbath worship, and that he has ignored the quite clear coupling of sabbath with new moon in the text. He says that the editor of the book of Isaiah 'bends the prophet's greatest thoughts to fit his orthodox schema', a criticism which could, with some measure of justice, be levelled at Smart himself.

Scholars who claim the dominance of sabbath worship seem oblivious to the equality of new moon and sabbath in this text—among others; that in some sense the two days are comparable, and can be considered together, part of the same complex of ideas, as they are repeatedly elsewhere in the Hebrew Bible, and not at all in opposition as far as the writer of Isa. 66 is concerned. Any claims for sabbath as the main day of Israelite worship must take account of the clear coupling of the two days. It would be equally illogical to claim from this text, and others like it, that new moon was the main day of Israelite worship.

If, however, Isa. 1.13 were indeed referring to regular sabbath worship at the Temple by ordinary Israelites, then it would be the only text in the Hebrew Bible to do so, apart from the references to future worship, either in Isa. 66.23, or in Ezekiel's vision to the people of the land worshipping at the gate of the future restored temple—neither of which can be a description of current practice. But this one text from Isaiah is not straightforward enough to be used on its own as evidence of regular communal worship by the Israelite populace. As part of a complex of similar texts it could be so used, but there are no others.

Cultic Calendars

The three lengthiest sections of text that deal with holy days and the practices required on them are Leviticus 23.2-43, Numbers 28.1–29.39 and Ezekiel 45.13–46.15. The passages share a more or less common understanding of the three annual feasts, similar to the

---

[73] Smart, *Second Isaiah*, p. 291.

descriptions in Deuteronomy 16, but they differ in the order in which they deal with the individual holy days, in the sacrifices prescribed and even in the selection of the holy days they present. The perspective from which the festivals are viewed in these calendars is that of the group in the Temple who operate the cult. There are no explanations of how ordinary worshippers might supply the sacrificial materials.[74]

Leviticus 23 details the holy days in order of their progression through the year, with a statement about the sabbath included at v. 3 between the general introduction to the appointed feasts and the details for the passover, and with an ambiguous reference to the sabbath, not connected in any way to the first reference, at v. 38. The sequence is sabbath, feast of unleavened bread, feast of weeks, first day of the seventh month, day of atonement, feast of booths. Of note is the fact that new moon is not mentioned at all. This list, along with the other cultic calendars, will be discussed in detail later in this Chapter.

In Numbers 28–29 the days on which sacrifices are to be offered are sequenced in order of their frequency throughout the year: daily, sabbaths, beginnings of months (new moons), feast of unleavened bread (passover), feast of weeks, day of atonement, feast of booths. The holy days and their rituals are individually described.

In Ezekiel 45–46 there is another set of instructions for the observance of holy days which deals with them in the order of passover, sabbath, new moon and appointed feasts; but the other two annual feasts are not mentioned by name although the general term 'feast' (חג) is there. It is surprising that the same section is also preceded by, or begins with, the list: feasts, new moon, sabbath, and all appointed feasts (45.17). There is no harmonising whatsoever of these two blocks because the list does not function in any way as an announcement of the substance to follow in the rest of the section.

Laying out these three cultic calendars side by side shows how little correspondence there is between them, though it is possible to identify a seven-part structure in each of the lists.

---

[74] In his discussion of sabbath actions as reported in the Damascus Rule and in the Mishnah, E.P. Sanders, *Jewish Law from Jesus to the Mishnah: Five Studies* (London: SCM Press, 1990), p. 11, concludes that since sacrificing is characterised as work, only priests were permitted to carry it out on the sabbath from his recognition that all the sources 'simply assume that individuals did not present sacrifices on the sabbath'.

Leviticus 23	*Numbers 28–29*	*Ezekiel 45–46*
sabbath	daily	day of atonement
passover	sabbath	passover
first fruits/weeks	new moon	feast (? weeks)
1st day of 7th month	passover	sabbath
day of atonement	weeks	new moon
booths	day of atonement	appointed feasts
sabbath	booths	daily
booths (repeated)		

The Numbers list has an obvious seven-part structure, with the days requiring sacrifices arranged by decreasing order of frequency in the year. Sabbath occurs at the logical place of second in such a list. The Ezekiel calendar has also a seven-part structure, but one which shows no immediately apparent logic of arrangement, with sabbath in the—apparently—central position of fourth in the list. The Leviticus text contains seven categories of holy day if one removes the repetitions, and sabbath appears near both ends of the list.

Numbers 28–29 [75]

daily	2 lambs
sabbath	4 lambs
new moon	2 bulls, 1 ram, 7 lambs, 1 goat
passover	2 bulls, 1 ram, 7 lambs, 1 goat, no work
first fruits	2 bulls, 1 ram, 7 lambs, 1 goat, no work
1st day of 7th month	1 bull, 1 ram, 7 lambs, 1 goat, no work, blow trumpets
10th day [atonement]	1 bull, 1 ram, 7 lambs, 1 goat, no work, 'afflicting oneself'
15th day [booths]	13 bulls, 2 rams, 14 lambs, 1 goat, no work
16th day of 7	12 bulls, 2 rams, 14 lambs, 1 goat
AND SO ON	decreasing by 1 bull until the 7th day, then
23rd day	1 bull, 1 ram, 7 lambs, 1 goat

---

[75] I have listed only the animal sacrifices as giving a simpler measure of the relative quantities and cost of sacrificial goods.

Ezekiel 45–46

1st day of 1st month	1 bull
passover	1 bull, then 7 bulls, 7 rams, 1 goat for 7 days
15th day of 7th month	the same as passover
sabbath	6 lambs, 1 ram
new moon	1 bull, 6 lambs, 1 ram
appointed feasts	general instructions
daily	1 lamb

The presentation in Numbers is most regular of the three cultic calendars. The sabbath offering is twice as great as the daily offering, but the new moon offering is very much greater than the sabbath offering, and identical in quantity to the passover offering.

In Ezekiel 45–46 sabbath and new moon were regarded as days of similar importance to the writer, but with the new moon having a clear edge over sabbath in terms of livestock slaughtered. Both days have much more importance than a weekday by this method of scoring, which was not the case in the Numbers material, where the sabbath sacrifice merely doubled the daily sacrifice of two lambs. And here both sabbath and new moon are of much less importance than passover, though the prescription for new moon bears some similarity to the passover prescription. There is more differentiation of the amounts of animals to be offered daily, on sabbaths, on new moons and on passover. But, of course, this list refers to the future restored temple where worship would be performed in a perfect way and whether anything similar took place in the Jerusalem temple is debatable.

Leviticus 23

sabbath	no sacrifice prescribed
passover	unspecified sacrifice for 7 days
first fruits	1 lamb
weeks	7 lambs, 1 bull, 2 rams, 1 goat, 2 lambs
1st day of 7th month	blow trumpets, do no work, unspecified offering
day of atonement	unspecified offering
booths (15th–22nd of 7th month)	unspecified offerings

A closer look at the material in Leviticus reveals two references to the sabbath—both without any content of detail or prescription for sacrifice—which look as if they have been added to an existing cultic sequence. The first describes sabbath as a day of solemn and holy rest, interrupting the preamble to the cultic calendar:

> The Lord said to Moses, 'Say to the people of Israel, "The appointed feasts of the Lord which you shall proclaim as holy convocations, my appointed feasts, are these. Six days shall work be done; but on the seventh day is a sabbath of solemn rest, a holy convocation; you shall do no work; it is a sabbath to the Lord in all your dwellings." These are the appointed feasts of the Lord, the holy convocations, which you shall proclaim at the time appointed for them (Lev. 23.1-4).

The second places sabbath in the middle of a reprise of general directions for holy days almost at the end of the calendar—which itself interrupts the lists of offerings—apparently in parenthesis to the word, 'day'.

> These are the appointed feasts of the Lord, which you shall proclaim as times of holy convocation, for presenting to the Lord offerings by fire, burnt offerings and cereal offerings, sacrifices and drink offerings, each on its proper day; besides the sabbaths of the Lord, and besides your gifts, and besides all your votive offerings, and besides all your freewill offerings, which you give to the Lord (Lev. 23.37-38).

Sabbath is included, almost at the end of the calendar, among a group of holy days on which sacrifices are made, as if the writer was forgetting that sabbath, in this list, does not have a set of sacrifices.

Notable also is the fact that, in this list, there is no reference at all to the new moon. Admittedly, on the first day of the seventh month rest, ritual act and sacrifice are laid down, but it is not stated that this is expected to happen on every new moon. New moon—as a holy day in its own right, with special, particular sacrifices—has been effectively eliminated from these proceedings; and although sabbath is included, it is without a sacrifice prescription. In this list of feasts the only feast that has a clear explanation of what is to happen to the various attendant flora and fauna is the feast of weeks.

In contrast with these three more or less complete cultic calendars, there is what appears to be a small section of another in Ezra 3—though it is only a list of some Israelite holy days, and without specific sacrifice prescriptions. The restoration of worship, at the beginning of the seventh month, is described, the cycle of worship on festivals and holy days beginning with twice-daily sacrifices, continuing with the feast of booths (3.4), and then with daily burnt offerings, 'the continual burnt offerings, the offerings at the new moon and at all the appointed feasts of the Lord ...':

Ezra 3
daily
booths
daily
new moons
appointed feasts

What is noteworthy about this list is the fact that sabbath is not mentioned at all, whereas new moon is explicitly named as a day with sacrifices.

Several commentators are troubled by this and believe, from comparison with lists of holy days in 1 and 2 Chronicles, Nehemiah, Judith and 1 Esdras,[76] where sabbath *is* present, that sabbath has dropped out of the list in Ezra 3.5 and should be replaced. Proposing the [re-]insertion of 'sabbaths' are Myers and Coggins, but demurring are Blenkinsopp, Williamson and Fensham.[77]

As it stands the Ezra block gives some currency to my proposal that certain texts give new moon higher status than sabbath, while others prefer to give the greater standing to the sabbath. In the three main cultic calendars sabbath seems to have less importance than new moon, and sabbath is completely missing from the listing in Ezra.

The details gleaned about new moon activities from these passages show that, compared with the sabbath, new moon had a greater, importance in the minds of some at least of the biblical writers. The sacrifice was always more magnificent—which means

---

[76] See above in this Chapter in lists and sequences of holy days.

[77] J.M. Myers, *Ezra. Nehemiah* (The Anchor Bible, 14; Garden City, NY: Doubleday, 1965), p. 25, R.J. Coggins, *Ezra and Nehemiah* (CBC; Cambridge: CUP, 1976), p. 21; demurring at its insertion are: J. Blenkinsopp, *Ezra–Nehemiah: A Commentary* (OTL; London: SCM Press, 1988), p. 98, H.G.M. Williamson, *Ezra, Nehemiah* (WBC, 16; Waco, TX: Word Books, 1985), p. 42, F.C. Fensham, *The Books of Ezra and Nehemiah* (New International Commentary on the Old Testament; Grand Rapids: Eerdmans, 1982), p. 60.

more costly—and a trumpet was sounded. As far as the priests were concerned, there was more work—and more worship—to be performed on a new moon than on a sabbath.

Discussion about the Cultic Calendars

From the gradations of quantities of livestock listed for sacrifice on the different occasions in Numbers 28–29, we can conclude that the writers of the cultic material valued the new moon a great deal more than the sabbath, regarding it as a festal day similar in importance to passover. The sabbath has no peculiar list of sacrifices, but merely has an extra dole of the daily offering.

The presentation of the cultic calendar in Ezekiel could, with some justification, be described as ragged, with dates left unclear and quite different specifications of sacrifice from those in Numbers. Among the commentators who discuss these differences,[78] Fisch notes the problems but merely re-iterates rabbinic conjectures for solutions to them. Cooke, on the other hand, blames the confusion on editings and updates to existing laws.[79] He believes that 'by the time when the present legislation was promoted, the ancient feasts had changed their character ... the laity assist at a distance, the priests alone carry out the sacrificial rites'.[80] This view recognises a distancing of the common people from the practice of worship, but the phrase 'assist at a distance' is irritatingly vague. One wonders at what distance such assistance would cease to have religious meaning—especially on sabbath when most Israelites would be eliminated by distance from attending the Temple at all.

Zimmerli rehearses the same points as the other commentators but also regards the process at work in the compilation of the Ezekiel text as one of levelling, where the great feasts are brought down to size, becoming less extravagant and more like one another in rituals and requirements.[81]

---

[78] S. Fisch, *Ezekiel* (Soncino Books of the Bible; Hindhead, Surrey: The Soncino Press, 1950), pp. 315-19; G.A. Cooke, *The Book of Ezekiel* (ICC; Edinburgh: T. & T. Clark, 1936), pp. 493-507; W. Zimmerli, *A Commentary on the Book of the Prophet Ezekiel*, II (Hermeneia; tr. J.D. Martin; Philadelphia: Fortress Press, 1983), pp. 480-86.

[79] Cooke, *Ezekiel*, p. 504; note the similarity to the conclusions of Haran above.

[80] Cooke, *Ezekiel*, p. 505.

[81] Zimmerli, *Ezekiel*, p. 484.

These latter commentators rightly, in my view, see the editing and reforming activities of groups in power in Israel as the source of the discrepancies and disturbances in the texts, and conclude that these groups had the power to change the value and importance of the different feasts when they inscribed them in the biblical texts.

And in consideration of the Leviticus passage it must be said that surprise at the placing of sabbath within the sequence of feasts is not new. Baumgarten, for example, describes the rabbinic question as to the intrusion of sabbath details at two places in this section of Leviticus, 'What place has the sabbath in the chapter dealing with festivals?'[82] Certainly, the two pieces about the sabbath jar badly with the rest of the material and seem like later additions to the text.[83] But why should the sabbath intrude itself in a list of feast days? The rabbi who asked that question must have considered the sabbath to be other than a feast day. And in whose interests would it have been to make the insertion? I conclude that the compilers of the Leviticus text revered the sabbath greatly as a holy day—though not as a feast day with sacrifices—and placed sabbath amongst the feast days, like an important latecomer being ushered to the head of a queue.

Certainly, the importance of the sabbath in the community that produced the book of Ezekiel has long been recognised,[84] and in Ezekiel 20–23 the concept of profanation of the sabbath is treated as if the sabbath itself were an entity that could be polluted, rather than implying the pollution—on a sabbath—of a physical entity, such as the sanctuary, with a physical pollutant, such as porcine blood. This ability of the sabbath itself to become polluted or profaned by peoples' actions or intentions is a theme that is developed more fully in the later writings of Maccabees and *Jubilees* and will be discussed in Chapter 2.

In Ezek. 44.24 there is a distinction of sabbath from the other feasts in terms of how one is meant to react towards the day, that is, there are rituals for the feasts, but there should be a proper attitude to the sabbath. Such a distinction indicates the development of a high

---

[82] J.M. Baumgarten, 'The Counting of the Sabbath', *Vetus Testamentum* 16 (1966), pp. 277-86 (278).
[83] See also comments in Andreasen, *Sabbath*, p. 76.
[84] Kraus, *Worship*, p. 87.

estimate of the value of the sabbath and suggests that there *was* nothing else to be done on the sabbath.

So we find that the search for sabbath worship on the part of ordinary people has not been advanced by a study of the Hebrew Bible texts about Temple worship. As far as sacrifices are concerned, there is nothing addressed to the laity for their execution; the calendars describe priestly activity. Even in those details there is inconsistency, one calendar gives the sabbath twice the daily offering, one gives it more and one gives no details of sacrifice for sabbath at all.

What emerges from the texts is that only the *priests* were actually involved in whatever sacrificing was done and it is not clear whether the people were involved in the sacrificial activity in any religious sense—apart from allegedly supplying the animals and agricultural products.

Conclusions about the Sabbath in the Hebrew Bible

All the pieces of evidence presented in this chapter encourage the view that the sabbath was not a sacred day with worship rituals for ordinary people in the period covered by the Hebrew Bible All the prescriptions for actual and particular behaviour on the sabbath are addressed to cultic officials, and not to the ordinary worshipper—save the implied providing of the material for the sacrifice.

The two texts that seem to state definitely that there should be worship on the sabbath (Ezek. 46.3; Isa. 66.23) both refer to a future glorious age. This suggests that while the authors of the texts wish sabbath worship to take place it is not, in their time, happening to the extent, or in the manner, that they desire.

Whether the king had either any sort of privileged access to the Temple (2 Kgs 16.18), or any extra responsibilities in the Temple (2 Chr. 31.3; Ezek. 46) on the sabbath is impossible to determine from the tantalising fragments of data provided by the texts of the Hebrew Bible; not least because the accounts are driven by their own agendas and do not set out to give answers to my questions. Answers to these questions could have given a picture of how a lay person, albeit a royal lay person, behaved on the sabbath in Jerusalem.

The regular religious commitment for non-priestly Jews, drawn from the evidence of the Hebrew Bible alone, is solely of a faithfully observed and revered sabbath of rest. Only the sabbath of the priests includes a set of rituals to be carried out in the Temple; only priests have to carry out extra religious activities on the sabbath.

CHAPTER TWO

SABBATH AS HOLY DAY OF THE JEWS:
EARLY JEWISH LITERATURE

Introduction   .

The texts of the Hebrew Bible show that the sabbath did not have a fixed, unchanging importance in the understanding of Jewish communities before the turn of the era. Some texts show a higher reverence for sabbath than others; some require sacrifices on the sabbath and others do not. The one feature common to all the texts about the sabbath is that they do not provide clear instructions for sabbath rituals for non-priestly Jews.

The gradual *development* of the importance of sabbath that was adumbrated in the biblical texts can be more fully identified in extrabiblical Jewish texts. There the various writers present their views of the sabbath as a religious entity with greater power to exact particular human behaviours than was evident in the Hebrew Bible. So, while some extra-biblical texts describe a sabbath with more stringent rules governing behaviour and thoughts, others demand from their followers further religious observances, and yet others require from their community a deeper attitude of reverence for the day itself. In each of the texts studied here the sabbath has been aggrandised in one or more of these aspects, but only the second type of response produces extra behaviour on the sabbath that might be evaluated as worship.

Not surprisingly, any such developments were not uniform throughout the writings of the period, so the different, although similar, trends can be seen more clearly if data from the Apocryphal and Deutero-Canonical works are presented together followed by data from the Dead Sea Scrolls and *Jubilees*. Then, from the different images of sabbath in the lives and thoughts of the different groups of Jews, conclusions can be drawn about sabbath praxis.

The Sabbath in the Apocryphal Literature

In some apocryphal texts the sabbath day has acquired a new character: it is no longer merely a day set aside for rest, once a week, but is a special time with some quality of holiness that it possesses intrinsically. This quality causes the sabbath both to affect life on other days as well and to have the power to exact more attention than was demanded from the believing community in the Hebrew Bible narratives. However, even though the sabbath might achieve a greater level of influence in Jewish community life, that would not entail the development of a set of religious practices.

In certain other apocryphal works, the sabbath is not mentioned at all, even where one might expect it to appear, as in the description of the piety of the young man, Tobit.[1] Also, although Ben Sira records the names of some holy days, and refers to the exalting and hallowing of certain (unspecified) days,[2] he does not mention the sabbath at all. Even Ben Sira's lengthy descriptions, in chs. 34–35, of the Temple cult and its sacrifices, and of the proper behaviour of one who keeps the law, make no mention of the sabbath by name.[3] The sabbath does not play an obvious part in what goes on in the Temple cult as he describes it. Ben Sira speaks of sacrifices, offerings of first fruits, of tithes and of prayer, but there is no reference to the sabbath.

The range of ways of regarding or ignoring the sabbath visible in the early Jewish texts, reinforces our earlier conclusion that different groups within Jewish society had different views of the value and role of the sabbath in Jewish life. The lack of interest in the sabbath displayed in texts such as Tobit and Ben Sira contributes little to our study, but a more detailed analysis of the texts that promote or honour the sabbath can show how the sabbath was regarded by the communities who preserved such texts.

---

[1] Tob. 1.3-9.

[2] Sir. 33.7-13; see also in Chapter 3 a discussion on the lack of references to 'synagogue' in Ben Sira.

[3] E. Rivkin, 'Ben Sira and the Nonexistence of the Synagogue: A Study in Historical Method', in *In the Time of Harvest: Essays in Honor of Abba Hillel Silver* (New York: Macmillan, 1963), pp. 320-54 (331-34).

Texts about the Sabbath

References to sabbath occur in Judith, 1 and 2 Maccabees and 1 Esdras.

In Jdt. 8.4-8, the beautiful and pious Judith is described as living as a widow for three years and four months, during which time she 'fasted all the days of her widowhood, except the day before the sabbath and the sabbath itself, the day before the new moon and the new moon itself, and the feasts and days of rejoicing of the house of Israel'. Apparently, both sabbath and new moon allow freedom from fasting because they are holy days, but both also occasion that freedom on one extra day, the day before. The holy ambience of both these days extends beyond the twenty-four hours of the day itself.

In 1 Macc. 1.20-50, there is a passage that describes the proscription of Jewish religious practices by Antiochus Epiphanes. There the sabbaths are described as having been 'turned into a reproach' (1.39) and 'profaned' (1.43, 45). These sabbaths are evidently more than a portion of time set aside for rest; they are religious or holy entities that can be besmirched in some way, as could an altar or shrine, by the actions of outsiders.[4]

In 1 Maccabees 2, a group of Jewish rebels is pursued by the Antiochus's soldiers who aim to attack them on the sabbath day (2.32). They refuse to profane the sabbath day by fighting on it (2.34); they are attacked on it (2.38), and perish. Later in ch. 2, the group of rebels under Mattathias decide to fight on the sabbath day on future occasions (2.41). The same issue arises again, when Jonathan is in charge (9.34, 43) and fighting on sabbath is again sanctioned.[5] The importance of keeping the day in the traditional way is set against the importance of many human lives, but the decision to give human lives the priority is not easily made. The respect for human life narrowly outranks the respect for the sabbath.

In 2 Macc. 12.38 keeping the sabbath is mentioned, with purification as a customary preparation, and in 15.3 the issue of fighting on the sabbath recurs. Nicanor orders his reluctant Jewish soldiers to fight, but he does not succeed in this aim.

---

[4] See also the use of this imagery in Ezek. 20–23, discussed in Chapter 1.
[5] See also full discussion on the issue of fighting on sabbath in Kubo, 'Sabbath in the Intertestamental Period', pp. 61-65.

The issue of the importance of feast days, including the sabbath, is addressed in 1 Macc. 10.34. All feast days are declared by King Demetrius, in a letter to the Jews, to be days of immunity from any exaction or annoyance. Extra days of immunity are given on the three days before a feast and the three days after; but there is no extension for sabbath or new moon, which are therefore presumably lesser in importance than the annual feasts, though important enough to merit one day of immunity each.

In 2 Macc. 5.21-26 there is described an incident in which Jews were slaughtered because they did not suspect there could be an attack on the sabbath. And 2 Macc. 6 describes how, after the replacement of the Jewish cult by the worship of Zeus, the Jews were no longer permitted to keep either the sabbath or the traditional feasts, and claims that some were burned to death for observing the sabbath secretly in caves.[6] This opaque reference will be discussed below.

2 Maccabees 8 includes a description of a Jewish victory and explains that pursuit of the fleeing enemy was discontinued because it was late on the day before the sabbath. Thereafter the victors 'kept the sabbath, giving great praise and thanks to the Lord' (8.27). After the sabbath they resumed distribution of the booty to the needy among them.

In 1 Esdras 5.52, the restoration of the Jerusalem cult at the time of Ezra is retold, and the days for sacrifices are listed: on sabbaths and at new moons and at all the consecrated feasts. This list differs interestingly from its source text in Ezra 3 where sabbath is not mentioned. Perhaps it indicates a developing reverence for the sabbath.[7]

Discussion of the Sabbath in the Apocryphal Literature

The change of perception of sabbath, from being a day like any other days, save that it was chosen and singled out as a day of rest, kept holy by the inaction of the people observing it, to being regarded as a holy entity in itself and of itself—possessing holiness intrinsically, can be seen throughout these Jewish writings. Jewish people now

---

[6] Cf. a parallel text in Josephus, *Antiquities* 12.274-77, in *Josephus*, VII (tr. R. Marcus; LCL; Cambridge, MA: Harvard University Press, 1961).

[7] See discussion in Chapter 1.

thought differently about the sabbath—but did they carry out any special activities on sabbath? And could these activities be classed as worship?

In the book of Judith the sabbath, and the day before it, are days when the pious widow in the midst of her mourning rites is free of the obligation of fasting. By affecting what she could or could not do on Fridays as well as Saturdays, the sabbath has extended its numinous quality through *time*.

This text describes Judith's 'religious character and practice', and, therefore, outlines what constitutes her religious practice on these holy days.[8] But all that is said is that she may eat rather than fast, and no particular religious rituals or observances are mentioned. All that may be discovered from this text is that the sabbath can affect the normal actions of daily life on another day as well as on sabbath.

In the more impassioned writings of 1 and 2 Maccabees, which share a similar evaluation of the importance of the sabbath in the life of their communities, there are multiple references to the sabbath in the discussion as to whether Jews should fight on the sabbath or not. This *more concentrated attention* indicates the extreme reverence with which the day of rest was regarded. The sabbath law had to be discussed by the community, and then interpreted, or re-interpreted, to exclude fighting from classes of work forbidden on the sabbath. Such an interpretation would aid the survival of those who wished to keep the sabbath week by week, thus guaranteeing continued observance of the sabbath.[9]

In recognition of the importance given to these discussions in the texts, attention is drawn to the fact that, as Goldstein puts it, 'Jason's efforts to show that Judas observed the Sabbath rigorously[10] are at least as massive as the efforts in 1 Maccabees to justify Mattathias' decision to permit warfare on the Sabbath (1 Macc. 2.39-41; cf. 9.43-49)'.[11] Goldstein sees further signs of the importance of the sabbath

---

[8] C.A. Moore, *Judith: A New Translation with Introduction and Commentary* (The Anchor Bible, 40; New York: Doubleday, 1985), pp. 185, 181.

[9] An account of these events can also be found in the works of Josephus: *War* 2.456-57, 517, 634, in *Josephus*, II (tr. H.St.J. Thackeray; LCL; Cambridge, MA: Harvard University Press, 1976); *Antiquities* 12.274-77; 13.10-13, 252-53, 337; 14.63-64, 226-46, in *Josephus*, VII (tr. R. Marcus; LCL; Cambridge, MA: Harvard University Press, 1961).

[10] 2 Macc. 8.25-28; 12.38; 15.1-5; cf. 12.31-32.

[11] J.A. Goldstein, *I Maccabees: A New Translation with Introduction and*

in his understanding of 1 Macc. 9.34 as a 'misplaced gloss',[12] for although the text represents the sabbath as the day on which Bacchides learned of the appointment of Jonathan as leader in place of his brother Judas, Goldstein believes that the phrase 'on the sabbath' originally earned its place in the margin of the text because of the importance of the issue of violating the sabbath by fighting. So, he convincingly argues, fighting on the sabbath was what was at issue, not whichever day it was that Bacchides learned about Jonathan's appointment.[13]

The three extra days of immunity given by Demetrius (1 Macc. 10.34) on either side of the main feast days can be thought of as enabling travel to and from Jerusalem at each of the three pilgrim feasts.[14] The sabbath, like new moon, has an immunity only for itself, since no travel is involved.

In 2 Macc. 6.1-11, we find the story of the suppression of Judaism, and the cameo picture of Jews assembling in caves to observe the sabbath secretly. Goldstein refers to these people eight times as 'Sabbath observers', and gives no synonyms for the phrase.[15] Perhaps he believes that there are no alternatives that would not affect the meaning he wishes to ascribe to the words. All that may be deduced is that whatever the observance was it could be recognised as subversive and so, had to be done in secret.

The thanksgiving offered to God on the sabbath (2 Macc. 8.24-29), leans heavily on the language of prayer in the Hebrew Bible. It does, however, represent communal praise and thanksgiving following a victory won with God's help—not the performance of a regular weekly sabbath ritual.[16] This is the only passage which gives evidence of worship of God on the sabbath, but, because there are no further details, and because of the way the section is introduced, it seems to be prompted by the victory rather than the sabbath. So, there is nothing here about regular sabbath worship.

Commentary (The Anchor Bible, 41; New York: Doubleday, 1976), p. 87.

[12] Goldstein, I Maccabees, pp. 378, 380-81, 385-86.

[13] See also J.R. Bartlett, The First and Second Books of the Maccabees (CBC; Cambridge: CUP, 1973), pp. 39, 121.

[14] Bartlett, Maccabees, p. 137; see also Josephus, Antiquities 13.52.

[15] J.A. Goldstein, II Maccabees: A New Translation with Introduction and Commentary (The Anchor Bible, 41a; New York: Doubleday, 1983), pp. 279-80.

[16] Goldstein, 2 Maccabees, pp. 336-37.

An important sign of Jason's reinforcing of the strict sabbath observance of Judas is the description of purification for the sabbath in 2 Macc. 12.38.[17] Goldstein points out that there is no scriptural warrant for this pre-sabbath purification. The description of it in the text as a 'custom' shows that the community whose interests are preserved in this text were extending the laws of Torah to display more reverence for the holiness of sabbath, in a way that involved the members in a cleansing process. Such a process requires time, provision of water and facilities, and the group's acquiescence in the ritual. We may conclude that members of this group believed that sabbath observance required this extra commitment. This is a description of an act preparatory to sabbath observance, but, of course, it is an act that takes place before the sabbath actually begins.

As for the addition of 'sabbath' to the list of holy days in 1 Esdr. 5.52; it is an interesting hint of the greater importance given to the sabbath in the time frame of the author of 1 Esdras. Myers, commenting on the Esdras text, does not refer to the disparity between the list of holy days given here and in the biblical book of Ezra, namely the inclusion of 'sabbaths' in the list along with new moons and appointed feasts.[18] This is disappointing, from the point of view of this discussion, and especially noticeable since at other junctures he is at pains to point out the closeness of the two textual traditions; this difference remains invisible or unnoticed.[19] The variation between Ezra and 1 Esdras seems to me quite crucial, indicating a possible change in perspective as to how sabbath was regarded by the two communities or within the two time zones. And this change goes some way towards confirming my belief that the sabbath had a much more definite and important place in the religious consciousness of the later groups who produced these texts.[20]

---

[17] Goldstein, 2 Maccabees, pp. 447-48.

[18] J.M. Myers, I and II Esdras: Introduction, Translation and Commentary (The Anchor Bible, 42; New York: Doubleday, 1974), p. 70.

[19] Myers, I and II Esdras, pp. 69, 70.

[20] Many commentators 'solve' the problem of the difference between the two texts by saying that the word 'sabbath' has been lost from the Ezra text; see discussion on Ezra 3.5 in Ch. 1.

Conclusions about the Sabbath in the Apocryphal Works

The pictures of the sabbath that may be uncovered from the apocryphal works are varied, but the day can be fairly described as a day with some compelling quality that attracts the loyalty of certain groups of Jews.

In the books of the Maccabees, sabbath-keeping is a key distinguishing factor of the group of resistance fighters who refuse to modify their behaviour in accordance with the edicts of the Seleucid rulers, but also a distinguishing factor they have to modify in order to survive. They agree, paradoxically, to re-interpret the sabbath restrictions on activity for the present in order to be free to keep the sabbath more faithfully in the future. However, in spite of the intensity of their commitment to the sabbath, as for instance in their custom of purification before the sabbath, nowhere is sabbath worship (or prayer) described or even mentioned as an activity these fervent Jews undertook on a regular basis.

In the book of Judith the waiving of mourning rituals on the sabbath is extended to Friday as well, producing the double result of extending the benefits of the sabbath and also of bringing the sabbath to mind a full twenty-four hours before it began. But the sabbath is nothing more than a day of freedom and rest for Judith; she carries out no special sabbath activities.

And in the heavily theological and pious discussions in the quite different world of the book of Tobit, the sabbath is never referred to at all, which is further evidence of how varied the attitudes to the sabbath were. For me, it is impossible to justify the belief—held by many scholars—that all those observant Jews undertook sabbath worship every week, though the texts never mention it.

To some Jews and to some Jewish writers the sabbath was important as an *ideal* that stirred the imagination and the blood. To other groups it was merely the day of rest, a day at variance with the other six only in the matter of what was *not* done on that special day. If people are described in the texts as faithful Jews, that does not apparently determine how they would regard the sabbath day. People with deep devotion to the sabbath and people who never mention it are both represented in the literature as members of the Jewish community of intertestamental times.

Texts about the Sabbath in the Dead Sea Scrolls

The traditional image of the weekly sabbath as a day with worship rituals especial to itself can be given more substance by a search among the Dead Sea Scrolls. In the Psalms Scroll (11Ps^a 27.4-8) we find a descriptive summary of the psalms and songs supposedly composed by David, namely three hundred and sixty-four daily psalms plus fifty-two for the sabbath:

> And he wrote 3600 psalms; and songs to sing before the altar over the whole-burnt *tamid* offering every day, for all the days of the year, 364; and for the *qorban* of the Sabbaths, 52 songs; and for the *qorban* of the New Moons and for all the Solemn Assemblies and for the Day of Atonement, 30 songs.[21]

The arithmetic confirms both a weekly sabbath, and the implied practice of singing an extra and particular sabbath psalm, in addition to the daily psalm. Compared with the one psalm designated specifically as 'for the sabbath' in the Hebrew psalter, the collection referred to here represents quite a development in sabbath worship.

Then, in the liturgical fragments known as 'The Words of the Heavenly Lights' (4Q504) there is a heading, 'Hymns for the Sabbath Day', which precedes a short exhortation to angels and to all other sentient beings to give praise and sing to God.[22]

Fragments of a text known as the 'Songs of the Sabbath Sacrifice' have been found at Qumrân and Masada.[23] The text is an angelic liturgy of heavenly praises for the first thirteen sabbaths of the year, listed sabbath by sabbath, e.g. 'the seventh Sabbath on the sixteenth of the second month'.[24] These texts imply sabbath worship by angels in the heavenly sanctuary; but the physical evidence of the scrolls is limited to the thirteen songs for the first quarter of the year.[25]

---

[21] J.A. Sanders, *The Psalms Scroll of Cave 11* (DJD, 4; Oxford: Clarendon Press, 1972), pp. 202, 210; Baumgarten, 'The Counting of the Sabbath', pp. 277-86.

[22] M. Baillet, *Qumrân Grotte 4*, III: *4Q482–4Q520* (DJD, 7; Oxford: OUP, 1982), pp. 137, 150-51; G. Vermes, *The Dead Sea Scrolls in English* (3rd edn; Sheffield: JSOT Press, 1987), pp. 217, 219-20.

[23] 4Q400-407; 11QShirShabb.

[24] C. Newsom, *Songs of the Sabbath Sacrifice: A Critical Edition* (Harvard Semitic Studies, 27; Atlanta: Scholars Press, 1985), p. 211; cf. also J. Strugnell, 'The Angelic Liturgy at Qumrân—4Q Serek Sîrôt 'Ôlat Haššabbāt', in *Congress Volume: Oxford 1959* (Vetus Testamentum Supplements, 7; Leiden: Brill, 1960), pp. 318-45 (320); Vermes, *Dead Sea Scrolls*, pp. 221-30.

[25] Newsom, *Songs of the Sabbath Sacrifice*, p. 5.

A more direct form of evidence of the esteem in which sabbath was held by the Qumrân community can be found in the Damascus Document (CD 11–12), where there are injunctions as to the purity and cleanliness of the community members on the sabbath—including elaborate guidelines for proper behaviour on the sabbath (with seventeen occurrences of the word sabbath and two quotations from Torah about the sabbath), such as would preserve the community member from defiling the sabbath by so much as thoughts about the morrow's work, or by any actions that deal with commerce, travel or work of any sort.[26] Altogether there are twenty-eight prohibitions of specific actions which might be done on the sabbath, innocently and thoughtlessly, if they were not kept firmly in mind as infringing sabbath law, for example, the prohibition addressed to child-minders to prevent them carrying a child on sabbath. But there are no particular requirements with respect to either individual or communal prayer or other activity of worship on the sabbath.

One of the stated sabbath requirements is the wearing of clean clothes, and after ten intervening sabbath regulations the point is made that no one unclean and in need of washing should enter the house of worship when a holy service of worship is taking place.[27] This rule is placed at the end of the section referring to sabbath and may well complete the section, but as it is also the transition to the next, and more general, section of the document it is not explicit that this does refer to the sabbath. If it does, then we have a correspondence with the purification custom described in 2 Macc. 12.38, and more importantly a reference to worship on the sabbath.

Earlier in the Damascus Document (CD 3.14-15), God's gifts to Israel through the covenant are listed as 'His holy Sabbaths and His glorious feasts, the testimonies of His righteousness and the ways of His truth'.[28] The sabbath is again seen as an entity, something given to Israel by God.

In the War Scroll (1QM 2.4), there is a list of holy days on which courses of sanctuary officiants are standing by, which reads, 'at their appointed times, on New Moons and on Sabbaths ...'[29]

---

[26] Vermes, *Dead Sea Scrolls*, pp. 12-13, 82, 95-96.

[27] Vermes, *Dead Sea Scrolls*, p. 96.

[28] Vermes, *Dead Sea Scrolls*, p. 85.

[29] Vermes, *Dead Sea Scrolls*, p. 106; or 'on their festivals, on their new moons and the sabbaths ...' (Y. Yadin, *The Scroll of the War of the Sons of Light against the Sons*

Two small fragments of a scroll from Cave 4 (4Q513.3-4 = 4QOrd[b]) refer to the waving of the Omer and the view of the writer that it should not have the power to take precedence over sabbath rest.[30] Baillet lines up these fragments together to read:

4	3
... convocation [sainte ...]	balancer (la) gerbe
... le jour du sabbath *pour* ...	sans compter ... sabbats ...
... célébrer un mémorial *po[ur*...]	l'erreur d'aveuglement de ...
... qu'*a* m[ont]ré *un augure* ...	et non de la Loi de Moïse ...
... et	

Discussion on the Sabbath in the Dead Sea Scrolls

The texts from the Dead Sea community indicate a progression of fifty-two weeks through the religious year punctuated by sabbaths which were held in considerable regard by members of the community. The weekly sabbath was a day both of observance and worship for the community members.

Those who framed the Damascus Covenant extended the strictness of the rules governing the sabbath beyond what is found the Hebrew Bible. The community took the sabbath very seriously indeed, and with so many curbs on their behaviour, the fact of the day's being the sabbath could not have been out of their consciousness for much time during the duration of the day.

Baumgarten expounds the text from Qumrân about waving of the Omer having no power to take precedence over sabbath rest as an indication that the Dead Sea community thought that 'the ruling of the Pharisaic sages that the harvesting of the Omer overrides the Sabbath was an "error of blindness" and was "not in accordance with the Law of Moses"'.[31] If this interpretation is correct, this is evidence of a higher valuing of the sabbath by the Qumrân community than by an unidentified group, perhaps influential Jews in Jerusalem, with the community being ready to take umbrage at those

---

of Darkness [tr. B. and C. Rabin; Oxford: OUP, 1962], pp. 202, 264).

[30] Baillet, *Qumrân Grotte 4*, pp. 289-90, and Plate 72; see also J.M. Baumgarten, 'Recent Discoveries and Halakhah in the Hellenistic-Roman Period', in S. Talmon, ed., *Jewish Civilization in the Hellenistic-Roman Period* (Sheffield: JSOT Press and Philadelphia: Trinity Press International, 1991), pp. 147-58 (148).

[31] Baumgarten, *Recent Discoveries*, pp. 147-58, esp. pp. 148-50.

who gave sabbath less status than they did.[32]

The list of holy days given in the War Scroll: appointed times, new moons and sabbaths, is surprising in the texts of a community that followed a solar calendar and which could be expected to think of the 'new thing' (חדש) as the beginning of the calendar month.[33] I suggest that, in order for the lists to have meaning, they must be recognised to be quotations from the Hebrew Bible, maintaining a link with the past practices of the Temple cult. That understanding would render the conflict of meaning of חדש between solar and lunar calendars irrelevant for the lists would not be referring to any feasts actually celebrated by the community at that time.

It is more valuable to draw conclusions about the community's view of sabbath from the texts that deal exclusively with sabbath, and to say that the Qumrân community did give sabbath great attention and accorded the *concept of the sabbath* power to dominate the actions of their lives and the content of their thoughts on every sabbath day.

It has been suggested that the sequence of special songs for the sabbath day are in some way a replacement for the sacrifices of the Temple cult.[34]

But more important still is the fact that the group worshipped together—as a community—on the sabbath in ways that included the singing of special songs.

Prayer at Qumrân

Prayer is believed to have been an important part of daily life at Qumrân so could be relevant in a consideration of sabbath worship there. But unfortunately the fragmentary state of the evidence makes definite conclusions impossible.

Yadin believes that the community at Qumrân, realising that they could not feel happy about participating in Temple sacrifices, had to

---

[32] Reading the two fragments together, as Baillet does, would not affect the essentials of this exegesis.

[33] This query was raised by P.R. Davies in a private discussion.

[34] S. Talmon, 'The Emergence of Institutionalized Prayer in Israel in the Light of the Qumrân Literature', in *Qumrân: Sa piété, sa théologie et son milieu* (Bibliotheca ephemeridum theologicarum lovaniensum, 46; Gembloux: Duculot; Leuven: Leuven University Press, 1978), p. 275.

'content themselves with prayers and special ceremonies at home'.[35] He also finds that many of the prayers in the War Scroll recall biblical prayers before, during and after battles and are similar in style to them. So it seems to me valid to make a connection between these prayers at Qumrân and the description of thanksgiving after the battle reported in 2 Macc. 10.38.[36]

If we recall from Chapter 1 that Talmon regards the prayer offered by Israel as being primarily offered by priests in the holy silence in the Temple,[37] we can imagine that any inheritors of those traditions could well be expected to regard prayer in this light, and so the members of the Qumrân community would believe that their role involved continuing that type of prayer in their community gatherings. There is evidence of daily prayers said in the morning and evening, and also of special prayers for festivals.[38]

Sanders takes these prayers as evidence of twice daily prayers by the Qumrân community,[39] but Baillet, the editor of the fragments, is more cautious and recommends that the month indicated in the texts by the phases of the moon be regarded as an 'ideal' month, rather than any particular month.[40]

So, the details of sabbath worship and activities from the texts available so far indicate no requirement to say particular prayers as part of sabbath worship.

Conclusions about the Sabbath in the Dead Sea Scrolls

There is a definite increase in the reverence and attention accorded to the sabbath by the members of the Qumrân community over against that evident in the texts of the Hebrew Bible.

From the evidence of the fragment about the waving of the Omer, we can surmise that the Qumrân community had a considered view

---

[35] Yadin, *War Scroll*, p. 201.

[36] Yadin links these two references, but makes no comment on them as parallels (*War Scroll*, p. 228); see also discussion above.

[37] Talmon, 'Institutionalized Prayer', p. 268.

[38] Baillet, *Qumrân Grotte 4*, pp. 105-36, presents the reconstructed fragments of daily prayers (4Q503), and on pp. 175-214 of the prayers for feast days (4Q507–4Q509), suggesting New Year and the pilgrim feasts as likely occasions for these prayers.

[39] Sanders, *Jewish Law*, p. 73.

[40] Baillet, *Qumrân Grotte 4*, p. 106.

of the importance of the sabbath. And there are many more rules restricting behaviour, and restricting it more severely than in the biblical texts.

On sabbaths there are gatherings of the community at which it seems likely that particular songs are sung by the community on the different, numbered, sabbaths through the year.

What is less easy to determine is whether the members of the community sang their special sabbath songs as a community of priests giving a sacrifice of song to God, or whether they can truly be described as non-priestly Jews gathering for worship on the sabbath. The texts give evidence of regular, communal sabbath worship, but whether the members of the community can be classed as ordinary Jews is not made evident.

Texts about the Sabbath in Jubilees

In *Jub.* 1.14, sabbath occurs in a list of days sacred to Yahweh, 'new moons, sabbaths, festivals, jubilees and ordinances', in the observing of which the reader is warned to take special care, and in 23.19 the people are threatened with punishment because 'they have forgotten the commandments and covenant and festivals and months and sabbaths and the jubilees and all of the judgments'.

In *Jub.* 2 we are told that the sun has been created as a sign for days, sabbaths, months, feasts and years,[41] and also that the 'angels of the presence and all the angels of holiness ... keep the sabbath day with him [God] in heaven and on earth'.[42]

Later in *Jub.* 2, there is a long passage on the significance of the sabbath as sign, day of rest and day on which the people are to eat and drink and bless the Creator.

Chapter 50, the closing chapter of *Jubilees*, is devoted to laws about the sabbath. It succeeds a long section dealing with Moses and passover and its opening section makes immediate links between the sabbath and law.

Here the sabbath laws are much stricter than in the Hebrew Bible or in the Qumrân texts and affirm, or re-affirm, the death penalty for

---

[41] *Jub.* 2.9, tr. O.S. Wintermute in 'Jubilees' in *The Old Testament Pseudepigrapha*, II (J.H. Charlesworth, ed., London: Darton, Longman & Todd, 1985), pp. 35-142 (56).
[42] *Jub.* 2.18.

infringing the sabbath, for example, by work, profanation, marital relations, discussing business plans or travel, drawing water, lifting or carrying anything, ploughing, lighting a fire, riding or other travelling, slaughtering or snaring animals, fasting or waging war.

What are permitted, and stated to be the purposes to which the sabbath should be put are, for the ordinary people: eating, drinking, being satisfied, and resting from all occupations; and for the priests, although they are not mentioned by name: burning incense, blessing God and offering gifts and sacrifices in the sanctuary. No activities that could be construed as worship are expected of the readers of *Jubilees*.

Discussion on the Sabbath in Jubilees

There seems to be a distinct ideology of sabbath in the book of *Jubilees*, a sharper and more authoritarian view of how the sabbath should be regarded and observed.

In his study of the book of *Jubilees*, VanderKam claims that the writer wished 'his fellow Jews to observe carefully the divine laws about sacrifice, festivals, sabbath and the cultic calendar in order to avert the sort of punishments that God had meted out to their ancestors'.[43] He also believes that, in *Jub.* 2, the writer of the book was purposely drawing parallels between Israel and the sabbath in terms of what I would call 'an alternating induced harmony': the Lord had blessed and sanctified both Israel and the sabbath, therefore 'keeping sabbath is a means by which Israel's holiness is marked and through which it finds expression'.[44] If VanderKam is right, then there is quite a new understanding of the sabbath embedded in this text. Here the sabbath has power to influence the cosmic harmony on behalf of Israel, and perhaps the proper keeping of the sabbath on earth has influence over God himself, encouraging him to act on behalf of Israel. This implies an alternating current of devotion to sabbath-keeping connecting heaven and Israel in a perpetual, reciprocal linking.

---

[43] J.C. VanderKam, 'The Book of Jubilees', in *Outside the Old Testament* (ed. M. de Jonge; Cambridge Commentaries on the Writings of the Jewish and Christian World 200 BC to AD 200, 4; Cambridge: CUP, 1985), pp. 111-44 (113).

[44] VanderKam, 'Jubilees', p. 119.

Taking a less psychological view of the function of the sabbath in this text, Charlesworth regards this text[45] as an assertion that these particular (important) groups of angels have kept the sabbath in this way since the first week of creation,[46] which clearly shows an extension of reverence for the sabbath to the cosmic domain. But, as with all other texts studied so far, there is no suggestion that any of the duration of the sabbath should be spent in worship activities, in heaven or on earth.

And when in *Jub.* 50.12 war on sabbath is prohibited, this looks like a presentation of an opposite viewpoint to that expressed in Maccabees, or like a description of the situation that prevailed at the beginning of the story of the Maccabees, but unaffected by the experiences and rethinking that they underwent and undertook.

The one activity that is enjoined for the sabbath appears to be a domestic one: in *Jub.* 2 readers are told to eat, drink and bless the one who created all things, and in *Jub.* 50, they are told to eat, drink, be satisfied, rest and refrain from all work. Perhaps these texts imply the celebration of a sabbath evening meal, which was certainly a recognised feature of Jewish life in Rome by the first century CE.[47]

The readers are expressly told that on the sabbath day they should not fast; they are told to eat, drink, bless the Creator and be satisfied. They are not told to do anything else.

Conclusions about Sabbath in Jubilees

In *Jubilees* there is an increase in the *thrall* of the sabbath as evidenced by the widening of application of the death penalty for breaking, defiling or polluting the sabbath, even by such acts as marital relations or planning the next day's journey. The sabbath was able to control more aspects of life than work alone, and the sabbath seems to have become more important to the community that produced *Jubilees* than it was to the writers of the Hebrew Bible, paralleling its increased importance also to the Qumrân community.

Heaven observed the sabbath and on earth the Jewish people were

---

[45] *Jub.* 2.16-18, 30.
[46] J.H. Charlesworth, *The Old Testament Pseudepigrapha*, II (London: Darton, Longman & Todd, 1985), pp. 38, 58.
[47] See discussion in Chapter 4.

supposed to follow suit. Sabbath observance was regarded as a privilege.[48] The same atmosphere of religious fervour and holy elevation of the sabbath can be discerned in Jubilees as was discernible in the books of the Maccabees and the Dead Sea Scrolls.

But there is nonetheless no exhortation towards, or description of, sabbath worship for lay people.

Conclusions about Sabbath in Early Jewish Literature

Clearly there was no longstanding stability in the views held about the sabbath, whether as day of rest or as day of worship, and its influence was still growing and extending at the turn of the era.

The sabbath shows signs of achieving prominence in the religious consciousness of the Jewish groups represented by the texts of this period. More interest in, and emphasis on, what is owed to the sabbath is expressed in many of the texts, expressed mainly through increased restrictions on activities and thoughts on the sabbath, the only injunction to positive action being found in *Jubilees* where the readers are instructed to eat and drink and be satisfied on the sabbath—though not necessarily *only* on the sabbath.

So, in spite of all the later elaboration of the status of the sabbath, these texts are, like the Hebrew Bible, concerned only with sabbath rest and observance, not with worship. There are only a few exceptions to be made to this general statements: the liturgical fragments from Qumrân (11QShirShabb) which point to a sabbath on which communal worship took place, as evidenced by the numbering and sequencing of the sabbaths through the year, and by the fifty-two songs for the sabbath day (11QPs^a 27).

While noting with interest these evidences of worship on the sabbath at Qumrân, we must, however, bear in mind that this community was far removed from mainstream Judaism, both geographically and theologically. Thus any practices celebrated there may have been quite alien to the activities of city- or country-dwelling Jews. And whether the members of the Qumrân community could be classed as ordinary, lay worshippers remains a moot point.

---

[48] Charlesworth, *Old Testament Pseudepigrapha*, II, p. 40, claims that the privilege was not open to Gentiles.

What this survey has revealed, then, is that, for the ordinary Jew, there are no prescriptions for sabbath activities, or for private or public worship on the sabbath in any of these extra-biblical texts. The sabbath is to be a day of rest and also of mental relaxation and enjoyment. Also, it has been shown that the sabbath was not a fixed unchanging institution, but increased in importance during the period reflected in this literature.

CHAPTER THREE

SABBATH AS DAY OF REST AND STUDY OF THE LAW: PHILO AND JOSEPHUS

Background

Philo and Josephus provide a wide range of literary evidence about the life of the Jewish communities they knew in Palestine, Italy, Egypt and elsewhere in the Diaspora in the first century CE.[1] Both mixed socially with Jews and non-Jews at all levels of society and were adept in the use of appropriate and persuasive language. Their writings display the intellectual ground common to Jews and non-Jews in the first century CE.[2]

As Philo lived in Alexandria, he was a Jew of the Diaspora, but because he wrote as an apologist, and since his writings have been preserved not in Jewish but in Christian collections, there is some hesitation in scholarly circles about regarding him as a typical Jew. What have been described as '"syncretistic" tendencies' have been noted in his work,[3] and Philo has been described as the Jews'

---

[1] The writings of Philo may be securely dated to the first part of the first century of the common era, since he was a member of the legation sent from Alexandria to Rome to treat with Gaius Caligula in 41 CE.

[2] The background history and geography for this study has been obtained from a broad range of sources: H.I. Bell, *Jews and Christians in Egypt* (London: The Trustees of the British Museum, 1924), pp. 10-29; A.Y. Collins, 'Insiders and Outsiders in the Book of Revelation', in *The Jews among Pagans and Christians* (London: Routledge, 1992), pp. 187-218; M. Grant, *The Jews in the Roman World* (London: Weidenfeld and Nicolson, 1973); E. Haenchen, *The Acts of the Apostles: A Commentary* (tr. B. Noble, G. Shinn and H. Anderson, rev. R.McL. Wilson; Oxford: Blackwell, 1971); A.R.C. Leaney, *The Jewish and Christian World 200 BC to AD 200* (Cambridge Commentaries on the Writings of the Jewish and Christian World 200 BC to AD 200, 7; Cambridge: CUP, 1984); E.M. Smallwood, *The Jews under Roman Rule: From Pompey to Diocletian* (Studies in Judaism in Late Antiquity, 20; Leiden: Brill, 1976); and M. Whittaker, *Jews and Christians: Graeco-Roman Views* (Cambridge Commentaries on the Writings of the Jewish and Christian World 200 BC to AD 200, 6; Cambridge: CUP, 1984).

[3] M. Hengel, *Judaism and Hellenism: Studies in their Encounter in Palestine during*

'propagandist' whose 'numerous literary works clothed Judaism in Greek dress'.[4] However, despite these critical comments on the use of Philo as a source, there is the fact that he was writing within a completely Jewish community, before the time of the existence of the Christian Church, and he was regarded by that Jewish community as a suitable envoy in their dealings with Rome.[5]

I prefer to regard Philo as a typical Jewish intellectual of his day, and to survey his writings to see what he relates, whether on purpose, or in the bygoing, about Jews and their activities on the sabbath. The activities he describes will be examined to decide whether they should properly be classed as worship.

Josephus's writings span the latter part of the first century CE, and are of various kinds: apologies, histories and autobiography.[6] With Josephus's writings, as with all writings, we are limited to what he as author wishes to convey to us, but occasionally some material useful to the purpose of this study is embedded in, or described as background to, the matters Josephus is explaining.

In spite of the value of Josephus's extensive writings, scholars have expressed doubts as to the veracity and reliability of what he relates. Grant judges that his 'fascinating works ... show him up as self-congratulatory to the point of thoroughgoing mendacity'.[7] But taking a more positive view, and although allowing that Josephus (and Philo too) exaggerate in their claims about the acceptability of Jewish practices in the Graeco-Roman world, Gager believes that they 'stand closer, far closer, to the truth than has commonly been assumed'.[8]

Taking these qualifications of Josephus as a reliable historian into account does not devalue him as an important source for the period in question, even though he expresses his view of the matters he dis-

---

the *Early Hellenistic Period*, 2 vols. (tr. J. Bowden; London: SCM Press, 1974), I, p. 114; cf. I, pp. 149, 165-66.

[4] Grant, *The Jews*, pp. 122, 126; see also pp. 127-28.

[5] A thumbnail sketch of Philo's social standing can be found in V.A. Tcherikover and A. Fuks, *Corpus papyrorum judaicarum*, I (Cambridge, MA: Harvard University Press, 1957), p. 67.

[6] J. Juster, *Les Juifs dans l'empire romain: Leur condition juridique, économique et sociale*, 2 vols. (Burt Franklin Research & Source Works Series, 79; New York: Burt Franklin, reprint, n.d.; first published Paris, 1914), I, p. 12.

[7] Grant, *The Jews*, p. 188.

[8] J.G. Gager, *The Origins of Anti-Semitism* (Oxford: OUP, 1985), p. 86.

cusses in ways that best serve his own purposes. What he wrote could well display bias, but it is nonetheless unlikely to have been unintelligible to his readers, or at odds with his readers' knowledge of the milieu in which they lived.

Since Philo belonged to the Diaspora, he wrote of the Temple as an institution that was far from his experience. He knew of προσευχαί as centres where local Jews congregated to arrange the everyday business of living as Jews in an alien culture; these he describes with ease and familiarity. Josephus, for different reasons, also writes as if divorced from the Temple. He knew of a *former* Temple and of present-day προσευχαί and συναγωγαί where communities of Jews gathered to deal with all matters of concern to them.

A preliminary issue that needs to be clarified is that there can be no easy equation of sabbath observance and sabbath worship; the existence of one cannot be assumed to imply the existence of the other. There is indeed in the scholarly literature a tendency to assume sabbath worship as part of sabbath observance, and to locate such worship in 'services' in 'synagogue' buildings. In this chapter, each step in the arguments necessary to reach that conclusion will be carefully weighed against the textual data supplied by Philo and Josephus.

So, because much of the discussion of what Philo and Josephus have to tell us is clouded by the unresolved question of the possible meanings of the word 'synagogue' in Palestine and the Diaspora during their lifetimes, it is relevant to recall that there are no references whatsoever to synagogues, whether as groups of people or as buildings, or to sabbath worship, in the Hebrew Bible, nor in any of the apocryphal works of the Bible, not even in those books which speak of pious, observant Jews and their religious practices.

In making this assertion I am by no means alone, Rivkin, for example, has pointed to the lack of reference to 'the synagogue' in Ben Sira,[9] giving the direct negative to the widely prevailing scholarly belief in the early establishment of the synagogue as both institution and building.[10] He goes so far as to describe the claim for the

---

[9] Rivkin, 'Ben Sira', esp. pp. 344-48.
[10] Clements, *God and Temple*, p. 130; M. Simon, 'Judaism: Its Faith and Worship', in *A Companion to the Bible* (2nd edn; ed. H.H. Rowley; Edinburgh: T. & T. Clark, 1963),

existence of the synagogue in the period of Ben Sira as a 'notorious' assumption, since although no pre-Hasmonaean sources mention the synagogue, 'scholars give *priority* to silence', and take 'for granted that Ben Sira lived in a society where there were synagogues—synagogues that had been in existence for several hundred years'.[11]

Rivkin rightly claims that the argument from silence has been overplayed. The silence of the sources cannot mean that synagogues—whether groups or buildings—definitely did not exist, but neither can silence be used to prove that they did. With some justice, he insists that a claim for the existence of some institution in society must have some positive evidence, and that, when faced with a lack of such evidence, scholars may only postulate the institution's existence and be ready to revise their hypotheses should new evidence be found.

I agree with much of what Rivkin says and believe that evidence for synagogues, either as groups of people or as buildings, is to be found only in writings later than Ben Sira. All the evidence from the period will be examined in this and the following chapters of this study.

What we *do* have evidence for are the προσευχαί, the prayer-houses of Diaspora Jews in many provinces of the Mediterranean world, and especially in Egypt, where this name for a building frequented by Jews is well attested in inscriptions and papyri from the third century BCE onwards, as well as in the writings of Philo. Josephus also uses the term at one point in his writings—in his description of a Jewish meeting-house in Tiberias.

---

pp. 381-417 (392-93); Snaith, 'Worship', pp. 544-45; J.C. Turro, 'Synagogue', in *New Catholic Encyclopedia* XII (Washington, DC: McGraw–Hill, 1967), pp. 879-80; Hengel, *Judaism and Hellenism*, I, p. 79; II, p. 54 (n. 165); S. Sandmel, *The First Christian Century in Judaism and Christianity* (New York: OUP, 1969), p. 72, notes, p. 102. However, I. Sonne, 'Synagogue', in *The Interpreter's Dictionary of the Bible*, III (Nashville: Abingdon Press, 1962), pp. 476-91 (478-80), and R. Posner, 'Synagogue', in *Encyclopaedia Judaica*, XV (Jerusalem: Keter Publishing House, 1972), pp. 579-95, express the prevailing view but give contrary views also, and A.J. Saldarini, 'Synagogue', in *Harper's Bible Dictionary* (ed. P.J. Achtemeier; San Francisco: Harper & Row, 1985), pp. 1007-1008, makes the ambiguity of the extant evidence regarding synagogues abundantly plain.

[11] Rivkin, 'Ben Sira', pp. 345-46.

Philo: Sabbath Practice

A search through Philo's literary corpus to find details of sabbath worship practices yields little in the way of positive evidence.

Assuredly, Philo regards sabbath rest as of the highest importance and makes what seems to the twentieth-century mind a somewhat illogical extension of sabbath rest to plants (since they could only be involved in a passive sense or at the most complicitly!), by recommending that his readers spare even the plant kingdom from involvement with work on the sabbath by refraining from plucking fruit from the resting trees.[12]

Philo declares that the sabbath has been given the name of rest because of all the numbers seven is the most peaceful.[13] He regards sabbath as a sacred day, like the other festivals and feasts,[14] belonging to God, and expatiates on the ways in which human ill-nature can undermine religious celebrations, as, for example, by lust, mischief and jeering.[15] But he says nothing specific about the way the sabbath should be honoured or about worship activities for the sabbath, merely implying the necessity for an appropriate attitude of mind.

Philo does indeed refer to sabbath practices outside the domestic setting. He several times refers to current gatherings of Jews on the sabbath, but he only twice gives a name (συναγώγια) to the gatherings. So, when he speaks of the efforts of a member of the ruling class in Egypt trying to 'disturb our ancestral customs and especially to do away with the law of the Seventh Day which we regard with the utmost reverence and awe', he refers to the Jews as meeting as 'conventicles' or συναγώγια.[16]

Elsewhere in his writings he gives a name to the place where the Jews met, but does not name the gathering. So, although while speaking about unnamed 'cities' in general he gives two descriptions

---

[12] Philo, *Moses* 2.21-22, in *Philo*, VI (tr. F.H. Colson; LCL; Cambridge, MA: Harvard University Press, 1935); this point is made by Kubo, 'Sabbath in the Intertestamental Period', p. 61.

[13] Philo, *Abraham* 28, in *Philo*, VI (tr. F.H. Colson and G.L. Whitaker; LCL; Cambridge, MA: Harvard University Press, 1935).

[14] Philo, *Special Laws* 2.41.

[15] Philo, *Cherubim* 87-101, in *Philo*, II (tr. F.H. Colson and G.L. Whitaker; LCL; Cambridge, MA: Harvard University Press, 1929).

[16] Philo, *Dreams* 2.123-28, in *Philo*, V (tr. F.H. Colson and G.L. Whitaker; LCL; Cambridge, MA: Harvard University Press, 1949); the other occurrence is at *Embassy* 311-13, see discussion below.

of sabbath gatherings of Jews, in only one does he state the name of the place or building.

First, he recounts the sabbath practice of the Jews, saying that they 'every seventh day occupy themselves with the philosophy of their fathers' in their 'places of prayer (προσευκτήρια) throughout the cities'. The activities in these he describes as being similar to the philosophical schools of the Greeks, in providing 'edification and betterment in moral principle and conduct' and as being 'schools of prudence and courage and temperance and justice and also of piety, holiness and every virtue by which duties to God and men are discerned and rightly performed'.[17] Philo is painting a picture of educational gatherings in προσευκτήρια where religious, social and moral topics are discussed.

In the second description, he speaks of the Jews' mandatory abstention from work and the contrary 'exercise of the higher activities' stating that

> ... the law bids us take the time for studying philosophy ... So each seventh day there stand wide open in every city thousands of schools of good sense, temperance, courage and justice and the other virtues in which scholars sit in order quietly with ears alert and full attention, so much do they thirst for the draught which the teacher's words supply.[18]

This picture is very similar to the one painted already, and again depicts a teacher–student ambience at the sabbath meetings of Jews. But here neither the place where they met nor the gathering is referred to by any specific term.

Although Philo rarely gives a name to the sabbath gatherings of Jews, he frequently names the building where Jews meet as a προσευχή which is usually translated either as 'prayer-house' or as 'meeting-house'. The word, of course, normally means 'prayer' and by metonymy can signify 'prayer-house' in Jewish contexts.[19]

---

[17] Philo, *Moses* 215-16.
[18] Philo, *Special Laws* 2.60-62.
[19] *A Greek–English Lexicon* (rev. H.S. Jones; Oxford: Clarendon Press, 1940), p. 1151; *A Greek–English Lexicon of the New Testament* (rev. W.F. Arndt and F.W. Gingrich; Cambridge: CUP, and Chicago: University of Chicago Press, 1957), p. 720; *A Patristic Greek Lexicon* (ed. G.W.H. Lampe; Oxford: Clarendon Press, 1961), p. 1169; *Theological Dictionary of the New Testament*, II, p. 808; also 3 Macc. 7.20 refers to the setting up by Jews of an inscribed pillar and dedicating a προσευχή at a place of celebration.

In the prayer-houses, as Philo describes them, civic activity, namely, veneration of the imperial family, takes place as well as study and discussion.

Evidence of Honouring Roman Rulers in Jewish Prayer-Houses

The term προσευχή appears six times in Philo's account of the anti-Jewish behaviour of an Alexandrian official called Flaccus, who indicated to the mob in the city, by not taking measures against their hostility to the Jews, that he was in some sense sanctioning it, being, according to Philo, 'crazy for fame'. Thereupon the crowd 'called out with one accord for installing images in the meeting-houses (προσευχαί)'.[20] The crowd made out that placing statues of the emperor in the Jewish meeting-houses was one of *their* ways of showing loyalty to the Roman emperor and that it sprang from a good-hearted intention to show support for the Roman government. Flaccus concurred with this plan in spite of the fact that it was illegal under Roman law and that, according to Philo, the one million Jews in Egypt would be sure to raise a stir.[21]

Philo regards the spreading of the report of what he calls 'the overthrowing of the meeting-houses'[22] as a very hostile act also, since he believes that the idea that such behaviour was possible might spread to other cities and regions of the empire, to 'the most prosperous countries of Europe and Asia both in the islands and on the mainland, and ... the Holy City', and feels that 'it was to be feared that people everywhere might take their cue from Alexandria, and outrage their Jewish fellow-citizens by rioting against their synagogues [sic][23] and ancestral customs'. Obviously Philo believed the same types of meeting-houses of Jews, open to the same types of abuse, existed in all these different locations, including Jerusalem.

He goes on to indicate how serious a loss would have been occasioned to the Jews by the invalidating of their buildings for use by having images installed in them. He says that Jews 'by losing their meeting-houses[24] were losing also what they would have valued as

---

[20] Philo, *Flaccus* 40-55, in *Philo*, IX (tr. F.H. Colson; LCL; Cambridge, MA: Harvard University Press, 1960).

[21] Philo gives this number for the Jewish population of Egypt.

[22] Colson (LCL) translates προσευχαί as 'synagogues'.

[23] Colson (LCL) translates προσευχαί as 'synagogues'.

[24] Colson (LCL) translates προσευχή here as 'meeting-house', in the same section

worth dying many thousand deaths, namely, their means of showing reverence to their benefactors since they no longer had the sacred buildings where they could set forth their thankfulness'.[25]

It is clever of Philo to use the same arguments to stop the installation of images as the crowd used to have them installed, namely the importance to loyal subjects of having ways of showing their reverence for their emperor and the imperial house—included among the benefactors of the Jews. But of course on each side there are hidden agenda: on the Alexandrian crowd's part a hostility to the other race inhabiting their city, and on Philo's part an attempt to persuade the Roman authorities to continue to ban the introduction of Roman images into Jewish prayer-houses. Philo had to tune his arguments finely to get leverage on this Roman dichotomy for, as Goldenberg neatly puts it, 'Roman law recognized and protected Jewish Sabbath-observance, just as Roman thinking deplored it'.[26]

Philo completes his case by showing how fundamental the προσευχαί are to the Jews in their expressions of loyalty to the state; he has the Jews saying to Flaccus and the crowd: 'You have failed to see that you are not adding to but taking from the honour given to our masters, and you do not understand that everywhere in the habitable world the religious veneration of the Jews for the Augustan house has its basis as all may see in the meeting-houses; and if we have these destroyed no place, no method is left to us for paying this homage'.[27]

To Philo, for the sake of this argument at least, the προσευχαί are the places where the Jews give publicly visible religious homage to the Roman imperial family, which places would be invalidated for such use by Jews by the introduction of Roman statues.[28] He regards any installation of images as 'seizing the meeting-houses'.[29] And the

---

where the two previous occurrences of the word were translated as 'synagogue'.

[25] Philo, *Flaccus* 48.

[26] R. Goldenberg, 'The Jewish Sabbath in the Roman World up to the Time of Constantine the Great', in *ANRW* II.19.1 (Berlin: de Gruyter, 1979), pp. 411-47 (412).

[27] Philo, *Flaccus* 49.

[28] In this understanding of the importance of showing loyalty to Rome in a physical or material way Philo has a parallel the thinking of Tacitus, *Histories* 5.4, in *Tacitus in Five Volumes*, III (tr. C.H. Moore and J. Jackson; LCL; Cambridge, MA: Harvard University Press, 1969), who comments on the fact that the Jews 'set up no statues in their cities, still less in their temples; this flattery is not paid their kings, nor this honour given to the Caesars'. Cf. the discussion in Chapter 4.

[29] Philo, *Flaccus* 53.

reason that this counts as destruction is that the Jews would no longer be able to enter those buildings and carry out the actions in them that they were accustomed to carry out.

The Religious Celebration of Jewish Success against Flaccus

Later in his treatise *In Flaccum*, Philo describes the worship offered to God by the thankful Jews once they hear that Flaccus has been arrested. This is not worship offered on a particular day of the week, but offered in response to a belief that God had rescued them from their enemy. He says that they:

> advanced from their houses ... [and] ... with hands outstretched to heaven they sang hymns and led songs of triumph to God who watches over human affairs. 'We do not rejoice, O Lord,' they said, 'at the punishment meted out to our enemy, for we have been taught by the holy laws to have human sympathy. But we justly give thanks to Thee because Thou hast taken pity and compassion on us and relieved our unbroken and ceaseless afflictions.' All night long they continued to sing hymns and songs of praise and at dawn, pouring out through the gates, they made their way to the parts of the beach near at hand,[30] since their meeting-houses had been taken from them, and standing in the open space cried aloud with one accord 'Most Mighty King of mortals and immortals, we have come here to call on earth and sea, and air and heaven, into which the universe is partitioned, and on the whole world, to give Thee thanks ...'[31]

The words of the hymns put into their mouths by Philo make forceful contributions to the arguments he was offering to Caligula but probably should not be taken as the Jews' actual or usual hymns—even though the language of praise and thanks to God is typical of similar thanksgiving hymns in the Psalms and in 2 Maccabees.[32]

The worship is offered in response to a rescue. It consists of the ritual actions of prayer and the singing of hymns and triumph songs. The people perform it both as they walk through the streets and later on the beach because 'their meeting-houses had been taken from them'. These actions do correspond to my description of worship, but here, as in 2 Maccabees 8, they happen as a 'one-off' response to

---

[30] Josephus, *Antiquities* 14.256-58, refers to the building of προσευχαί 'near the sea, in accordance with their native custom', but it is not clear how generally prevalent this practice was.

[31] Philo, *Flaccus* 120-23.

[32] 2 Macc. 8.27, 29.

a particular perceived intervention of God on behalf of the Jews. I
have found no accounts of this type of worship taking place in a
Jewish meeting-house (προσευχή) described anywhere in the
writings of Philo. Regular sabbath worship is a far cry from an
unusual ceremony like this

Evidence from Other Incidents in Prayer-Houses in Alexandria

A second account of attacks on προσευχαί enlarges our understanding both of their role in the Jewish community and of their physical
appearance, for Philo gives a detailed and vivid account of the
hostile behaviour meted out by the Alexandrians towards the Jews.
Roman emperors intensely disapproved of civil unrest and could be
expected to punish those who has caused it. So Philo presents the
Jews as the innocent sufferers and reports that the Alexandrian mob

> collected great bodies of men to attack the meeting-houses, of which
> there are many in each section of the city. Some they ravaged, others
> they demolished with the foundations as well, others they set fire to
> and burnt regardless in their frenzy and insane fury of the fate of the
> neighbouring houses, for nothing runs faster than fire when it gets
> hold of something to feed it. I say nothing of the tributes to the
> emperors which were pulled down or burnt at the same time, the
> shields and gilded crowns and the slabs and inscriptions, considera-
> tion for which should have made them spare the rest ... The meeting-
> houses which they could not raze or burn out of existence, because so
> many Jews lived massed together in the neighbourhood, they out-
> raged in another way, thereby overthrowing our laws and customs.
> For they set up images of Gaius in them all and in the largest and
> most notable a bronze statue of a man mounted on a chariot and four.

We may conclude from this passage: that there were many meeting-houses in Alexandria, some free-standing, others abutting domestic dwellings, and at least one was large enough, and had a large
enough entrance portal, to accommodate a sculpture of a man driving
a chariot and four horses. On the walls[33] were tributes to the emperor: shields, gilded crowns, slabs and inscriptions, which in some
way related to the Jews acknowledging publicly the esteem in which
they held the Roman imperial family. Also important is the fact that
none of *these* items caused offence to the Jews, profaned their meeting-houses or rendered them in any way unacceptable to Jews.

---

[33] Whether inside or outside is not made clear.

Imperial Protection of Prayer-Houses

Philo continues his case by speaking of the time of Gaius's imperial predecessor, Tiberius, when there was no violence or illegality practised against the meeting-houses in Alexandria,[34] and there had been no efforts made to introduce statues, busts or paintings of the emperor into meeting-houses.[35] It appears, therefore, that the inclusion of any of these three types of object would have made the meeting-house unusable, although display of shields, gilded crowns, slabs and inscriptions apparently did not.

A third significant passage follows shortly thereafter, when Philo turns his attention to Rome. He discusses how the Jewish community in Rome fared there during the rule of Tiberius,[36] during which time there was in that city also no occurrence of violence or illegality against the Jews. He writes approvingly of Tiberius

> He was aware that the great section of Rome on the other side of the Tiber is occupied and inhabited by Jews, most of whom were Roman citizens emancipated. For having been brought as captives to Italy they were liberated by their owners and were not forced to violate any of their native institutions. He knew therefore that they have houses of prayer[37] and meet together in them, particularly on the sacred sabbaths when they receive as a body a training in their ancestral philosophy. He knew too that they collect money for sacred purposes from their first fruits and send them to Jerusalem by persons who would offer the sacrifices. Yet nevertheless he neither ejected them from Rome nor deprived them of their Roman citizenship because they were careful to preserve their Jewish citizenship also, nor took any violent measures against the houses of prayer, nor prevented them from meeting to receive instruction in the laws, nor opposed their offerings of the first fruits. Indeed so religiously did he respect our interests that supported by wellnigh his whole household he adorned our temple through the costliness of his dedications, and ordered that for all time continuous sacrifices of whole burnt offerings should be carried out every day at his own expense as a tribute to the most high God.

---

[34] Philo, *Embassy* 152.

[35] Philo, *Embassy* 141-54.

[36] Philo, *Embassy* 155-58.

[37] In this section dealing with Rome, although immediately following the section about Alexandria where προσευχή was consistently translated as 'meeting-house', Colson (LCL) translates προσευχή consistently as 'house of prayer', but reverts to 'meeting-house' when the narrative again refers to Alexandria. The rationale behind this alteration escapes me as Philo has no interruption at all in his flow of thought throughout the complete section. But readers of the English text might well imagine that two different words or institutions are indicated by the change of term.

Philo then rounds off his argument by praising Tiberius for the freedoms he allowed to the Jews in the exercise of their faith, and also the accommodations he made to Jewish religious scruples, such as avoiding doling out free corn to the populace on the sabbath, when Jews would be unable to benefit.[38]

So, to summarise, in this section of *The Embassy to Gaius*, from lines 132 to 165, concerning the Jewish meeting-houses in Alexandria and Rome, the word προσευχή appears nine times,[39] and in each case it represents a building in which Jews met on the sabbath to learn their laws and 'ancestral philosophy' from those of their number who could act as teachers. These premises were also places where homage was paid to the Roman imperial house and the walls of these buildings were adorned with inscriptions and carved designs which expressed this honouring permanently. But the buildings could lose their status as προσευχαί through profanation by forbidden items such as statues, busts or paintings of the emperor.

As the final salvo in this part of his submission to Gaius Caligula,[40] Philo refers to the pro-Jewish words and actions of another great emperor, this time Augustus, in whose tradition he could reasonably expect Caligula to wish to stand. He harks back to the time when Augustus instructed his Asian governors that

> the Jews alone should be permitted by them to assemble in συναγώγια. These gatherings, he said, were not based on drunkenness and carousing to promote conspiracy, but were schools of temperance and justice where men while practising virtue subscribed the annual first-fruits to pay for the sacrifices which they offer and commissioned sacred envoys to take them to the temple in Jerusalem.[41]

Perhaps Philo gilds the Emperor Augustus's words a little in this eulogy about the Jews as ideal citizens, but what he says must, in the main, reflect Jewish practice at the time and so provides details of the

---

[38] Philo, *Embassy* 156-58.

[39] And elsewhere, the word crops up three more times in re-iteration of the same arguments, at *Embassy* 191, 346, 371, making a total of eleven uses of the word προσευχή to describe the buildings where the Jews met.

[40] Philo, *Embassy* 311-13.

[41] The Loeb edition here translates συναγώγια as 'synagogues', whereas in *Dreams* 2.127, the same word is rendered 'conventicles'. The use of the word 'gatherings' in the next sentence, where the Greek noun does not appear, suggests that that is the meaning which should be understood in this passage.

functions of Jewish gatherings. They were sober affairs where dues
were collected prior to dispatch to Jerusalem.

Details about the Sabbath Activities of Jews from Philo's writings

In his more overtly apologetic writing, Philo describes how the sabbath of the Jews is spent valuably and not in idleness.[42] To help his
readers to form a clearer picture of what happened at the regular sabbath assemblies, Philo says that those present sat 'together in a
respectful and orderly manner' and heard 'the laws read so that none
should be in ignorance of them'. They sat in silence except for
adding something to signify approval of what was read.[43] A priest or
elder who was present read and expounded the holy laws to them.
The males thus informed were expected to pass on their understanding to their wives, children and slaves, which implies that those
groups of people were not present at these sabbath sessions.

Thus it appears that, in Alexandria at the time of Philo, the sabbath had become a day of (male) gathering for study and contemplation as well as a day of rest. But study and contemplation are by no
means the same as worship. The Jewish men[44] came to a building
called a προσευχή (or once, προσευκτήριον) where they could sit, to
receive and exchange instruction, offer homage to their Roman rulers
in ways unspecified by Philo, but possibly merely by including the
honorific material in the stonework of the building. There are no
indications that they held a regular sabbath service of worship to
God.

Sabbath Activities of the Therapeutae
When we turn to Philo's *Contemplative Life* and to his description of
Jews who devote themselves more completely to the religious
aspects of life, there we find, for the first time, activities that may
properly be called worship. Philo's description of the daily religious
life of the Therapeutae shows that they read the holy scriptures,
interpreting them allegorically, and also composed sacred songs to
God.

---

[42] Philo, *Hypothetica* 7.9-13, in *Philo*, IX (tr. F.H. Colson; LCL; Cambridge, MA:
Harvard University Press, 1960).

[43] Possibly interpolating 'Amen'.

[44] None of Philo's writings makes clear—or even implies—that females attended.

> Twice every day they pray, at dawn and at eventide ... The interval
> between early morning and evening is spent entirely in spiritual exer-
> cise. They read the Holy Scriptures and seek wisdom from their
> ancestral philosophy by taking it as allegory ... but [they] also com-
> pose hymns and psalms to God in all sorts of metres and melodies
> which they write down.[45]

This is described as *daily* worship. Whether it takes place on sabbath
also is not clear, for their sabbath meetings are described in terms
indistinguishable from those Philo gives of other Jews in the
προσευχαί. Here Philo describes how the Therapeutae assemble
together on the seventh day, how they

> sit in order according to their age in the proper attitude, with their
> hands inside the robe, the right hand between the breast and chin and
> the left withdrawn along the flank. Then the senior among them who
> also has the fullest knowledge of the doctrines which they profess
> comes forward and with visage and voice alike quiet and composed
> gives a well reasoned and wise discourse ... [which] ... passes
> through the hearing and into the soul and there stays securely ... [A]ll
> the others sit still and listen showing their approval merely by their
> looks and nods.[46]

This is close to what has been described before as normal practice
in the προσευχαί, apart from the description of the sitting posture of
the Therapeutae, and it, strikingly, includes none of the worship
practices that are described as the daily behaviour of the
Therapeutae.

The meeting-place of the Therapeutae is amply described by
Philo:

> This common sanctuary (σεμνεῖον) is a double enclosure, one
> portion set apart for the use of the men, the other for the women. For
> women too regularly make part of the audience with the same ardour
> and the same sense of their calling. The wall between the two
> chambers rises up from the ground to three or four cubits built in the
> form of a breast work, while the space above the roof is left open.
> This arrangement serves two purposes: the modesty becoming to the
> female sex is preserved, while the women sitting within earshot can
> easily follow what is said since there is nothing to obstruct the voice
> of the speaker.[47]

This is rather like the popular image of the synagogue building of

---

[45] Philo, *Contemplative Life* 27-29, in *On the Contemplative Life*, in *Philo*, IX (tr.
F.H. Colson; LCL; Cambridge, MA: Harvard University Press, 1960).
[46] Philo, *Contemplative Life* 30-31.
[47] Philo, *Contemplative Life* 32-33.

the Jews at the beginning of the Christian era, but here in Philo this description is attributed solely to the Therapeutae, and unfortunately he gives neither the building, nor the gathering held there, a specific name, using only the general term 'sanctuary'. I cannot agree with the unargued statement of Vermes and Goodman that the gathering described is 'the formal religious service on the Sabbath'.[48] To my mind it bears none of the characteristics of a worship service and remains a meeting for study, explanations and exhortation—an additional meeting to those held daily for worship. However, uncharacteristically among the writings of the time, women are specifically stated to be present and participating enthusiastically at this meeting of Therapeutae, in this sanctuary.

Sabbath Activities of the Essenes in their Synagogue
The word 'synagogue' (συναγωγή) is used by Philo only once, and once only, when he describes the meeting-place of the Essenes, whose sabbath gatherings are similar to those of other Jews he describes.

> on the seventh day ... [they] abstain from all other work and proceed to sacred spots which they call synagogues.[49] There, arranged in rows according to their ages, the younger below the elder, they sit decorously as befits the occasion with attentive ears. Then one takes the books and reads aloud and another of especial proficiency comes forward and expounds what is not understood. For the most part their philosophical study takes the form of allegory ...[50]

It is important to notice that, from the way Philo introduces the word, συναγωγαί, 'which they call synagogues', it is evident that the word 'synagogue' is not his own word; rather, he describes *their institution* by the name *they* give it—synagogue. And this is the only occasion that Philo uses the word 'synagogue' to mean either an assembly of Jews or a building in which they met. Even here, the context leaves ambiguous whether a building is indicated or not, for the sitting in rows could happen in the open air and it is only the taking of the books for reading aloud that suggests a permanent structure of some sort. Whatever the name of their meeting-place, it

---

[48] G. Vermes and M.D. Goodman, *The Essenes: According to the Classical Sources* (Oxford Centre Text-Books, 1; Sheffield : JSOT Press, 1989), p. 15.
[49] οἳ καλοῦνται συναγωγαί.
[50] Philo, *Every Good Man is Free* 81-83, in *Philo*, IX (tr. F.H. Colson; LCL; Cambridge, MA: Harvard University Press, 1960).

is essential to recognise that Essene sabbath gatherings are no different from those of other Jews: as Hoenig says Philo is 'describing the
study of the Law by the Essenes, but not prayer-worship'.[51] There
are sabbath gatherings: there is *no* sabbath worship.

Other Jewish Gatherings on Sabbath

Earlier, attention was drawn to Philo's use of the term συναγώγια
(gatherings) for the meetings of the Jews. One usage occurs in his
account of the permission, given by Augustus, for Jews to come
together in gatherings, which were 'schools of temperance and justice', and which opened their doors to outsiders.

In the other account of these 'gatherings' he describes a member
of the ruling class in Egypt railing at the Jews in the hope of persuading them that they had no good reason to persist in sabbath rest. The
man hypothesises, for the purposes of his argument, a sudden attack
on the gathered community, presumably—but not necessarily on the
sabbath, by enemies, flood, fire or other natural disaster and supposedly asks the Jews

> ... will you stay at home perfectly quiet? Or will you appear in pub-
> lic in your usual guise, with your right hand tucked inside and the left
> hand held close to the flank under the cloak lest you should even
> unconsciously do anything that might help to save you? And will you
> sit in your conventicles (συναγώγια) and assemble your regular
> company and read in security your holy books, expounding any
> obscure point and in leisurely comfort discussing at length your
> ancestral philosophy? No, you will throw all these off and gird your-
> selves up for the assistance of yourselves, your parents and your chil-
> dren, and the other persons who are nearest and dearest to you, and
> indeed also your chattels and wealth to save them too from annihila-
> tion.[52]

The picture of sabbath activities portrayed in this text is a quiet
and leisured reading of holy books followed by discussion, which
mirrors exactly Philo's other accounts. The Jews' sabbath inaction is
contrasted with the vigorous movements and actions that would be
taken by 'other, sensible' men in the face of disaster. And it appears
to be the males of the community who are being addressed in this
rhetorical way about the unlikelihood of them doing anything useful

---

[51] S.B. Hoenig, 'The Ancient City-Square: The Forerunner of the Synagogue', in
ANRW II.19.1 (Berlin: de Gruyter, 1979), pp. 448-76 (452), n. 26.
[52] Philo, *Dreams* 2.123-28.

if they must keep their hands tucked inside their clothes.

It must be said that this description of the disposition of the Jews' hands and arms in their clothes is uncannily like the description given elsewhere by Philo of the posture of the seated Therapeutae at their sabbath gathering, but here it appears to refer to the generality of Jews. Is Philo representing the practice of Jews generally, or has he extended the practice of the Therapeutae for greater rhetorical effect?

Summary of Philo's Evidence
The texts cited above show that the name for the gatherings of Jews on the sabbath and/or the name for the building in which they gathered were not applied unequivocally when Philo was writing. For he used συναγώγιον, for sabbath assemblies of Jews, προσευκτήριον, for the gathering place used by Jews, συναγωγή, for the Essenes' place of gathering and προσευχή for the name of any prayer-house building,[53] for, where a building is definitely indicated, for example, if it were burned down by an angry mob or had a statue put inside, it is always called a προσευχή. And the only worship that Philo describes for ordinary Jews, as distinct from the daily worship of the Therapeutae, takes place out of doors and in response to a saving act of God towards the people, namely the arrest of Flaccus.

When Jews assemble on the sabbath, it is not to worship, but to read, study and discuss Torah.

Josephus: Sabbath Practice

A very similar picture of sabbath activities can be found in the writings of Josephus: he makes several references to Jewish abstention from work or other activity on the sabbath, explains the biblical sabbath to his readers,[54] and describes sabbath gatherings in which political discussions took place,[55] or in which the Law was studied.[56]

---

[53] Apart from one occasion when he uses προσευκτήρια.

[54] Josephus, *Apion* 2.175-83, in *Against Apion*, in *Josephus*, I (tr. H.St.J. Thackeray; LCL; Cambridge, MA: Harvard University Press, 1926); *War* 2.147; *Antiquities* 3.237-38, in *Josephus*, IV (tr. H.St.J. Thackeray; LCL; Cambridge, MA: Harvard University Press, 1930).

[55] Josephus, *Life* 271-89, in *Josephus*, I (tr. H.St.J. Thackeray; LCL; Cambridge, MA: Harvard University Press, 1926).

[56] Josephus, *War* 2.289-92.

For Josephus, sabbath inactivity was a key feature of the day, and in this context he describes the sometime refusal of Jews to fight on the sabbath, saying also that it is 'a day on which from religious scruples Jews abstain from even the most innocent acts'.[57] Describing the Essenes, he reports that they 'are stricter than all Jews in abstaining from work on the seventh day', thus making plain his understanding that inaction is the main characteristic of the sabbath of all Jews everywhere.[58]

As part of his explanation of Jewish religious behaviour, Josephus claims that Moses ordained 'that every week men should desert their other occupations and assemble to listen to the Law and to obtain a thorough and accurate knowledge of it ...'[59], and in obedience to this requirement, he, and Jews everywhere, give 'every seventh day over to the study of our customs and our law, for we think it necessary to occupy ourselves, as with any other study, so with these through which we can avoid committing sins'.[60] There is no indication here that the study is in any way a worship activity; rather it is pursued as an acceptable occupation of the mind which does not infringe, and even supports the execution of, sabbath law.

Josephus regards Judaism as being perfectly at home in the Roman empire and frequently draws attention to the legal protection given to Jews wishing to exercise their religion in the cities of the empire,[61] freedom to gather together for sacred and holy rites, to make offerings for sacrifices, to decide community affairs and to observe the sabbath. But, unfortunately, he gives no direct account of what he considers to be proper 'observance' of the sabbath.

Community Activities in the Jewish Prayer-House at Tiberias

One of our best insights into the range of activities that could take place in a προσευχή comes from Josephus's autobiography. In a

---

[57] Josephus, *War* 2.456; see also *War* 2.517, 634; *War* 7.52, in *Josephus*, III (tr. H.St.J. Thackeray; LCL; Cambridge, MA: Harvard University Press, 1928); see also *Antiquities* 13.252-53; 14.63-64, 226-46 for other references to sabbath rest.

[58] Josephus, *War* 2.147.

[59] Josephus, *Apion* 2.175.

[60] Josephus, *Antiquities* 16.42-44, in *Josephus*, VIII (tr. R. Marcus; LCL; Cambridge, MA: Harvard University Press, 1963).

[61] Josephus, *Apion* 2.72; *Antiquities* 14.232-49, 260-64; 16.27-28, 42-44, 168; 19.304, 306.

sustained piece of first-person narration, Josephus describes a series of events in which he was directly involved and which took place in a large prayer-house (προσευχή) in Tiberias. The events recounted last from the morning of a sabbath till the following Monday morning and include an exciting series of confrontations.[62] This is the longest extant piece of writing that describes Jews assembling in a communal building, and so merits our closest attention. According to Josephus, a deputation of Jonathan and others, 'from the lower ranks and adherents of the Pharisees',[63] has been sent from Jerusalem to oppose Josephus, with the remit of sending him to Jerusalem alive, or of killing him if he resists.[64]

He writes that on the sabbath morning 'there was a general assembly in the Prayer-house, a huge building, capable of accommodating a large crowd'. A heated political discussion took place—at which Josephus was not present—about whether the Jews of the town were better off under Josephus as general or would be better taking orders from four of their own number and Josephus remarks that 'a riot would inevitably have ensued, had not the arrival of the sixth hour, at which it is our custom on the Sabbath to take our midday meal, broken off the meeting'. At noon on the sabbath the discussions ceased, although unfinished, for the time-honoured lunchtime meal. There is no reference in the passage to any purpose in the Jews' being together on that Saturday morning other than discussing this vital piece of community business. The meeting did not continue in the afternoon—but early on the Sunday morning. Presumably the requirement for sabbath rest now supervened.

Arriving at 7 am the next morning, presumably at the time when he expected the discussion to resume, Josephus 'found the people already assembling in the Prayer-house, although they had no idea why they were being convened'. This indicates that other people had been asked to attend, people who had not been there on the Saturday morning, people who were willing to obey, and who perhaps were accustomed to receiving, such a summons. However, Josephus could not remain to listen to the discussions as he was decoyed away from Tiberias by the delivery of a spurious message of danger on the fron-

---

[62] Josephus, *Life* 272-303.
[63] Josephus, *Life* 197.
[64] Josephus, *Life* 197, 202-203, 217.

tier, which delivery had been arranged by the inimical local leaders.

Josephus later returned to the prayer-house to defend himself against the verbal attacks of his opponents, which he expected to have been delivered during his absence; he says that he 'found the whole of the council (βουλή) and populace in conclave,[65] and Jonathan and his associates making a violent tirade against me, as one who lived in luxury and neglected to alleviate their share of the burden of the war'. The Jewish leaders produced more letters allegedly from persons requesting assistance on the Galilee frontier. The Tiberian citizens, believing the letters, became angry with Josephus, who countered by acting as if he also believed in the letters and outlined plans of campaign which would involve Jonathan (a leading citizen) and his friends in immediate action. This caused a check to their enthusiasm for a swift response to the bogus letters.

But one of their group suggested that on the next day—Monday—a public fast should be called and that 'they should reassemble at the same place and hour, without arms, in order to attest before God their conviction that without his aid no armour could avail them'. This proposal indicates to the modern reader that the προσευχή was regarded as a place in which it was suitable to state allegiance to God and make vows, yet also a place that one might attend wearing weapons; but to Josephus it implied that his enemies wished to have him and his friends present at the meeting in a 'defenceless condition'.

So to avoid falling into any trap that might be in preparation, Josephus put on sword and breastplate 'as little conspicuous as possible' and went to the prayer-house with two of his most reliable bodyguards wearing hidden daggers. Only these two of Josephus's party were allowed by Jesus [the chief magistrate of Tiberias[66]] to enter with him. Josephus continues that the assembly was 'proceeding with the ordinary service and engaged in prayer when Jesus rose and began to question me about the furniture and uncoined silver which had been confiscated', asking also the whereabouts of another twenty pieces of gold. Josephus explains to the assembly that he has used it to pay the expenses of the Jewish deputation to Jerusalem, but agrees to reimburse the costs out of his own pocket.

---

[65] Only maled seem to be implied by this text.
[66] Josephus, *Life* 271, 294.

Following that statement, the crowd at the meeting began to incline more to Josephus's position and the leaders saw that it was in their interests to remove the crowd and continue the business with the council alone present, especially as the assembly in the prayer-house was now 'tumultuous'. Then, in a last desperate attempt to regain control of the situation, Jonathan attempted to persuade the assembled Jews that Josephus deserved to die, and he and his party laid hands on Josephus—who fully expected to be murdered. But the two bodyguards of Josephus drew their swords to protect him and he escaped.

This account of exciting and violent events in a προσευχή in Tiberias belies any image we may have of a quiet and orderly 'house of prayer'. That prayer at a public fast, by a large group of assembled Jews, could be interrupted for such matters as these, and that prolonged, heated political discussion could take place in the prayer-house on Saturday mornings and on other days passes without comment by Josephus. Such activities were apparently part of the proper functioning of a προσευχή.

Popular Reactions to Three Jewish Synagogues

The meeting places of Jews on sabbaths are also called 'synagogues' by Josephus. He refers to a 'synagogue' on three occasions, each time meaning a Jewish building with religious and community functions, buildings located in Antioch, Caesarea and Dora.[67] The descriptions of these buildings and the activities—religious or otherwise—associated with them are in close agreement with Philo's descriptions of προσευχαί, and can easily be understood as referring to the same type of building.

1 Writing about the distribution of the Jewish population of Syria, Josephus claims that they were particularly numerous in Antioch, and that the successors of Antiochus Epiphanes 'restored to the Jews of Antioch all such votive offerings as were made of brass, to be laid up in their synagogue'—which later attracted 'richly designed and costly offerings' as well.[68] Josephus continues his praise of the Jews

---

[67] See references in the following paragraphs.
[68] Josephus, War 7.43-45. The synagogue is referred to in parallel as a 'shrine' or 'temple' (ἱερόν)—which has caused some difficulty in translation and understanding; see footnotes in the Loeb edition.

in Antioch by saying that they 'were constantly attracting to their religious ceremonies multitudes of Greeks, and these they had in some measure incorporated with themselves'. The synagogue building in Antioch thus seems to have been large, richly endowed and prestigious enough in official eyes to take possession of returned religious artefacts and also to attract the approving notice of local townspeople.

2 Josephus elsewhere paints a vivid picture of activities in and near a synagogue building in Caesarea where the Jews were being harassed by the local people.[69] The synagogue building adjoined a plot of ground owned by a non-Jew and though the Jews had frequently tried to buy that land, offering much more than the market value for it, he had refused to sell. And rather than accept their money, the owner, intending to annoy, built workshops on the land and left only a narrow passage for access to the synagogue building.

Thereupon, some young hotheads among the Jews attacked the builders and tried to stop the work, but the governor Florus stopped the violence. The Jews bribed Florus to arrange for the building work to stop, but having taken their money he reneged on the bargain and left the two parties to 'fight the matter out'.

Josephus continues the story: 'On the following day, which was a sabbath, when the Jews assembled at the synagogue, they found that one of the Caesarean mischief-makers had placed beside the entrance a pot, turned bottom upwards, upon which he was sacrificing birds'. Obviously the Caesareans were aware that chicken entrails and blood spattered over the narrow entrance passageway would make it difficult or impossible for Jews to go in to the synagogue. There was some discussion among the more peaceable Jews, but the young bloods on both sides were spoiling for a fight. Thus, in spite of the intervention of Jucundus, a cavalry commander, who came and removed the offending pot and tried to calm things down, a scuffle took place, after which the Jews 'snatched up their copy of the Law and withdrew to Narbata'.

Florus managed to evade responsibility for this fiasco by putting the Jewish deputation who complained to him in custody on the flimsy charge of 'having carried off the copy of the Law from

---

[69] Josephus, *War* 2.284-92.

Caesarea'.

When we compare Josephus's accounts of the synagogue at Caesarea and the προσευχή at Tiberias with our knowledge of προσευχαί from Philo, we find common material in the descriptions of both types of building: we find that Jews assemble in both on the sabbath, that a copy of the Law is available in both and that raised tempers and physical violence among those attending are not at all unknown.

3 Thirdly, Josephus recounts an incident that took place in 'the synagogue of the Jews'[70] at Dora, when zealous young citizens brought into it an image of Claudius, in flagrant contradiction of the rights granted to Jews by Roman law.[71] The Roman governor of Syria, Petronius, took up the Jews' case and ruled that the introduction of the statue, apart from being contrary to an imperial edict, 'prevented the Jews from having a synagogue', implying that its acceptability to Jews as a place of assembly was what made it into a synagogue. The term συναγωγή occurs three times in this account of events.

Here we see the same concept of 'preventing the Jews from having a synagogue' as was expressed in the writings of Philo in the phrase 'losing their meeting-houses', the risk on both occasions being caused by the introduction of a statue of a Roman emperor. Josephus does not follow this account with a description of alternative veneration of the emperor taking place in the building, as Philo does, resting his case simply on the rights of freedom in matters of religion given to the Jews by Roman edicts.[72] But elsewhere he presents a picture of Jewish loyalty to the Roman state,[73] and also refers to the 'payment of homage of another sort, secondary to that paid to God, to worthy men; such honours we do confer upon the emperors and people of Rome'—as opposed to erecting statues to the emperors.[74] He specifies the honours as offering perpetual sacrifices daily in the Temple at the expense of the whole Jewish community.[75] And

---

[70] This phrase also occurs in Acts 13.5; 14.1; 17.1, 10, although with a different word order in Greek; see discussion in Chapter 5.

[71] Josephus, *Antiquities* 19.301, in *Josephus*, IX (tr. L.H. Feldman; LCL; Cambridge, MA: Harvard University Press, 1965).

[72] See Goldenberg, 'Jewish Sabbath', pp. 415-18.

[73] Josephus, *Apion* 2.68-74.

[74] Josephus, *Apion* 2.73-78.

[75] Cf. the comments of Philo, *Embassy* 155-58, noted above.

he affirms that this signal honour was reserved for the Roman emperors only and for no one else.

Jewish Prayer

Writing on the Jewish attitude and commitment to prayer, Josephus affirms that the offering of prayer twice daily, at dawn and before retiring, was expected of all Jews.[76] He describes the position of the arms as outstretched during prayer,[77] the attitude Philo ascribed to Jews marching through the streets singing hymns of thanksgiving to God.[78]

To be sure, Josephus speaks of prayer at 'the ordinary service' being held in the prayer-house in Tiberias, but this is *daily* prayer, and though he also speaks of the holding of a 'a public fast' there on a Monday, he gives no details of what was done to celebrate the fast. As for *worship*, Josephus depicts worship taking place only in the Temple. He states that the Jews have 'but one temple for the one God', and says that sacrifices and prayers for the community are offered there.[79]

Jewish Religious Practice in the Home on Sabbath

The only reference Josephus makes to (presumably) domestic sabbath practice, is to the lighting of lamps on the sabbath, but he does not say where, or at what particular juncture, they were lit.[80]

Jewish Religious Practice outside the Home on Sabbath

Josephus's descriptions of communal gatherings of Jews on sabbath, therefore, provide corroborative evidence for many of the activities described by Philo for προσευχαί and συναγώγια, but Josephus attributes them, in the main, to buildings and/or groups he calls 'synagogues'. However, we must remember that the multi-faceted,

---

[76] Josephus, *Antiquities* 4.212; though it is not clear whether women are included in this requirement.

[77] Josephus, *War* 5.388.

[78] Philo, *Flaccus*, 120-23.

[79] Josephus, *Apion* 2.193; also a complete description of the sacrificial system is given at Josephus, *Antiquities* 3.236-54. But note that in spite of Josephus having written some of his works after the destruction of the Temple, he makes no reference to any transfer of the responsibility or practice of worship to any other place or institution.

[80] Josephus, *Apion* 2.282-83.

and, no doubt, highly unusual, session at Tiberias, incorporating a complex mixture of religion and politics, celebration of a public fast, discussion and physical violence, took place in a προσευχή, and that the prayers of the 'ordinary service' held there were on the Monday of a public fast. In the whole of Josephus's writings there is no reference to prayers or to any other worship activity on the sabbath.

Comparison of the Data Gained from Philo and Josephus

There are many items common to the descriptions of the gatherings of the Jews in the writings of Philo and Josephus. There is the weekly sabbath gathering of the adult males of the community with the stated purpose of becoming thoroughly knowledgeable about Jewish laws and customs. The buildings in which Jews meet are of different size and status, some being large and prestigious, others closely crowded among houses and shops. The introduction of objects considered to be 'graven images' instantly invalidates the gathering place as far as the Jews are concerned, but the buildings enjoy legal protection under Roman law as part of the sanctioned freedom of the Jews to meet and practise their religion undisturbed in the cities of the Roman empire. Violent arguments and scuffles can apparently take place in the meeting place without in any way profaning or invalidating it.

The points on which the two literary sources differ are the name they give to the building, and in the greater emphasis Philo gives to the importance of the building as a public focus for expressing the Jews' loyalty to the emperor. But the proffering of veneration to the imperial house through the prayer-houses is not ruled out by anything Josephus says, rather it is not directly addressed.

Another important difference is that, while Josephus gives particulars of synagogues in Antioch, Caesarea and Dora, and of a προσευχή in Tiberias, Philo describes Jewish meeting-houses in two cities, Alexandria and Rome, and makes the assumption that other cities where Jews lived, including Jerusalem, have identical institutions.

Discussion on the Evidence from Philo and Josephus

Much of the ground that I have discussed in depth in this chapter is briefly outlined by Kee in his article about the changing nature and role of the synagogue in the first two centuries CE.[81] Kee reports with disfavour how previous scholars have conflated the evidence of Philo and Josephus incorporating also details gleaned from the Mishnah and Talmud—the whole then being labelled with the title 'the ancient synagogue'. And trying to find a more acceptable credible account of the origin of the synagogue, he adopts the view of Zeitlin 'that many institutions of a purely religious character 'came into existence as a result of social and economic forces'.[82] Zeitlin believes that the synagogue was 'initially a secular meeting house in post-exilic Judaism', and that 'it was only after 70 CE that the synagogue began to emerge as a distinctive institution with its own characteristic structure'.[83] Accepting this leads Kee to the conclusion that Philo cannot have known synagogues as such, but describes their fore-runner, the meeting-house; and that Jesus and Paul could only have known gatherings on the sabbath like those described by Philo.[84] With these views I wholeheartedly concur.

Zeitlin's precise analysis of the data from Philo and Josephus leads him to conclude that they both describe the Jewish house of worship, by the same two Greek terms, but that Philo uses mainly προσευχή and Josephus uses mainly συναγωγή.[85] Zeitlin draws the conclusion that the Jewish communities had assemblies to discuss communal matters, and that these assemblies *later* acquired religious characteristics.[86] This agrees with my findings but the facts are seldom stated so succinctly and accurately elsewhere.

An attempt to analyse the way that Philo uses the word προσευχή has been made by Rivkin, but he has been handicapped by his

---

[81] H.C. Kee, 'The Transformation of the Synagogue after 70 CE: Its Import for Early Christianity', *NTS* 36 (1990), pp. 1-24 (1-7).

[82] S. Zeitlin, 'The Origin of the Synagogue', *PAAJR* 1 (1930–31), pp. 69-81 (70).

[83] Kee, 'Transformation', pp. 3 (following Zeitlin, 'Origin'), 7 (following Hoenig, 'City Square').

[84] Kee, 'Transformation', pp. 17-18.

[85] Zeitlin, 'Origin', p. 73; bearing in mind that Philo uses συναγωγή only of the sabbath gathering of the Essenes and uses συναγώγια when referring to gatherings of more typical Jews.

[86] Zeitlin, 'Origin', pp. 74-78, my emphasis.

assumption that 'Philo wrote at a time when there is abundant evidence that synagogues were flourishing'.[87] He seems to me to confuse the issue by classifying Philo's προσευχαί into two sorts: one identical with synagogues (though he does not give details of the synagogues to which he refers) and, a second group, those which were 'nonsubversive meeting houses ... symbols of loyalty to the emperors ... erected by the Jews from the time of the Ptolemies as evidence of Jewish loyalty to the "divine" monarchs ... offered to, and accepted by, the Ptolemies as a substitute for the erection of statues of the emperors and for the refusal to worship them as gods'.

Rivkin has correctly identified the two strands occurring together in Philo's descriptions of προσευχαί, and his perception of the building replacing a statue as a material expression of the people's loyalty to the emperor could be helpful.[88] But the idea of προσευχαί having one meaning in *Flaccus* and another in *The Embassy to Gaius* is, I feel, both unhelpful and unnecessary.[89] The one word and the one building could have carried out the two functions described by Philo.

Conclusions about the Evidence from Philo and Josephus

In contrast with the writings of Philo, where the meeting-house of the Jews is consistently referred to as the προσευχή, in the works of Josephus the word συναγωγή is used to describe three buildings and the word προσευχή once. Neither Philo nor Josephus ever reports or describes a sabbath worship service in such a building.

I am not alone in highlighting the difficulties in conflating the pictures of Jewish sabbath activities described in Philo and Josephus. They are not identical, though they do have common aspects. It can be convenient to explain the grosser differences between them either as a by-product of Philo's wish to paint the Jews in a favourable light

---

[87] Rivkin, 'Ben Sira', pp. 350-51.

[88] Inscriptions can give this impression of the purpose of construction of the building; see Chapter 7.

[89] See L.L. Grabbe, 'Synagogues in Pre-70 Palestine: A Re-Assessment', *JTS* n.s. 39 (1988), pp. 401-10, esp. pp. 401-402, n. 2 where this point is raised; also Sandmel, *The First Christian Century*, p. 102, n. 17, where Rivkin is taken to task for hypothesising an unnecessary distinction between *proseuche* and synagogue in order to strengthen his own argument.

to Caligula by stressing the amount of homage expressed towards the Emperor via the προσευχαί, or as a consequence of the differences to be expected between the central Mediterranean regions, including Rome and Alexandria, and the eastern Mediterranean regions of Palestine and its environs. Of course, some of the differences could also be attributed to the passage of fifty years or so between the times of Philo and Josephus. But the pictures they present have a such a large amount in common that their combined evidence gives a reliable view of the sabbath religious activities of Jews.

Hence we may conclude from the evidence we have examined up to this point that Jews, the adult males at least, throughout and up to the end of the first century CE, did many things at their meetings in prayer-house or synagogue, not all of them religious or pacific. The name usual in Philo for the buildings in which they met is προσευχαί, although in the writings of Josephus, referring to Palestine and Syria, the alternative name συναγωγή is also used.

For communal Jewish worship on the sabbath there is simply no evidence.

CHAPTER FOUR

SABBATH AS DOMESTIC CELEBRATION: GRAECO-ROMAN NON-CHRISTIAN SOURCES

Introduction

This study of the origins and location of Jewish sabbath worship will now be placed in a wider cultural context by surveying what was said about the Jews and their sabbaths in the writings of classical authors (Roman mainly, with a few Greek) from roughly 100 BCE to 150 CE, where the Jews and their institutions are described by non-Jews.[1] All the literature studied in the other chapters of this book has been written by Jewish or Christian authors, but these classical authors can be expected to understand Jewish religious affairs from quite a different knowledge base. Their perception of Jews depends on how the practice of Judaism affects Roman society; to them Judaism is one more among the many strange, imported ways of life that co-exist within the Roman Empire. They are observers who are also outsiders.

For these writers, Jews are indeed part of their world—both actual and literary—sometimes as exotic travellers or merchants from far away lands, telling tales of the Salt Sea and of the bitumen pits, or selling dates and flax of the highest quality. But Jews were also immigrants of the poorest sort, scraping a living on the fringes of Roman society.[2] They might also be slaves, perhaps bought as slaves

---

[1] M. Stern, ed., *Greek and Latin Authors on Jews and Judaism. I. From Herodotus to Plutarch* (Jerusalem: The Israel Academy of Sciences and Humanities, 1976); M. Stern, ed., *Greek and Latin Authors on Jews and Judaism. II. From Tacitus to Simplicius* (Jerusalem: The Israel Academy of Sciences and Humanities, 1980); M. Whittaker, *Jews and Christians: Graeco-Roman Views* (Cambridge Commentaries on the Writings of the Jewish and Christian World 200 BC to AD 200, 6; Cambridge: CUP, 1984).

[2] Martial, *Epigrams* 12.57.7-14, in Martial, *Epigrams* (tr. W.C.A. Ker; LCL; Cambridge, MA: Harvard University Press, 1919; rev. edn, 1968); Juvenal, *Satires* 3.12-16; 6.542-47, in *Juvenal and Persius* (tr. G.G. Ramsay; LCL; Cambridge, MA: Harvard University Press, 1940); Cleomedes, *De motu*, 2.1.9,1 in *Cléomède: Théorie*

elsewhere and brought to Rome, perhaps captured in a military campaign,[3] although such slaves may have been few in number due to the alleged Jewish practice of ransoming their co-religionists as soon as possible.[4] There were also Jews who were former slaves, emancipated by their masters, and thus Roman citizens.[5]

These classical writers take different stances and use different tones in their comments on, and descriptions of, Jews. They may show respect, misunderstanding, envy or disgust. The full range of emotions can easily be discovered—although sometimes they are voiced more strongly in the translation than in the original text.

Some of the texts studied are moral discourses, historical or geographical treatises and contain what are, as far as we can tell, misapprehensions about Jews along with valid material. But many of the texts are written in a less didactic mode: law court orations, love poetry, satire. In these, irony, exaggeration and invective all abound. 'Jews', presenting their more notable—to Roman eyes—characteristics in stereotyped ways, are used as a sort of shorthand to create an image in the mind of the reader. In order to take 'information' from such texts we have to absorb and take the measure of the writer's stance in the production of the text.[6] So, some texts about Jews that are unrelated to the topic of sabbath worship are included and discussed here to help in getting the measure of the writers' comments about Jewish sabbaths and Jewish meeting-houses.

Certain themes and topics recur through all the texts and should be borne in mind as being constitutive of Jews to the Roman mind, or at least typical of Jews as they appear in metaphors, or as

---

Harvard University Press, 1940); Cleomedes, *De motu*, 2.1.9,1 in *Cléomède: Théorie élémentaire: De motu circulari corporum caelestium* (tr. R. Goulet; Librairie Philosophique; Paris: J. Vrin, 1980) and in *Cleomedis de motu circulari corporum caelestium* (tr. H. Ziegler; Leipzig: Teubner, 1891); Artemidorus, *Dreams*, 53, in Artemidorus, *The Interpretation of Dreams: Oneirocritica* (tr. R.J. White; Noyes Classical Studies; Park Ridge, NJ: Noyes, 1975).

[3] Petronius, *Satyricon* 68.6, in *The Satyricon of Petronius* (tr. W. Arrowsmith; Ann Arbor: University of Michigan Press, 1959), *Petrone: Le Satyricon* (tr. A. Ernout; Paris: Les Belles Lettres, 1950) and *The Satyricon of T. Petronius Arbiter* (tr. W. Burnaby, 1694; ed. C.K. Scott Moncrieff; The Abbey Classics: London, n.d., ca 1961); Philo, *Embassy* 155.

[4] Grant, *The Jews*, p. 62.

[5] Philo, *Embassy* 155.

[6] All the writers studied are male, so non-inclusive language may be used without any erroneous implications.

'character parts' in the more rhetorical forms of discourse.[7] These elements are: the oddity of circumcision, Jewish lechery or lustfulness, Jewish abstention from pork, Jews as beggars, fortune-tellers and dream interpreters, Jews wasting one day in seven in idleness, Jews making up a close-knit separatist community with laws and moral standards of its own. As Goldenberg says, 'Judaism remained *for the Roman élite* an exotic Oriental importation ... [T]o observe the sabbath meant to enter a world of lower-class ignorant Jews, half-Jews and gentile fellow travelers.'[8] This description represents the perceived image of Jewry for educated Romans.

Texts and Writers from before the Common Era

At this period the writers were aware of the Jews as a part of Roman life, but there seems to be no particular singling out of the Jewish nation for the purposes of ridicule, nor is there any animus directed against the Jewishness of Jews.

Meleager

Meleager, a Gadarene of the first century BCE, wrote several love poems to a woman named Demo, and in one of them tortures himself by imagining that he has been displaced in love by a passionate Jew.

> *The Greek Anthology*, V, 160
> White-cheeked Demo, someone hath thee naked[9] next him and is taking his delight, but my own heart groans within me. If thy lover is some great Sabbath-keeper, no great wonder. Love burns hot even on cold Sabbaths.[10]

He knows that Jews light no fires on the sabbath, but also knows that even on the sabbath the lustful Jews do not abstain from love.

---

[7] S. Robinson, *Sixteen Satires upon the Ancient Harlot* (Manchester: Carcanet, 1983), p. 49, defines rhetoric as: the public use of words and gestures to produce an emotion in the listener which the speaker does not feel himself, although he seems to.

[8] Goldenberg, 'Jewish Sabbath', pp. 441-42 (my emphasis).

[9] The translation of Stern has, by mistake, 'named' for 'naked'.

[10] Meleager, *Anthology* 5.160, in *The Greek Anthology*, I (tr. W.R. Paton; LCL; Cambridge, MA: Harvard University Press, 1916); also P. Whigham and P. Jay, *The Poems of Meleager* (London: Anvil Press, 1975), pp. 21, 22.

Cicero

Cicero's only reference to Jews occurs in his speech *Pro Flaccus* from 69 BCE. Flaccus, a public official, has been arraigned for preventing, while governor of Asia, the sending of the Jews' annual collection to the Jerusalem temple and for condoning the subsequent seizing of the money in a number of Greek cities in the province.[11] Cicero sets about defending him in the time-honoured way, by discrediting the witnesses and supporters of the opposing side.

> *Pro Flacco* 28.66-67
> 66 Then there is that unpopularity over the Jewish gold. This is presumably why this case is being heard not far from the Aurelian[12] steps. It was for this particular charge, Laelius, that you sought this site and that crowd. You know how vast a throng it is, how close-knit, and what influence it can have in public meetings. 67 To oppose this outlandish superstition was an act of firmness, and to defy in the public interest the crowd of Jews that on occasions sets our public meetings ablaze was the height of responsibility.[13]

Cicero feels somewhat out-manoeuvred by his young opponent Laelius, who has set the trial in a very public place, where Jews were able to attend and make their views heard.[14] (Cicero was, politically speaking, in the other party from that supported by the generality of Jews.[15]) So he tries to disarm the Jews' influence, by speaking of it at the outset. But if I remove the edge from his voice, what does he say about Jews? They are numerous, they are united, they are influential. These descriptions can be either positive or negative, depending on one's point of view.

Much is made in the scholarly literature of the fact that Cicero describes Judaism as a *barbara superstitio*, outlandish superstition.[16] So, commentators feel able to write of Cicero's 'unfriendly remarks'[17] and to describe them as milking the 'natural prejudice of the Romans against a people who had been subdued by Roman arms

---

[11] Grant, *The Jews*, p. 55.

[12] Pun on *aurum*, 'gold'.

[13] Cicero, *Pro Flacco* 28.66-69, in *Cicero*, X (tr. C. MacDonald; LCL; Cambridge, MA: Harvard University Press, 1977); this Flaccus has no connection with the Flaccus addressed by Philo.

[14] But note the contradictory view of Grant, *The Jews*, pp. 55, 62, that Cicero exaggerated the size and power of the Jewish community in Rome.

[15] See the extended discussion of this incident in Leon, *Ancient Rome*, pp. 5-8.

[16] Cicero, *Pro Flacco* 28.67.

[17] Gager, *Anti-Semitism*, p. 41.

only a few years previously'.[18] But Cicero is not being particularly unfriendly to Jews, he defends Flaccus, in the same aggressive way that he defends others, by attempting character assassination of those bringing the charges, those who allege they have been damaged by the defendant.

Flaccus, while acting as a Roman magistrate, had removed or flouted the Jewish privilege of collecting money annually for the Jerusalem temple, so Cicero defends him by making out that 'the Jews are a tiresome people whose "superstition" it is a virtue to oppose'.[19] But this is clearly Cicero's way of obscuring the central issue, for the Jews had gained this special privilege of being able to send money out of the province of Asia and it is that privilege that Cicero chooses to attack indirectly, by mockery, rather than attempt to prove that Flaccus's actions are honourable or justifiable. It must be noted, however, that the worst he says about the Jews is that they are influential and passionate in debate.

Denigrating the national character of opponents was a common practice of Cicero's in his defence speeches. His remarks about Gauls as credible witnesses in the trial of Fonteius are no less unpleasant. He asks: '[I]s any the most honourable native of Gaul[20] to be set on the same level with even the meanest citizen of Rome ...?' And he is no kinder to Sardinians during the trial of Scaurus when he says: 'See now, gentlemen, to what families, how foul, how polluted, how degraded, you are called upon to surrender the family of Scaurus'.[21] The Jews are the subject of no worse insults than many other non-Romans.

I would characterise Cicero's attitude as he directs his prepared remarks 'at' the Jews in the crowd, as healthy respect tinged with envy, for he states quite plainly that the Jews are influential at public meetings. No doubt, if the Jews had been his supporters, their qualities would have been a source of much praise and not censure.

---

[18] H.J. Leon, *The Jews of Ancient Rome* (Philadelphia: The Jewish Publication Society of America, 1960), p. 7; see also S. Bacchiocchi, *From Sabbath to Sunday: A Historical Investigation of the Rise of Sunday Observance in Early Christianity* (Rome: The Pontifical Gregorian University Press, 1977), p. 173.

[19] Smallwood, *Roman Rule*, pp. 126-27.

[20] Cicero, *Pro Fonteio* 26 in *Cicero*, XIV (tr. N.H. Watts; LCL; Cambridge, MA: Harvard University Press, 1972); the translation is quoted correctly.

[21] Cicero, *Pro Scauro* 13, in *Cicero*, XIV (tr. N.H. Watts; LCL; Cambridge, MA: Harvard University Press, 1972).

Horace

Horace, in the latter half of the first century BCE, draws upon several Roman stereotypes of Jews: Jewish enthusiasm and insistence bring in converts; Jews are credulous; and Jews do not transact business on the sabbath.

> *Satires*, I, 4. 139-43
> we [poets], like the Jews, will compel you to make one of our throng.
>
> *Satires*, I, 5. 96-104
> Apella, the Jew may believe it, not I ...
>
> *Satires*, I, 9. 60-78
> 'Today is the thirtieth day, a Sabbath. Would you affront the circumcised Jews?' 'I have no scruples', say I 'But I have. I am a somewhat weaker brother, one of the many.'[22]

In the third extract Horace describes a situation when he is caught in the street on a sabbath by a frightful bore, and pretends to another passing friend, Fuscus, that he wishes to talk some private business with him, in the hope of being rescued from the bore. But his malicious friend gives an unhelpful reply, saying that since it is the sabbath they must not talk business for it would give offence to any Jews who might observe them. In the by-going he does speak in offensive language, 'affront' being a euphemism,[23] about how the putative conversation of Horace might insult Jews, showing by this low kind of humour that the excuse is bogus, and that the Jewish sabbath is of little real value to him, but also showing that he believed sabbath rest to be of such high importance to Jews that to disparage it would cause them affront.

Some writers on Jewish–Roman relations read this passage very negatively. Thus, Bacchiocchi says that Horace makes 'sneers and jibes' at Jews,[24] and Simon accuses Horace of employing sarcasm against Jews.[25] But other commentators, of whom Michael is typical,

---

[22] Horace, *Satires* 1.4, 139-43; 1.5, 96-104; 1.9, 60-78, in *Satires, Epistles and Ars Poetica* (tr. H.R. Fairclough; LCL; Cambridge, MA: Harvard University Press, 1970); Horace's confusion of 'the thirtieth' and 'a sabbath' is unresolvable; scholars understand it either as a mistake or a garbled conflation of sabbath and new moon.

[23] *Oppedere* is 'to break wind at' (*A Latin Dictionary* ed. C.T. Lewis and C. Short; Oxford: Clarendon Press, 1962]); 'to fart in the face of' (*Oxford Latin Dictionary* [ed. P.G.W. Glare; Oxford: Clarendon Press, 1982], *s.v.*).

[24] Bacchiocchi, *Sunday*, p. 173.

[25] M. Simon, *Verus Israel: A Study of the Relations between Christians and Jews in the Roman Empire 135–425* (tr. H. McKeating; Oxford: OUP, 1986), p. 280.

find rather a hint that many Romans know of Jewish sensibilities about the sabbath for, they claim, Fuscus's throw-away line could have no meaning if the Jewish sabbath was not common knowledge.[26]

Both these readings miss the mark, however; for Fuscus's reason for resisting conversation is intended to be a bogus one. No Roman foreswore business on the Jewish sabbath out of respect for the Jews; but neither can we infer that the Jewish custom was a laughable one. What Fuscus implies is that many Romans are 'weak' enough to kowtow to Jewish sensibilities.

An interesting point about these three references to Jews in Horace is that they are each at the end of the satire in which they appear. They are each part of the climax of the pieces—almost a closing leitmotif, or a signal that he is reaching a satirical punchline. The funny story or comment about Jews is the signal to smile and to applaud the final flourish of the satire.

Pompeius Trogus

As Gager argues, the historian Pompeius Trogus, writing in the first century BCE, was 'capable of writing about them [the Jews] in a dispassionate, sympathetic, and occasionally admiring manner',[27] and was aided in doing so by the fact that he cast his history in a strongly aetiological mould, which allowed portrayal of the Jews as unsociable or even misanthropic without any sense of hostility being attached to those descriptions—even, by this means, presenting the Jews as thoughtful and considerate towards their neighbours. Thus his writings contributed to the 'positive image of Judaism projected during Augustus's reign by various Greek writers'.[28]

Pompeius Trogus, contributing to a recurring misunderstanding of Jewish habits, describes Moses as having consecrated the sabbath as a perpetual fast day, hallowed for all time.

> Preserved in Justinus, *Historiae Philippicae, Epitoma* 36, 2.14-16
> ... he (Moyses), for all time, consecrated the seventh day, which used to be called Sabbath by the custom of the nation, for a fast

---

[26] J.H. Michael, 'The Jewish Sabbath in the Latin Classical Writers', *AJSL* 40 (1924), pp. 117-24 (118); cf. Goldenberg, 'Jewish Sabbath', p. 438.
[27] Gager, *Anti-Semitism*, pp. 72.
[28] Gager, *Anti-Semitism*, pp. 71-72, 86-87.

day ... [T]hey took care, in order that they might not become odious,
from the same cause [fear of spreading infection], to their neighbours,
to have no communication with strangers; a rule which, from having
been adopted on that particular occasion, gradually became a religious institution ... and ever afterwards it was a custom among the
Jews to have the same persons both for kings and priests; and, by
their justice combined with religion, it is almost incredible how
powerful they became.[29]

The confusion of the ban on cooking with a requirement to fast is
common in many of the writings of the time.[30] But Pompeius Trogus
does conceive of the day as being held sacred.

In my opinion this confusion over sabbath and fasting could possibly be visible in, or have arisen from, the writings of Josephus, for,
in a section describing how the Jews have had many imitators, he
says:

The masses have long shown a keen desire to adopt our religious
observances; and there is not one city, Greek or barbarian, nor a single nation, to which our custom of abstaining from work on the seventh day has not spread, and where the fasts and the lighting of lamps
and many of our prohibitions in the matter of food are not observed.[31]

This passage, whether by chance or on purpose, definitely links sabbath rest, fasting, the lighting of lamps and food rules—though, as
far as we know, there was no requirement to fast on the sabbath.

Pompeius Trogus remarks on the Jews' separatism, explaining it
by an aetiology. He says it began as a Jewish way of protecting
themselves against odium being occasioned by their having spread
contagion to neighbouring tribes, but it remained as a religious
embargo. He comments on the Jews' singularly successful and powerful mode of government, namely, having the same people as rulers
and priests, this being a more than usually effective system because
both religion and justice are administered by the same persons. None
of this comment could be called pejorative.

---

[29] Pompeius Trogus, *Epitoma 36*, 2.14-16, preserved in Justinus, *Historiae
Philippicae*, in *Justin Cornelius Nepos and Eutropius* (tr. J.S. Watson; London: George
Bell and Sons, 1902).
[30] Goldenberg, 'Jewish Sabbath', pp. 435-42, has a thorough discussion of this confused understanding of sabbath praxis—although he does not refer to the passage from
Josephus discussed below; see also Michael, 'Jewish Sabbath', pp. 122-24.
[31] Josephus, *Apion* 2.282-83.

Ovid

Ovid, writing around the turn of the era,[32] also knows the sabbath as a weekly day held sacred (*sacra*) by Jews (or Palestine Syrians, a synonym for Jews[33]), and twice refers to it in light-hearted vein as a day as suitable as any other for finding a new sweetheart. He lists all the places, weathers and occasions that might wrongly be considered unsuitable for finding a sweetheart—including the sabbath as a an example of a time that some might avoid. But in his view the sacredness of the day to the Jews should not cause any Roman male to curtail his amatory pursuits, in fact he regards the sabbath as more suitable than a woman's birthday—a day when an appropriate and beguiling present could very well be expected from the would-be lover.[34]

> *Art of Love*, 1.75-78
> Nor let Adonis bewailed of Venus escape you, nor the seventh day that the Syrian Jew holds sacred. Avoid not the Memphian shrine of the linen-clothed heifer: many a maid does she make what she was herself to Jove.

> *Art of Love*, 1.413-17
> You may begin on the day on which woeful Allia flows stained with the blood of Latin wounds, or on that day, less fit for business, whereon returns the seventh day feast that the Syrian of Palestine observes. But hold in awful dread your lady's birthday ...

Goldenberg is unwilling to regard as neutral Ovid's persistent use of 'foreign' or 'Syrian' when describing the sabbath, and sees it as a pejorative reference to the Jews' holy day.[35] It seems to me, on the other hand, that Ovid uses colourful imagery from all the cultural richness of Roman society, and is not using these descriptions to demean those who follow foreign cults.

A quite different evaluation of Ovid's attitude is taken by Leon, who considers Ovid to go so far as to recommend the sabbath as 'a

---

[32] Ovid, *The Art of Love*, 1.75-70, 413-16, in *Ovid*, II (tr. J.H. Mozley, rev. G.P. Goold; LCL; Cambridge, MA: Harvard University Press, 1979).

[33] Stern, *Authors*, I, pp. 348-49; Simon, *Verus Israel*, pp. 204.

[34] A similar point, though the reference is specifically to Saturn's sacred day, is made by the poet Tibullus writing in the late first century BCE; see Tibullus, *Elegies* 1.3.15-18, in G. Lee, *Tibullus, Elegies: Introduction, Text, Translation and Notes* (2nd edn; Liverpool Latin Texts [Classical and Mediaeval], 3; Liverpool: Frances Cairns, The University of Liverpool, 1982), pp. 36-37, 113; see also Stern, *Authors*, I, pp. 318-20; also cf. discussion on Seneca below.

[35] Goldenberg, 'Jewish Sabbath', p. 436.

favourable time for courting a girl'.[36] But Michael, begging the question of the existence at that time of either synagogue buildings[37] or sabbath worship services, goes further and insists that Ovid means that the hopeful lover should go to sabbath synagogue services and look for a young Roman woman there:[38] he says '[W]hat meaning is there in the counsel unless Roman maidens were wont to attend those services?'[39] Michael apparently also assumes that the generality of Roman women spent the sabbath in rest or idleness.[40] Perhaps he is merely unable to conceive of women being courted while about their daily tasks because, from his perspective, courtship belongs to one's leisure hours, and therefore the young Roman women of the poet's imagination must have had leisure on the sabbath. This is speculation run riot.

All we can conclude from Ovid is that a knowledge of the Jewish sacred day can be assumed for his audience. He knows that Jews do not do business on it—but more we cannot say.

Conclusions about the Writings from before the Common Era and at the Turn of the Era

Meleager, Horace and Ovid use references to Jews to enliven or colour their poetry, Pompeius Trogus respects the Jews, and Cicero has a healthy respect for them. The Jewish sabbath is to them a day held sacred, with no fires, and no cooking—and so construed as a day with no eating either. The Jews' avoidance of everyday activities on their sabbath attracts comment, but there are no hints of activities special to the sabbath in which Jews participate.

Texts and Writers of the Common Era

Apart from Seneca and Frontinus, who are fairly neutral in their comments, the writers of the later first century CE found the Jews

---

[36] Leon, *Ancient Rome*, p. 13.
[37] See Stern, *Authors*, II, discussion on Artemidorus, p. 330.
[38] Michael, 'Jewish Sabbath', p. 119.
[39] Grant, *The Jews*, pp. 62-63, repeats these same conclusions, but, unfairly in my view, puts them in the mouth of Ovid himself.
[40] Michael, 'Jewish Sabbath', p. 120.

somewhat more threatening, no doubt because Jews were more respectable now, both ideologically and socio-economically. There is an edge of discomfort discernible in what is written because the Jews show signs of outshining or supplanting Romans in situations that really matter to them. The Jews are 'put in their place' by mockery at all levels of severity, from gentle jibes to bitter sarcasm; yet more knowledge about Jewish religious habits can be discerned in these writings.

Seneca

The philosopher Seneca, in his *Moral Letters*, speaking about how one's intentions condition the value of one's actions, discusses the necessity in life of striving to do one's duty and seeking the Supreme Good. Following this passage he makes critical comments about the different, and in his view inadequate, ways in which people worship gods.

> *Moral Letters* 95.47
> Precepts are commonly given as to how the gods should be worshipped. But let us forbid lamps to be lighted on the Sabbath, since the gods do not need light, neither do men take pleasure in soot. Let us forbid men to offer morning salutation and to throng the doors of temples; mortal ambitions are attracted by such ceremonies, but God[41] is worshipped by those who truly know him.[42]

Commentators note that he refers to the Jewish practice of lighting lamps on Friday evening when the sabbath is welcomed into the home, but they have not noticed that Seneca regards this as the way Jews *worship* God, and that he thinks it is too trivial a way to worship any god worthy of the name.[43]

Leon, among the commentators, comes close to realising that Seneca has this misapprehension but he uses a phrase more appropriate to Roman worship—'paying homage to one's gods'—of Seneca's understanding of the lamp lighting,[44] rather than recognising in Seneca's description a Roman perception of what counts as

---

[41] Or 'a god' (my translation).
[42] Seneca, *Moral Letters* 95.47, in *Ad Lucilium epistulae morales* (tr. R.M. Gummere; LCL; Cambridge, MA: Harvard University Press, 1925); see also the phrase 'lighting of lamps' in Josephus already quoted above.
[43] See the discussion of the worship of gods in their temples by Rattray in 'Worship'.
[44] Leon, *Ancient Rome*, p. 245.

Jewish worship of the one God.

Seneca sees the Jews involved in these practices, as Jews going about the business of worship, but he cannot see that any of it is of value to God. He is not 'railing against the customs of this "accursed race"', as Bacchiocchi avers,[45] but rather, as Whittaker puts it, 'Seneca is deprecating any ritual which might seem to belittle the transcendence of God'.[46]

But why should Seneca regard these homely ritual activities as worship? The only reason can be that these things are the answer to some question such as: 'What different things do Jews do to celebrate their holy day, the sabbath?' And Seneca lists what he knows. He knows only of lighting sabbath lamps, offering morning, i.e. every morning, salutations and thronging the doors of 'temples';[47] so these are the actions he criticises. He knows nothing of services of worship, nothing of prayers or psalms, nothing of reading, expounding and discussing the Law of Moses—as described by Philo, Josephus and New Testament authors.[48] He ascribes nothing specifically to the sabbath except the lighting of lamps. And although it is not absolutely clear from the text, he may also know of, and be describing, the gathering of Jews for daily services of morning prayers.

A further passage of Seneca's about the Jews is preserved only in Augustine's *City of God*.

> Augustine, *City of God* 6.11, quoting Seneca *On Superstition*
> Along with other superstitions of the civil theology Seneca also censures the sacred institutions of the Jews, especially the sabbath. He declares that their practice is inexpedient, because by introducing one day of rest in every seven they lose in idleness almost a seventh of their life, and by failing to act in times of urgency, they often suffer loss ... But when speaking of the Jews he says: 'Meanwhile the customs of this accursed race[49] have gained such influence that they are

---

[45] Bacchiocchi, *Sunday*, pp. 173-74, unfairly conflating the two pieces of Seneca's writings about Jews; see discussion below.

[46] Whittaker, *Views*, p. 72.

[47] Possibly these last two practices are not Jewish, but in Mk 12.38, the voice of Jesus, in a similar way, censures the scribes for salutations in the market place.

[48] Philo, *Embassy* 157; *Moses* 2.216; *Special Laws* 2.59-64; *Hypothetica* 7.9-13; *Contemplative Life* 27-33; *Dreams* 123-28; Josephus, *Antiquities* 16.40-46; *Life* 272-303; Mk 1.21; 6.2; Acts 15.21; 18.4.

[49] Seneca's phrase 'sceleratissimae gentis' can equally be translated 'of the most rascally race' [my translation]; *sceleratissimus* (superlative of *scelerus*) is capable of many translations: bad, impious, wicked, accursed, infamous, vicious, flagitious, hurtful,

now received throughout all the world. The vanquished have given laws to their victors.' He shows his surprise as he says this, not knowing what was being wrought by the providence of God. But he adds a statement that shows what he thought of their system of sacred institutions: 'The Jews, however, are aware of the origin and meaning of their rites. The greater part of the people go through a ritual not knowing why they do so.'[50]

Augustine relates that Seneca censured the Jews for wasting a seventh of their lives in sabbath rest, but he also preserves Seneca's respectful reference to certain qualities of Jews, namely their deep commitment to, and thorough education in, their religion. So, although he apostrophises the Jews as the most pernicious, or unhappy, or unfortunate race, Seneca is apparently quite impressed by them. He comments on the fact that, while the Jews have been vanquished by other races, their laws—perhaps sabbath observance is being alluded to here—have been adopted 'throughout all the world',[51] and also that the Jews are 'aware of the origin and meaning of their rites', which awareness he contrasts with most people's ignorance of such matters.

It is interesting that Josephus, writing at a time very close to Seneca, makes a similar comment when he writes:

> The masses have long since shown a keen desire to adopt our religious observances; and there is not one city, Greek or barbarian, nor a single nation, to which our custom of abstaining from work on the seventh day has not spread and where our fasts and the lighting of lamps and many of our prohibitions in the matter of food are not observed.[52]

Of course, this belief in the popular acceptance of a weekly rest day on Saturday could be wishful thinking on Josephus's part, but there is some support for his claim in the work of the poet Tibullus who suggests that he had on occasions thought travel to be inauspicious on the day of Saturn,[53] the same day as the Jewish sabbath and often

---

harmful, noxious, pernicious, unhappy, unfortunate, calamitous, etc.; cf. *A Latin Dictionary*, p. 1640.

[50] Seneca, *On Superstition*, preserved in Augustine, *City of God*, 6.11, in *The City of God against the Pagans*, II (tr. W.H. Green; LCL; Cambridge, MA: Harvard University Press, 1963).

[51] Leon, *Ancient Rome*, pp. 42, 250, understands this as referring negatively to Jewish proselytising activity; see also Gager, *Anti-Semitism*, p. 60.

[52] Josephus, *Apion* 2.282-83, already quoted above in reference to fasting.

[53] Tibullus, *Elegies* 1, 3.15-18, in a poem written on his sick bed far from home, remembers the excuses he used to delay his departure from his lover, Delia: 'I myself,

regarded as synonymous with it.[54]

Josephus also reports that the Jews in Antioch 'were constantly attracting to their religious ceremonies multitudes of Greeks, and these they had in some measure incorporated with themselves'.[55] These two writers, Josephus and Seneca, from very different backgrounds, share a common belief in the spread of Jewish customs and a common knowledge of the lighting of lamps and of sabbath rest. But, in my opinion, both are reporting, not criticising, the spread of the customs.

Goldenberg is of a different opinion. He claims, that, by the way Seneca refers to the adoption of Jewish customs and laws by non-Jews, he shows that he 'was anxious to keep the practice from spreading'.[56] With this view of Seneca's concern Grant concurs,[57] for he detects in Seneca a 'strongly anti-Jewish attitude' and says that: '[t]he smoking lamps on the Sabbath, and the wastefulness of this institution in losing one seventh of man's labour, caused Seneca great annoyance, and he complained that "the customs of that most criminal nation ... have now been received in all lands"'.

But, in the text of *On Superstition*, Seneca writes only of the spread of Jewish laws, not of the spread of the sabbath evening domestic habits, and it is unfair of Grant to conflate the comment about the 'smoking lamps' from one piece of writing with the comment on the widespread reception of Jewish 'customs' from the other, especially bearing in mind that one has been preserved by another writer, in this case Augustine.

I also find it hard to agree with Stern's criticism that 'Seneca was the first Latin writer to give vent to deliberate animadversions on the Jewish religion and its impact on Roman society',[58] and more readily endorse the views of Gager who finds that neutral or positive evidence of Roman attitudes towards Jews 'is simply overlooked', as they wish to make the case that 'the ancient world in general, and the

---

her comforter, when I had already given my commissions, was still anxious and sought lingering delays. I alleged either birds or evil omens or that the day sacred to Saturn had held me back'; translation, Whittaker, *Views*, p. 65.

[54] Cf. Lee, *Tibullus*, pp. 36-37, and p. 113, n. 18 where the identity of Saturn's day and the Jewish sabbath are assumed.

[55] Josephus, *War* 7.43-45.

[56] Goldenberg, 'Jewish Sabbath', p. 434.

[57] Grant, *The Jews*, p. 176.

[58] Stern, *Authors*, I, p. 429.

early Roman Empire in particular, disliked Jews'.[59] This negative view is most clearly expressed by Grant, when he says that 'all the old Roman prejudices against the Jews still remained actively rampant' and indicts Juvenal, Plutarch and Epictetus, among others, for 'reviving the time-worn attacks against Jewish imageless monotheism, abstinence from pork, circumcision, Sabbath observation and mendicant fortune telling'.[60] In my opinion, Grant has read all these writers through a particular lens of sensitivity to slights to Jews and has seen much negativity expressed in the texts which is not visible to other commentators or to me.

Seneca seems to me to pass a variety of comments on the Jews, some praising and some deflating the value of Judaism as a religion, but none expressing hostility to Jews or to customs and laws of Jewish origin, *merely* because of their Jewishness; I do not believe he invents unpleasant comments out of spite or pique. If he criticises behaviours it is for something in the behaviour itself, rather than for that one aspect, its ethnic origin. So, I am able to regard Seneca's comments as reflecting what he really thought the Jews actually did to celebrate their religion and worship on their holy day, the sabbath, that is, they lit lamps and they stopped work.

Persius

The poet Persius (34–62 CE)[61] wrote to 'promote the world view of Stoicism' yet gives an evocative picture of the sabbath which is 'vivid and true to the reality of the sabbath celebrated by the Jews'.[62]

> Satires 5. 176-84
> And that white-robed wheedler there, dragged open-mouthed by his thirst for office—is he his own master? Up with you before dawn and deal out showers of chick peas for the people to scramble for, that old men sunning themselves in their old age may tell of the splendour of our Floralia. How grand. But when the day of Herod comes round,

---

[59] Gager, *Anti-Semitism*, pp. 67-88, esp. p. 82.

[60] Grant, *The Jews*, p. 240.

[61] Persius, *Satires*, in *The Satires of A. Persius Flaccus* (tr. J. Conington; Oxford: Clarendon Press, 1893), pp. 118-19; in *Juvenal and Persius* (tr. G.G. Ramsay; LCL; Cambridge, MA: Harvard University Press, 1940), pp. 386-89; *Persius: The Satires* (tr. J.R. Jenkinson; Warminster: Aris & Phillips, 1980), p. 53, and see especially Jenkinson's analysis of the complexity of Persius's rhetoric in the notes at pp. 91-92; also R.A. Harvey, *A Commentary on Persius* (Mnemosyne Supplements, 64; Leiden: Brill, 1981), pp. 176-78.

[62] Stern, *Authors*, I, p. 435.

when the lamps wreathed with violets and ranged round the greasy
window-sills have spat forth their thick clouds of smoke, when the
floppy tunnies' tails are curled round the dishes of red ware, and the
white jars are swollen out with wine, you silently twitch your lips,
turning pale at the sabbath of the circumcised.[63]

In this satire, Persius suggests that those who believe themselves
to be free are, in fact, merely unaware of the force, or forces, controlling their lives. He illustrates this theme by depicting a man torn
between the joys offered by working hard in response to Avarice and
the pleasures of lolling in idleness under the influence of Luxury.

Following shortly after this portrayal, he focusses his attention on
a man caught in the grip of ambition, who steadfastly follows all the
moves in the political game, hoping for advancement; but who also
succumbs to the appeal of superstitious rituals. To illustrate this
conflict of ambition and superstition Persius transfers his narration
from the public arena of the Forum to a description of the beginning
of sabbath in a Jewish home as seen from the street by a passer-by,
followed by a few brief references to other superstitions which command responses.

Our main interest in the passage is with the description of Jewish
sabbath activities, and here, as in Seneca, the only sabbath activities
described are those which happen in the home on Friday evening:
there is the lighting of lamps, followed here by a meal of fish and
wine and accompanied by some unidentified recitation. The items
conceived as belonging to the Jewish sabbath are domestic and ordinary—culinary items—not items set apart for religious use only.[64]

But the very last phrase of this piece immediately attracts and
holds the reader's attention, for it alters the mood of the recital,
seemingly referring to some prayer or other ritual spoken by a person
who is, or becomes, pale. Commentators suggest various meanings
for this enigmatic phrase.

Here, as in his reading of Seneca, Goldenberg interprets Persius's
picture as less than sympathetic to the observed sabbath activities of

---

[63] Persius, *Satires*, 5.132-60.

[64] Harvey, *Persius*, pp. 177-78, regards the fish tails and the red dishes as a sign of
Jewish poverty, describing them as 'poor fare and poor ware', fish tails being the poorer
cut, but Conington, *Persius*, p. 120, nn. 182, 183, thinks that having the fishes' tails
curled round the dish indicates the buying of whole tunnies, surely a sign of reasonable
financial circumstances. This is another good example of how the interpreter's attitudes
can completely alter the perceived meaning of the texts.

Jews because he finds it paints the atmosphere of the sabbath as 'one of dread, of unpleasant mystery, sordid ugliness, disgusting superstition'.[65] Goldenberg uses seven negative word images to transmit his understanding of Persius's picture of the sabbath and decides that Persius writes out of 'hostility' and 'unfamiliarity with the activities described'.[66]

An alternate view of the dynamics of the last line of Persius's description is given by Harvey, who suggests that the person described might be showing 'the unreasoning terror of the superstitious man on festal days (as opposed to the faith of the religious man)',[67] but here Harvey also seems to carry some religious freight of his own, in the point of view expressed parenthetically.

Abandoning the search for a specifically Jewish meaning for the phrase, Jenkinson argues that '[f]lowers and silent prayer, however, do not seem to belong especially to Jewish ritual either in fact or elsewhere in the ancient imagination',[68] so he regards the phrase about the violet-wreathed lamps as unrelated to actual Jewish practice, thus endorsing Goldenberg's perception of Persius as revealing unfamiliarity with Jewish practices.

The meaning of the phrase *labra moves tacitus recutitaque sabbata palles* will vary depending on whose lips it is placed, and to what emotion is being portrayed.[69] And that is a vexed question. Conington regards the passage as dealing with the lack of freedom experienced by people in the thrall of either ambition *or* Judaism.[70] But Conington contradicts himself as to whether the passage implies that one person is a slave to the different superstitions one after the other,[71] or whether different people with one strong superstition each are being described in turn.[72]

Leon takes the reference to be to the prayer of the one observed

---

[65] Goldenberg, 'Jewish Sabbath', p. 435; also R. Goldenberg, 'The Sabbath in Rabbinic Judaism', in *The Sabbath in Jewish and Christian Traditions* (ed. T.C. Eskenazi, D.J. Harrington and W.H. Shea; New York: Crossroad, 1991), pp. 31-44.

[66] Goldenberg, 'Rabbinic Judaism', p. 37.

[67] Harvey, *Persius*, p. 178, n. 184.

[68] Jenkinson, *Satires*, p. 92, n. 42.

[69] Jenkinson, *Satires*, p. 53: 'then you mutely move your lips in dread of the circumcised sabbath'.

[70] Conington, *Persius*, p. 118, nn. 176-88.

[71] Conington, *Persius*, p. 120, n. 185.

[72] Conington, *Persius*, p. 118, nn. 176-88; see also Bacchiocchi, *Sunday*, p. 174.

rather than to the reaction of the observer for he translates the phrase as 'the awed prayer of silently moving lips on the "circumcised Sabbath"'. In my view, Leon has grasped part of the meaning of the phrase, for he locates the emotion—in his view, awe—within the person reciting the prayer.[73]

Persius himself provides ambiguous clues as to which meaning the word *palles* should carry. Early in the satire he praises his tutor whose 'delight' it has been 'to grow pale over nightly study, to till the minds of the young',[74] and later he suggests that someone might be 'uneasy' with a certain judge.[75] The word seems to me to carry the sense of a changed, or suddenly sobered countenance, associated with a sense either of uneasiness or of responsibility.

But I further believe that the difficulties of understanding the phrase and its role in the passage as a whole can be resolved if one considers the possibility that the political aspirant is the *same person* as the observer of, and then participant in, the Jewish sabbath. Suppose the man seeking preferment in Rome is a Jew. Then after all his fine parading in public places in a 'blanco'ed toga',[76] and, in spite of his courting favour in the usual manner of Romans—driven by ambition, he still, in private on Friday evenings, is drawn home by a need for security. He returns to the environment of familiar Jewish customs and family relationships, and reverts to the customs of his forefathers, which are rather low-class customs—from a Roman perspective, of course.

Persius provides the man's internal dialogue as he reviews his day of jockeying for status with the populace of Rome and then forcedly assumes a quite different persona when he returns home to join in the weekly sabbath meal of fish and wine, prefaced by the saying of prayers and blessings. Possibly he arrives late, and hurriedly, looking in the window to see if he has missed the beginning of the ritual, just after the lamps are lit and the first blessing said. At the door, I believe, he sheds his public Roman identity, resumes his private Jewish existence and joins in the sabbath recitations. He loses his buoyant mien and adopts a sober and humble demeanour, which is

---

[73] Leon, *Ancient Rome*, pp. 38, 24-45.
[74] Persius, *Satires*, 5.62; *inpallescere* 'to grow pale'.
[75] Persius, *Satires*, 5.80; *palles* 'you turn pale'.
[76] Jenkinson's literal translation of *cretata* (Jenkinson, *The Satires*, p. 91, n. 41).

how I understand the reference to pallor or unease.

This is my reading of the stanza; it allows for the mood change to happen in the mind of the man, and for the reader to be taken through the same disorientating shift from high, Roman, ambition back to humble, ethnic background.

This section of the satire could be Persius's piquant way of warning Roman society that Jews are no longer merely immigrants and underlings, but are ready to take important roles in society, while still persisting in their own separatist and thus 'inferior' ways—always a great infamy in Roman eyes.[77]

Petronius

Petronius, a contemporary of Seneca and Persius, wrote a vulgar and humorous novel, *The Satyricon*, about the fortunes of three rather ramshackle travellers. In the first extract their conversation flows very smoothly from the description of a slave as being circumcised, through his likeness to Venus, and on to lust and lechery—seemingly a common view of Jews, and one used here to paint a vivid and slightly denigrating picture of this apparently attractive slave.

> *Satyricon* 68.8
> He has only two faults, and if he were rid of them he would be simply perfect. He is circumcised and he snores. For I do not mind his being cross-eyed; he has a look like Venus. So that is why he cannot keep silent, and scarcely ever shuts his eyes. I bought him for three hundred denarii.[78]

In the second extract the three rascals seize on circumcision as one possible mode of disguise in a tight corner, an alternative to chalking their faces to the rarely tanned whiteness of Gauls or piercing their ears to be like Arabians.

> *Satyricon* 102.14
> and please circumcise us too, so that we look like Jews ...[79]

---

[77] As noted above for the satires of Horace, the reference to Jews heralds the close of the satire.

[78] Petronius, *Satyricon* 68.8, in *The Satyricon of Petronius* (tr. W. Arrowsmith; Ann Arbor: University of Michigan Press, 1959); *Petrone: Le Satyricon* (tr. A. Ernout; Paris: Les Belles Lettres, 1950); *The Satyricon of T. Petronius Arbiter* (tr. W. Burnaby, 1694; ed. C.K. Scott Moncrieff; The Abbey Classics: London, n.d., ca 1961) and *Petronius* (tr. M. Heseltine; Cambridge, MA: Harvard University Press, 1975).

[79] Petronius, *Satyricon* 102.14.

Again there is a kind of flavour of pantomime about the importation of Jewish characteristics into the mental images conjured up by the three prospective disguises. But a third extract, though only a fragment, and couched in fairly offensive language, does add a bit to our knowledge of how Jews and their sabbaths were perceived.[80]

> *Fragments, 37*
> The Jew may worship his pig-god and clamour in the ears of high heaven, but unless he also cuts back his foreskin with the knife,[81] he shall go forth from the people and emigrate to Greek cities, and shall not tremble[82] at the fasts of Sabbath imposed by the law.[83]

Because of their known abstention from eating pork, the Jews are erroneously—or perhaps mischievously—described as venerating the pig; but circumcision is quite clearly understood as an absolute 'must' for being a Jew. So, to me, the offensiveness of these remarks lies more in the extravagance of the language used in the descriptions than in any distortion of Jewish praxis.

The clause about emigration is quite enigmatic. Stern thinks of forced expulsion as the reason implied for the Jewish removal to Greek cities,[84] but it is possible that some other issue of Jewish status or proselytism is being alluded to here.

The last line of the fragment deals tantalisingly, but rather unintelligibly, with sabbath law. Many adopt the emendation of Bücheler which reads: 'and shall not tremble at the fasts of Sabbath imposed by law'.[85] This implies that, as well as demanding fasting, the sabbath inspires dread in those subject to it. The original, however, reads, 'where he will cease to oppress the Sabbath with his fasting law'.[86]

---

[80] Grant, *The Jews*, p. 176, regards Petronius, like his contemporary Seneca, as sneering at the sabbath, but I believe that Grant is detecting an author's intention of racism on the basis of the extravagant language of poetry.

[81] We should add at this point 'and unties its tightly-knotted head', my translation of a line omitted by the translator in the LCL.

[82] The translation 'tremble' presupposes the reading *tremet*—Bücheler's emendation. The translation of Michael follows the original text: 'he will be driven from among his people and will migrate to the cities of Greece where he will cease to oppress the Sabbath with his fasting law'.

[83] Petronius, *Fragmenta* 37.

[84] Stern, *Authors*, I, p. 444.

[85] Bacchiocchi, *Sunday*, p. 174, adopts and comments on this translation, but I am unable to trace a translation of Fragment 37 by M. Heseltine, as quoted by Stern, and have relied on the French translation of Ernout and my own translation.

[86] Michael, 'Jewish Sabbath', p. 123.

This seems to imply that there might be an 'unoppressed' sabbath that did not include a fasting law, but was a day of rest and happiness. Or it could imply that there was some type of semi-Jew, or quasi-Jew, who worshipped God and shouted to him in highest heaven, but was not willing to be circumcised and went to Greek cities where there was no compulsion to 'oppress' the sabbath by insisting on fasting. So this description could refer to a sympathiser with Judaism who had been attracted to its teaching and precepts but was not prepared to be circumcised or fast on the sabbath. It could also be alluding to early Jewish Christians.

Petronius, of course, expresses the common Roman misunderstanding of the sabbath as a day of fasting. He makes no mention of any public sabbath activities for Jews—the only reference to the sabbath is linked to refraining from eating.

Frontinus

Frontinus, in his book of military strategy written in the late first century CE, offers a religious understanding of sabbath observance, by stating that it was 'sinful' (*nefas*) for Jews to do business on the sabbath.

> *Stratagems* 2.1.17
> The deified Augustus Vespasian attacked the Jews on the day of Saturn, a day on which it is sinful for them to do any business ...[87]

This interpretation of sabbath observance as a moral or religious obligation is a more sympathetic view of Jewish abstention from work than the common accusation of idleness.

Martial

Martial was a most pungent humorist, his poetry being often both cutting and obscene. For the latter reason it has been difficult to find adequate translations of his works, for previous to the Loeb edition of 1968,[88] translators were willing to convert the more explicit

---

[87] Frontinus, *Stratagems* 2.1.17, in *The Stratagems and the Aqueducts of Rome* (tr. C.E. Bennett, rev. M.B. McElwain; LCL; Cambridge, MA: Harvard University Press, 1980).
[88] Martial, *Epigrams* (tr. W.C.A. Ker; LCL; Cambridge, MA: Harvard University Press, 1919; rev. edn, 1968).

poems into either French[89] or, rather more commonly, Italian,[90] or to leave them untranslated.[91] This lack of accurate—and explicit—translations has led to a lack of understanding of Martial's writings in the scholarly community.

Martial has been treated like a hostile witness and the worst possible construction put on his acrid comments, because, as Sullivan has claimed, Martial's flattery of Domitian, and his obscenity in writing, 'have blinded the supposedly neutral and value-free interpreter ... and prevented a proper appreciation of Martial's value as a poet and a witness of his times'.[92] The more liberated mores from the sixties onwards have allowed a fresh look at Martial's picture of Roman society and have prompted a fresh reading of his works.

In a vivid epigram, he abuses a woman, Bassa, because of her body odours (female body odours were obnoxious to Martial[93]), and he says that, among other things, he would prefer the breath of fasting Sabbatarian females (the Latin is feminine), fasting Jewish women, one might say, to her smell.

> *Epigrams* 4.4
> The stench of the bed of a drained marsh; of the raw vapours of sulphur springs; the putrid reek of a sea-water fishpond; of a stale he-goat in the midst of his amours; of the military boot of a fagged out veteran; of a fleece twice dyed with purple; of the breath of fasting Sabbatarian women (Jews: Ker 1968); of the sighs of depressed defendants; of filthy Leda's lamp as it expires; of ointment made of dregs of Sabine oil; of a wolf in flight; of a viper's lair—all these stenches would I prefer to your stench, Bassa. [94]

This does not tell us *necessarily* that Jews fasted on sabbath, *pace* Stern,[95] though it does tie in with that Roman misconception. What it does make plain is that Jewish women when fasting, had some sort of smell that Martial could expect his readers to recognise and to agree was unpleasant, which indicates that the Jews had alien food

---

[89] Martial, *Epigrammes* I–II (tr. H.J. Izaac; Paris: Les Belles Lettres, 1930).

[90] Martial, *Epigrams*, in *The Epigrams of Martial* (London: Bohn, 1860).

[91] *Martial: The Twelve Books of Epigrams* (tr. J.A. Pott and F.A. Wright; London: George Routledge & Sons, n.d., ca 1921–1936), p. 207.

[92] J.P. Sullivan, 'Synchronic and Diachronic Aspects of Some Related Poems of Martial', in *Contemporary Literary Hermeneutics and Interpretation of Classical Texts* (ed. S. Kresic; Ottawa: Ottawa University Press, 1981), pp. 215-25 (215).

[93] Sullivan, 'Synchronic and Diachronic Aspects', p. 223.

[94] Martial, *Epigrams* 4.4.

[95] Stern, *Authors*, I, p. 521.

habits, which produce differently scented sweat, and allowed the 'other' to be identified by smell. It tells us that the two cultures were separate and that the Jews were, or were thought to be, in a socially inferior position, where they could safely be described, even insulted, in this way.

Elsewhere in Martial's epigrams,[96] the 'circumcised Jews' are listed in the company of powerful sexual athletes from all over the Eastern Mediterranean who delight Caelia and who leave her with little enthusiasm for Romans—such as Martial himself—as lovers.

> *Epigrams* 7.30
> You grant your favours to Parthians, you grant them to Germans, you grant them, Caelia, to Dacians, and you do not spurn the couch of Cilicians and Cappadocians; and for you from his Egyptian city comes sailing the gallant (poker: Ker, 1968) of Memphis, and the black Indian from the Red Sea; nor do you shun the lecheries (groin: Ker, 1968) of circumcised Jews, and the Alan on his Sarmatian steed does not pass you by. What is your reason that, although you are a Roman girl, no Roman lewdness (prick: Ker, 1968) has attraction for you?

This exclusion of Romans in favour of foreigners points to Jews being successful in an arena to which Martial has not even been invited. He upbraids the Roman woman because she does not regard Roman men as equivalent in appeal to these exotic outsiders. The woman Caelia becomes the target of his rhetoric, because she can give a particular favour to men whom he would exclude from the competition.

Another extract has produced misleading commentary,[97] Leon, Stern and Gager all stating that the epigram refers to a circumcised Jew among Martial's slaves.[98]

> *Epigrams* 7.35
> A slave, girt around the groin with a black covering of dressed leather, waits on you while you are being caressed all over by warm water. But my slave, to say nothing of myself, has a Jewish load beneath bare skin; but bare are the young men and old men who wash themselves in your company. Is your slave's prick the only true one? Do you, O matron, follow at all after feminine recesses, and do you, O lower end, wash yourself secretly in water of your own? (tr. Ker)

---

[96] Martial, *Epigrams* 7.30.
[97] Martial, *Epigrams* 7.35.
[98] Leon, *Ancient Rome*, p. 39; Stern, *Authors*, I, p. 525; Gager, *Anti-Semitism*, p. 56.

As may be seen from this translation, Martial, addressing in satirical vein a woman who has a slave as a lover, claims that he has a
slave who is as well-hung as a Jew, though not necessarily a Jewish
slave, and also arrogates the same attribute to himself as well. This is
another envious reference to the lustiness of Jews.

Martial's remark smacks more of sexual jealousy than 'ridicule of
Jews' as Leon has it.[99] And in another witticism, Martial again hints
at Jews being well endowed sexually. This kind of remark is hardly
ever an insult when penned by a male author.

> *Epigrams* 7.82
> Menophilus' person (penis: Ker, 1968) a sheath (brace: Ker, 1968)
> covers so enormous that it alone would be sufficient for the whole
> tribe of comic actors. This fellow I had imagined—for we often bathe
> together—was solicitous to spare his voice; but while he was exercis-
> ing himself in the view of the people in the middle of the exercise
> ground, the sheath unluckily fell off: lo, he was circumcised.[100]

In another epigram, Martial is in an exquisite frenzy of jealousy
over a Jewish poet, who is a strong and successful rival, not alas only
in poetry, but also in the matter of Martial's favourite boy.

> *Epigrams* 11.94
> Your overflowing malice, and your detraction everywhere of my
> books, I pardon: circumcised poet, you are wise. This, too, I disre-
> gard, that when you carp at my poems you plunder them: so, too,
> circumcised poet, you are wise. What tortures me is this, that you,
> circumcised poet, although born in the very midst of Solyma
> (Jerusalem: Ker 1968), outrage my boy. There! you deny it, and
> swear to me by the Thunderer's Temple. I don't believe you: swear
> circumcised one, by Anchialus.[101]

This Jew strikes Martial too close to home for him to ridicule him
dispassionately. He is really stung by the Jewish poet's success, and
uses the most visually explicit word, of the four possible in Latin, to
describe the poet's circumcised state.[102]

---

[99] Leon, *Ancient Rome*, index entry for Martial, p. 372.

[100] Martial, *Epigrams* 7.82.

[101] Martial, *Epigrams* 11.94.

[102] The word used is *verpus* which describes the colour and condition of the glans
penis as opposed to *recutitus*, *curtus* or *circumcisus* which reflect the circumcision process. All the Latin words for 'circumcised' except 'circumcisus' are regarded by Smith
in *A Smaller English–Latin Dictionary* (ed. W. Smith, London: John Murray, 1970) as
having a *scornful* connotation, and these are the words used by Horace, Martial and
Juvenal; but such a connotation is not mentioned in the dictionaries of Lewis and Short
or Glare. This attribution of scorn, which could well have arisen by means of a circular

Less close to Martial's pride and his person is the Jew described below, a beggar taught to be such from his mother's knee, a Jew of quite a different social class and background from the 'circumcised poet', and just one in the list of noisy nuisances of the Roman streets.

Epigrams 12.57.7-14
On this side the money-changer idly rattles on his dirty table Nero's coins, on that the hammerer of Spanish gold-dust beats his well-worn stone with burnished mallet; and Bellona's raving throng does not rest, nor the canting ship-wrecked seaman with his swathed body, nor the Jew taught by his mother to beg, nor the blear-eyed huckster of sulphur-wares.[103]

Is this proof of anti-semitism? There is a fine line to be drawn between dislike of all foreigners and dislike of Jews in particular, and I agree with Gager, who thinks that the former, more than the latter, is in evidence. He characterises Martial as belonging to 'a closed circle of like-minded spirits bent on defending "the old ways"',[104] and discerns in his writing the stamp of xenophobia which in turn gives rise to anti-semitism. Simon takes a stronger line and believes that there was anti-semitism, which arose out of the separatism occasioned by the Jews' religion and had nothing to do with 'race', a notion he describes as 'quite foreign to the ancient way of thinking'.[105] Bacchiocchi opines that Martial thinks that the 'circumcised Jews and their Sabbath are a synonym of degradation'.[106]

I disagree that we have evidence of anti-semitism here. I find that the negativity expressed towards Jews by Martial is neither on such a grand scale nor so specifically directed at the Jewishness of Jews. It is a petty and domestic dislike—to do with amours and vanity. Martial, as a satirist, finds that although Jews are treading on his toes socially, they make useful butts for his humour. He is able to make his audiences laugh with what he says about Jews. His caricatures are near enough to the mark to be funny, a well-worn way of releasing tension when another social group threatens one's own privileges. He depicts Jews as exotic foreigners who practise circumcision, great

---

argument based on translators' own opinions as to the Roman writers' evaluations of Jews, has evidently been incorporated into some scholars' understanding of Horace, Martial and Juvenal.

[103] Martial, *Epigrams* 12.57.7-14.
[104] Gager, *Anti-Semitism*, p. 65.
[105] Simon, *Verus Israel*, pp. 202-207 (202).
[106] Bacchiocchi, *Sunday*, p. 175.

lovers and—only just—his social inferiors.

In all important matters Jews stood very close to Martial, ready perhaps to step into his shoes. But he regards them as an intriguing race, not as a religious group. He knows nothing about their sabbaths or their religion.

Epictetus

Epictetus, writing in Greek at the end of the first century or beginning of the second, in one passage strangely speaks of a Jew as having been 'baptised'.

> Preserved in Arrian, *Dissertations* 2.9.19-21
> Sit down now and give a philosophical discourse upon the principles of Epicurus, and perhaps you will discourse more effectively than Epicurus himself. Why then do you call yourself a Stoic, why do you deceive the multitude, why do you act the part of a Jew, when you are a Greek? Do you not see in what sense men are severally called Jew, Syrian, or Egyptian? For example, whenever we see a man halting between two faiths, we are in the habit of saying, 'He is not a Jew, he is only acting the part'. But when he adopts the attitude of mind of the man who has been baptised and has made his choice, then he both is a Jew in fact and is also called one. So we also are counterfeit 'Baptists', ostensibly Jews, but in reality something else, not in sympathy with our own reason, far from applying the principles which we profess, yet priding ourselves upon them as being men who know them.[107]

It is not quite clear to what he is referring, for he speaks of someone who 'takes up the commitment of one who has been immersed and won over'.[108] Scholars are divided as to whether the person is being baptised in some way into Judaism,[109] or whether Epictetus does not properly distinguish between Christians and Jews.[110] Commentators generally consider such a distinction to be earlier than the writings of Epictetus, but I do not accept that the differentiation took place early on; so I do not find the confusion at all surprising. For John Chrysostom, for example, in fourth-century Antioch, was

---

[107] Epictetus, *Discourses* 2.9.19-21, in *The Discourses of Epictetus* (tr. W.A. Oldfather; LCL; Cambridge, MA: Harvard University Press, 1980); Epictetus, *The Discourses of Epictetus* (tr. G. Long; London: George Bell and Sons, 1890); and Epictetus, *Moral Discourses: Enchiridion and Fragments* (tr. E. Carter; London: J.M. Dent & Sons, 1910).

[108] My translation of ὅταν δ' ἀναλάβῃ τὸ πάθος τὸ τοῦ βεβαμμένου καὶ ἡρημένου.

[109] See discussion in Stern, *Authors*, I, pp. 541-44.

[110] Long, *Epictetus*, p. 126; Whittaker, *Views*, p. 89.

still urging his Christian congregation to give up attending the synagogue there.[111]

Plutarch

Plutarch, writing literary and theological works in Greek at the end of the first century,[112] is a man for whom 'moral concern and learning go hand in hand'.[113] That Plutarch's religious practices, as a priest at Delphi, were, in his own perception anyway, much more serious and pious than Judaism, is suggested by Russell when he concludes that Plutarch 'belongs to the continuous tradition of Hellenic piety and Hellenic scepticism, not much affected by the great changes in religious feeling which he could sense in the world around'.[114] So while Plutarch might be ignorant of Judaism he was a widely read and thoughtful man. As such, his comments are, in my view, valuable, though Grant sees in Plutarch's writings a malign intention, more inimical than merely a state of blinkered complacency and self-satisfaction, and groups him with writers he regards as hostile to Jews.[115]

Certainly, as Plutarch writes from a position of strong bias towards the unchallenged superiority of all things Hellenic, he does ride somewhat roughshod over Jewish sensibilities and Jewish aspirations to be taken seriously as a religion when he lists some follies of superstition.

> De Superstitione 3
> ... because of superstition, such as smearing with mud, wallowing in filth, keeping of the Sabbath, casting oneself down with face to the ground, disgraceful besieging of the gods, and uncouth prostrations.

It is hard to understand how keeping the sabbath can fit into that

---

[111] Gager, *Anti-Semitism*, pp. 118-19; Simon, *Verus Israel*, pp. 326-27, and *passim*.

[112] Plutarch, *De superstitione*, in *Plutarch's Moralia*, II (tr. F.C. Babbitt; LCL; Cambridge, MA: Harvard University Press, 1928); *De la superstition* in *Plutarque: Oeuvres morales*, II (tr. J. Dafradas, J. Hani and R. Klaerr; Paris: Les Belles Lettres, 1985); *Quaestiones conviviales* (tr. H.B. Hoffleit), in *Plutarch's Moralia*, VIII (tr. P.A. Clement and H.B. Hoffleit; LCL; Cambridge, MA: Harvard University Press, 1969); *Propos de table* in *Plutarque: Oeuvres morales*, VIII (tr. F. Fuhrmann; Paris: Les Belles Lettres, 1978).

[113] D.A. Russell, *Plutarch* (London: Duckworth, 1973), p. 83.

[114] Russell, *Plutarch*, p. 83.

[115] Grant, *The Jews*, p. 240; see above text at note 41; see also Bacchiocchi, *Sunday*, p. 175.

list in any logical way, as the others all refer to extreme body movements and involve contact with mud or other semi-solid substance.
And there is no evidence that Jews were believed to do any of those
things on the sabbath.

It is much easier to see how the image of 'immersions' would fit
into Plutarch's sequence—though that change removes the reference
to sabbath.[116] This is perhaps the reason that in translating this text
Stern follows the French edition of Dafradas and retains 'keeping of
the Sabbath' rather than the emendation 'immersions'.

Plutarch is, however, one of the few Graeco-Roman writers to
mention the taking of wine on sabbath; Persius indeed referred to the
flask full of wine, visible through the window of Jewish homes on
Friday evenings, but Plutarch describes the consumption of wine by
Jews as proving a connection with the cult of Dionysius. However,
the information Plutarch gives is far from clear, for the Greek of the
comment[117] is amenable to quite different translations.

Quaestiones Conviviales 4.6.2
I think that the sabbath festival too is not entirely without a Dionysiac
element ... They themselves attest the theory, for whenever they celebrate sabbaths they challenge one another to drinking and drunkenness and, when some more important business prevents this, they
make a habit of tasting at least a little neat wine.[118]

I believe that even the feast of the Sabbath is not completely unrelated to Dionysius ... The Jews themselves testify to a connection
with Dionysius when they keep the Sabbath by inviting each other to
drink and enjoy wine; when more important business interferes with
this custom, they regularly take at least a little sip of neat wine (tr.
Hoffleit).

Whittaker translates in a way that denigrates the wine-drinking as
drunkenness, whereas Hoffleit regards it as merely enjoyment. In one
translation Plutarch is offensive and, in the other, sympathetic.[119] The

---

[116] Stern resists the emendation of Bentley which reads "immersions' in place of
"keeping of the Sabbath': βαπτισμούς for σαββατισμούς; see also other occurrences
of σαββτισμός in A.T. Lincoln, 'Sabbath, Rest, and Eschatology in the New
Testament', in *From Sabbath to Lord's Day: A Biblical, Historical and Theological
Investigation* (ed. D.A. Carson; Grand Rapids: Zondervan, 1982), pp. 197-220 (213).

[117] ὅταν σάββατα τελῶσι, μάλιστα μὲν πίνειν καὶ οἰνοῦσθαι παρακαλοῦντες
ἀλλήλους, ὅταν δὲ κωλύῃ τι μεῖζον ἀπογεύσθαί γε πάντως ἀκράτου νομίζοντες.

[118] Whittaker, *Views*, pp. 72-73.

[119] Goldenberg, 'Jewish Sabbath', pp. 435-36, is quite certain in his mind for he
states that Plutarch compares the sabbath to 'a bacchanalian orgy, at which the
participants ply each other with wine until they are drunk'; and Dafradas, *Plutarque IX*,

reader has to decide whether the sabbath domestic celebrations include the taking of a little—or a great deal—of wine.

As with other writers of the time, Plutarch knows only of gustatory celebration of the sabbath.

Tacitus

Tacitus, at the end of the first century CE, writes rather sharply about Jews, but I don't accept that Tacitus maltreated the Jews by what he wrote. As will become evident, Tacitus gives a fairly accurate description of the behaviour and attitudes of Jews.

Histories 5.4.3–5.5

4.3 By frequent fasts even now they bear witness to the long hunger with which they were once distressed, and the unleavened Jewish bread is still employed in memory of the haste with which they seized the grain. They say that they first chose to rest on the seventh day because that day ended their toils; but after a time they were led by the charms of indolence to give over the seventh year as well to inactivity. Others say that this is done in honour of Saturn, whether it be that the primitive elements of their religion were given by the Idaeans, who, according to tradition, were expelled with Saturn and became the founders of the Jewish race, or is due to the fact that, of the seven planets that rule the fortunes of mankind, Saturn moves in the highest orbit and has the greatest potency; and that many of the heavenly bodies traverse their paths and courses in multiples of seven.

5.1 Whatever their origin, these rites are maintained by their antiquity; the other customs of the Jews are base and abominable, and owe their persistence to their depravity; for the worst rascals among other peoples, renouncing their ancestral religions, always kept sending tribute and contributing to Jerusalem, thereby increasing the wealth of the Jews; again the Jews are extremely loyal to one another, and always ready to show compassion, but towards every other people they feel only hate and enmity. 5.2 They sit apart at meals and they sleep apart, and although as a race, they are prone to lust, they abstain from intercourse with foreign women; yet among themselves nothing is unlawful. They adopted circumcision to distinguish themselves from other peoples by this difference. Those who are converted to their ways follow the same practice, and the earliest lesson they receive is to despise the gods, to disown their country, and to regard their parents, children, and brothers as of little account. 5.3 However, they take thought to increase their numbers; for they regard it as a crime to kill any late-born child, and they believe that the souls of those who are killed in battle or by the executioner are immortal:

---

p. 43, follows the same idea by saying 'puisqu'ils s'exhortent avant tout les uns les autres à boire et à s'enivrer'.

hence comes their passion for begetting children, and their scorn of
death ... 5.4 ... [T]he Jews conceive of one god only, and that with
the mind only ... Therefore they set up no statues in their cities, still
less in their temples; this flattery is not paid their kings, nor this
honour given to the Caesars. 5.5 But since their priests used to chant
to the accompaniment of pipes and drums and to wear garlands of
ivy, and because a golden vine was found in their temple, some have
thought that they were devotees of Father Liber, the conqueror of the
East, in spite of the incongruity of their customs. For Liber
established festive rites of a joyous nature, while the ways of the Jews
are preposterous and mean.[120]

Before looking in detail at what Tacitus has to say about Jews,
there is on interpretational crux that requires a closer look at the text
in Latin. In this passage, the standard translations of § 5.5.1 require
the understanding of several words or referents that are not present in
the text. The key phrase is: *Nam pessimus quisque spretis religion-
ibus patriis tributa et stipes illuc <con>gerebant, unde auctae
Iudaeorum res.* Moore,[121] and Church and Brodribb,[122] regard the
'pessimus' as describing a person of other race—not originally
Jewish—who has given up the religion of that race in order to send
money to Jerusalem. They regard this phrase as evidence of successful Jewish proselytism in Rome.[123]

But it is better to read the text as saying that the Jews are in general the worst of people, *because* they have renounced 'the ancestral
religions' (i.e. the Roman religion) and are instead sending money to
support Judaism in Jerusalem, which means out of Roman coffers.
This is no doubt true. Tacitus is equally cognisant of Jewish practice
in § 5.4 where he explains why the Jews do not set up statues to
important public figures in their cities or 'temples'.[124]

But if we may set on one side Tacitus's evident xenophobia and
unquestioning belief in the superiority of all things Roman, his
account displays the following knowledge about Jews: they always

---

[120] Tacitus, *Histories* 5.4.3–5.5, in *Tacitus in Five Volumes*, III (tr. C.H. Moore and J.
Jackson; LCL; Cambridge, MA: Harvard University Press, 1969).
[121] Translator of the LCL edition.
[122] *The History of Tacitus* (tr. A.J. Church and W.J. Brodribb; London: Macmillan,
1927).
[123] To my understanding, Jewish proselytising is more clearly indicated in 5.2, which
points to noticeable numbers of men being willing to accept circumcision as their entry
into the Jewish faith.
[124] Simon, *Verus Israel*, p. 40, assumes that the word 'temples' means 'synagogues'.
Perhaps 'prayer-houses' would be a better substitution.

send money to Jerusalem, they are loyal to each other, always ready to show compassion to each other, but keep apart from other people for sitting, sleeping and eating. They are lusty but keep to Jewish women. They are circumcised. Their converts reject the Roman pantheon and put God before their non-Jewish relatives. Jews do not kill infants or procure abortions, and even enjoy having children.[125] They will not make statues of public figures either to adorn their cities or 'temples' or to honour secular rulers. They celebrated rituals in the past in their temple with singing, music and garlands of ivy, but they are not joyful in religion, but are rather unusual, namely non-lavish, in their festal rites.

Most of this is quite accurate and faithful to the Jewish way of life. Jewish religious festivals were indeed likely to be sober affairs by Roman standards. Jews did not wish to become assimilated into Roman society and that the Romans regarded as enmity. Tacitus mentions several distinctive features of Jewishness familiar to us from other writers, e.g. Josephus. But in all his account of Jews Tacitus says nothing about distinctive Jewish behaviour or worship on the sabbath, though he does refer to sabbath observance.

Juvenal

Juvenal, younger than Martial by about fifteen years, wrote satires in a similar, powerful vein.[126] He shows a 'nightmare obsession with poverty and degradation' in his earlier satires which contain 'lethal invective'.[127] He avoids direct obscenity in his comments about Roman life, but, as Highet puts it, can turn one's stomach in three words.[128] Yet he more often shows wryness about his place in the social life of the city, and adopts the voice of his friend, or possibly his own poetic persona, Umbricius,[129] when he describes the 'squalid and humiliating life of a déclassé hanger-on',[130] who lives by

---

[125] Cf. the similar description of Jewish views and practice on these matters in Josephus, *Apion* 2.198-203.

[126] Juvenal, in *Juvenal and Persius* (tr. G.G. Ramsay; LCL; Cambridge, MA: Harvard University Press, 1940); S. Robinson, *Sixteen Satires*; *The Sixteen Satires* (tr. P. Green; Harmondsworth, Middlesex: Penguin, 1967).

[127] Green, *Sixteen Satires*, p. 13.

[128] G. Highet, *Juvenal the Satirist: A Study* (Oxford: Clarendon Press, 1954), p. 215.

[129] Highet, *Juvenal*, pp. 68-69, n. 254.

[130] Green, *Sixteen Satires*, p. 22.

scrounging meals at rich men's houses.

As for his attitude to Jews, I find him no more negative about Jews than about many other groups. Occasionally he is more brutal about Romans than about Jews, as for instance when he speaks of a man who 'has first defrauded his ward, and later [d]ebauched the boy as well'.[131] Jews are never accused of behaviour of that sort either by Juvenal or by any of the Roman writers. Roman women fare no better, for Juvenal warns the worthy men of Rome to watch their step in the morning as they pass the Temple of Chastity in the Forum of Boarium for their wives regularly stop their litters there late at night and use the shrine as a public toilet.[132] No Jewish woman is ever referred to in such terms.

In the following passage, Juvenal, declaiming against the difficulties of making a reasonable living in Rome, describes the groups of Jewish beggars in the grove at the Porta Capena, near the main gate to the Circus Maximus.

> *Satires* 3.12-16
> Here Numa held his nightly assignations with his mistress; but now the holy fount and grove and shrine are let out to Jews, who possess a basket and a truss of hay for all their furnishings. For as every tree nowadays has to pay toll to the people, the Muses have been ejected, and the wood has to go a-begging.

These Jews lived in the open air, having only the minimum of belongings and being ready, at a moment's notice, to beg or hawk among the crowds attending events at the city's main stadium.

Green translates this passage as 'But today Egeria's grove and shrine and sacred spring are rented to Jewish squatters, their sole possession a Sabbath haybox'.[133] There is a measure of interpretation there, as the Jews are called 'squatters', emphasising their poverty, and their truss of hay becomes a way of keeping food warm for their sabbath meal. But the word 'sabbath' is not present in the Latin text, and this translation is, therefore, an interpretation.

All through Satire 3, writing about life in a big city, Juvenal catalogues the petty economies and indignities of people like himself, the out-at-elbow and the shabby genteel, making do with little and pre-

---

[131] Green, *Sixteen Satires*, p. 66.
[132] Juvenal, *Satires* 6.306-13.
[133] Green, *Sixteen Satires*, p. 87.

tending to others that it is sufficient and acceptable. So, later in Satire 3, he speaks of the hazards for someone like himself walking home through the city at night: waggons thunder past, he is jostled by a litter carrying a wealthy parvenu, tiles or rubbish fall on him, and a thwarted bully-boy, balked of richer prey, vents his spleen by insulting Umbricius.

> *Satires* 3.292-96
> 'Where are you from?' shouts he; 'whose vinegar, whose beans have blown you out? With what cobbler have you been munching cut leeks and boiled wether's chaps?—What sirrah, no answer? Speak out, or take that upon your shins. Say, where is your stand? In what prayer-house shall I find you?'

What commentators do not notice is that this bully-boy *mistakes* the speaker, Umbricius, for a Jew, or treats him as a Jew, suggesting that he could be found in a *proseucha*.[134] Courtney thinks that Umbricius, who loathes immigrants, would be insulted to be accused of begging at a *proseucha*.[135] If suggesting he is a beggar is an insult to the Roman male, it would be more of an insult to accuse him of being a Jew. What is crucial for understanding this passage is to recognise that throughout it Umbricius is being treated as a Jew.

And so something more is discovered about Roman 'knowledge' of Jews. Jews drink vinegar, or perhaps cheap wine mixed with water, eat beans and boiled sheep's heads with onions. This would indeed be kosher food. They have convivial evenings with their low-class cronies, for example, a cobbler. They may safely be threatened with a kicking as they go home carrying one little candle.[136] And they smell unpleasant or noticeable because of what they eat. This is similar to the point made by Martial about Jewish women.

All this is no expression of anti-Jewish feeling. If it were, how could Juvenal possibly write of being mistaken for a Jew, without

---

[134] Here I use the Latin word *proseucha* for the meeting-house or prayer-house of the Jews (see *A Latin Dictionary*, p. 1475), assuming it to have the same meaning as προσευχή (see *Theological Dictionary of the New Testament*, ed. G. Kittel and H. Greeven; Grand Rapids: Eerdmans, 1964, pp. 807-808), reserving the word 'synagogue' for the congregation of Jews, as previously discussed in Chapter 2; see also Stern, discussion on Artemidorus, *Authors*, II, p. 330; and also in Chapter 8 the inscription which gives 'at the rampart by the *proseucha*' as the business address of a Roman fruit vendor.

[135] E.H. Courtney, *A Commentary on the Satires of Juvenal* (London: The Athlone Press, 1980), pp. 191-92.

[136] *Satires*, 3.285-88.

some immediate denial of that allegiance from Umbricius, rather than his description of how painfully impossible it was to either answer the bully's taunts or escape in silence. He writes as if he has regularly had to accept the insults that would also have been meted out to Jews, for he was in many ways their like, eking out his existence on the margins of high society, not entirely poor but of the 'rootless middle-class'.[137] And these would be the Jews who could be found inside or hanging about outside a prayer-house. Perhaps also, Juvenal is bemoaning the fact that a man like himself can be mistaken for a Jew.

Juvenal constructs a mosaic picture of the Jews he knew as being, in many ways, like himself, although they were not Romans and had no roots in the city's social structures. They would hang about their *proseuchae*, rather than the Forum.

The third extract from Juvenal is a piece of 'the gigantic and virulent Sixth Satire directed against women',[138] in which Juvenal makes fun of the Roman matron who is swayed and controlled by the whims of superstitious religious practices. And he also makes fun of the aged Jewess who offers to tell dreams for a small coin.

> *Satires* 6.542-47
> No sooner has that fellow departed than a palsied Jewess, leaving her basket and her truss of hay, comes begging to her secret ear; she is an interpreter of the laws of Jerusalem, a high priestess of the tree, a trusty go-between of highest heaven. She, too, fills her palm, but more sparingly, for a Jew will tell you dreams of any kind you please for the minutest of coins.

Considering how nasty Juvenal is about Roman women in this and other satires, he describes the Jewish woman in quite a gentle way, merely as palsied and begging, descriptive rather than pejorative terms. For elsewhere in this satire he reviles many Roman women for all sorts of lewdness and vulgarity, as well as, in one case, for murdering her own children at the meal table.[139] His remarks on the Jewish woman are mild and delicate by comparison.

Satire 8 descries all that is wrong with social life in Rome. In it Juvenal paints a thumb nail sketch of an all-night tavern, run by a Jew. The bar-maid rushes to offer her wine bottle, and Green's trans-

---

[137] Highet, *Juvenal*, p. 68.
[138] Green, *Sixteen Satires*, p. 12.
[139] Green, *Sixteen Satires*, pp. 129-41, 151.

lation gives more than a hint of venery as well on offer. Here again
we find the linking of Jews and lust.

> *Satires* 8.158-62
> And when it pleases him to go back to the all-night tavern, a Syro-
> Phoenician runs forth to meet him—a denizen of the Idumaean gate
> perpetually drenched in perfumes—and salutes him as lord and prince
> with all the airs of a host; and with him comes Cyane, her dress
> tucked up, carrying a flagon of wine for sale[140] (tr. Ramsay).

> At the all-night taverns; when he shows up, mine host—
> Some greasy Syrian from the Jewish quarter, with slicked-back,
> Pomaded hair—runs out, greets him obsequiously,
> Calls him 'M'lord' and 'Your Honour', while the barmaid gives
> A hitch to her skirts, and uncorks her bottle for action.[141]

In another satire Juvenal, with less than his usual particularity of
observation, also uses a Jewish stock character to kick at.

> *Satires* 14.96-106
> Some who have had a father who reveres the Sabbath, worship noth-
> ing but the clouds and the divinity of the heavens, and see no differ-
> ence between eating swine's flesh, and that of a man; and in time they
> take to circumcision. Having been wont to flout the laws of Rome,
> they learn and practise and revere the Jewish law, and all that Moses
> handed down in his secret tome, forbidding to point out the way to
> any not worshipping the same rites, and conducting none but the cir-
> cumcised to the desired fountain. For all which the father was to
> blame, who gave up every seventh day to idleness, keeping it apart
> from all the concerns of life.[142]

Simon makes an interesting analysis of this extract, finding in it
evidence of frequent instances of Roman conversions to Judaism in
the time between the two Jewish wars.[143] Roman fathers, in his reading, are described as being on the fringes of Judaism, accepting
monotheism, keeping the sabbath and avoiding pork, with their sons
taking matters further, becoming fully converted and accepting circumcision. Simon regards this description of Juvenal's as a
vehement denunciation of the Jews and their increasing grip on
Roman society, and records it as another example of Juvenal's
spitefulness towards Jews. But it is difficult to see where the
spitefulness occurs in this text.

---

[140] Ramsay, *Juvenal and Persius.*
[141] Green, *Sixteen Satires,* pp. 182-83.
[142] Stern, *Authors,* II, pp. 102-103.
[143] Simon, *Verus Israel,* pp. 280-82, 285, 375.

A similar reaction to this text comes from Goldenberg, who claims that Juvenal 'attributed the growing number of non-Jewish Sabbath-observers to their laziness, as though the Sabbath gave them an excuse to pass every seventh day without having to give any attention to life's serious concerns'.[144] Goldenberg's comments combine maximisation both of the number of Jewish proselytes and of the insult expressed towards the Jews, both points he is at pains to make. But the text seems to me to tease rather than insult, particularly in the way the ban on eating pork is expressed.

However, a comparison of this piece with the fragment of Petronius shows that both texts have almost parallel content and perspective about Jews. Both list the numen of heaven, pork avoidance, circumcision, keeping the sabbath and the law. The writers share a negative evaluation of the Jews' enclave mentality and sabbath prohibitions. This reads like a standard package describing Jews. And again we find that no activities special to sabbath are described: it is simply rest from public work that characterises the Jewish sabbath.

Juvenal has been, in my view, much maligned for his bitter treatment of Jews. He was hard on all sorts and conditions of people, and did not single out the Jews for insult. I find that he is often kinder in his descriptions of Jews than of fellow Romans—as Martial was not—and that he has experienced the oppression undergone by Jews at the hands of bully-boys and felt it as a parallel victim himself.

So from Martial we learn that Jews were rather too significant on the Roman scene. And, from Juvenal, although we learn nothing more about sabbath practice, the building *proseucha* is mentioned for the first time, as a place where Jews congregated.

Suetonius

Suetonius adds little to the Roman picture of the Jewish sabbath, reporting only that Augustus claimed that he fasted as scrupulously as Jews did on the sabbath.[145] The misunderstanding about Jewish fasting seems to have extended to all ranks of Roman society.

The Deified Augustus 76.2
Once more: 'Not even a Jew, my dear Tiberius, fasts so scrupulously

---

[144] Goldenberg, 'Jewish Sabbath', p. 430.
[145] Suetonius, *The Lives of the Caesars*, II, in *Suetonius*, I (tr. J.C. Rolfe; LCL; Cambridge, MA: Harvard University Press, 1914), pp. 240-41.

on his sabbaths as I have today; for it was not until after the first hour of the night that I ate two mouthfuls of bread in the bath before I began to be anointed',

From other references to Augustus's eating habits,[146] and his care to eat in private and toy with food in public, we may conclude that this text refers to the Emperor's efforts to maintain the public image of his fastidiousness, rather than to any religious attitude.

Later Graeco-Roman Writers

The last four authors to be studied seem to have a different set of interactions with Jews. The heat in the debate has cooled, and Jews seem to be strangers again rather than near or would-be intimates and rivals. The writings of three of these authors were in Greek originally, though some exist now in Latin translation only, and the details the four writers supply are about the discussions in groups of Jews and about their gathering in their προσευχαί.

Cleomedes

The extract from Cleomedes (dates uncertain) is somewhat difficult to unravel, but he is deriding the florid over-elaborated style of discourse of Epicurus; he associates it with brothel clients and prostitutes, women at the Thesmophoria festivals and Jewish beggars in the courtyards of προσευχαί.[147]

> De motu 2.1.91
> Since, in addition to other things, his style [scil. Epicurus] is also a corrupt motley, making use of expressions like 'stable states of the flesh' and 'hopeful hopes' concerning it, and calling tears 'glistenings of the eyes' and having recourse to phrases like 'holy screechings' and 'ticklings of the body' and 'wenchings' and other bad mischiefs of this kind. One may say that these expressions derive in part from brothels, in part they are similar to those spoken by women celebrating the Thesmophoria at the festivals of Demeter, and in part they issue from the midst of the synagogue (προσευχή) and the beggars in its courtyards. These are Jewish and debased and much lower than reptiles.[148]

---

[146] Suetonius, *Lives*, pp. 240-43.
[147] Stern, *Authors*, II, pp. 157-58; see also Cleomedes, *De motu* (tr. R. Goulet), p. 150.
[148] Stern, *Authors*, II, pp. 157-58. We should, of course, translate προσευχή 'prayer-house', not 'synagogue'.

Cleomedes here implies three things about Jews: they speak in flowery, and possibly noisy, circumlocutions, they gather in buildings called προσευχαί, which are large enough to have courtyards, and they are or can be beggars. This points to a more flourishing Jewish community and an image of Jews as having particular speech patterns or rhythms—perhaps flowery or ingratiating language.

Apuleius

Apuleius describes a woman who has rejected the Roman gods in favour of one single god, although he says that she also consumed alcoholic drink in large quantities and pursued lechery.[149]

> *Metamorphoses* 9.14
> Furthermore she scorned and spurned all the gods in heaven, and, instead of holding a definite faith, she used the false sacrilegious presumption of a god, whom she would call 'one and only', to invent meaningless rites to cheat everyone and deceive her wretched husband, having sold her body to drink from dawn and to debauchery the whole day (tr. Hanson).

The Latin of the phrase 'whom she calls the one and only' (*quem praedicaret unicum*) can be translated in such a way as to indicate that the woman would declaim to this one and only god. Could this be a reference to the opening line of the Shema, 'Hear, O Israel, the Lord our God is one'? It is possible. Certainly, commentators agree that Christianity or Judaism is implied in this passage, although only a very garbled description of either can be drawn from this passage.

Galen

Galen, in one of his medical works from the latter part of the second century,[150] contrasts a proper way of discussing and proving a thesis with the way he finds in the 'school of Moses and Christ'.[151]

> *De pulsuum differentiis* 2.4
> Thus one would not, at the very start, as if one had come into the

---

[149] Apuleius, *Metamorphoses* 2.9.14, in *Metamorphoses* (tr. J.A. Hanson; LCL; Cambridge, MA: Harvard University Press, 1989).

[150] Galen, *De pulsuum differentiis*, in M. Stern, ed., *Greek and Latin Authors on Jews and Judaism*, II. *From Tacitus to Simplicius* (Jerusalem: The Israel Academy of Sciences and Humanities, 1980).

[151] This is reminiscent of Horace's view of Jews as credulous, since it refers to their mode of accepting ideas as proposed to them.

school of Moses and Christ, hear about laws that have not been demonstrated, and concerning a matter where it is least appropriate.[152]

Most commentators see here a reference to the two religious groups of Jews and Christians, but I see rather a reference to, either the as yet undifferentiated group of Christians and Jews, or the group of Jews who followed Christ, namely the early Christians.

The second extract is similar,[153] but can read as referring to either one or two groups of thinkers and talkers. It is another very interesting hint that Jews and Christians were not separated, either in fact, or in the popular perception of them as a religious group, until later than has usually been suggested.

De pulsuum differentiis 3.3
One might more easily teach novelties to the followers of Moses and Christ than to the physicians and philosophers, who cling fast to their schools. So that in the end I determined to spare myself much idle talk by not discussing anything at all with them.[154]

These passages go some way to confirming Cleomedes' view of the modes of argumentation of Jews.

Artemidorus

In Artemidorus's work on the interpretation of dreams, the paragraph on προσευχαί is, strangely, sandwiched between one on dunghills and one on keys.[155] Arranging the paragraphs like that does suggest some sort of unflattering connection between dunghills and the Jewish place of assembly. But the section on keys is quite neutral in character, so perhaps the arrangement of paragraphs is merely random.

He does, however, associate dreaming of προσευχαί with images of beggars and misery of various description. He has nothing good to say about προσευχαί.

Oneirocritica 53
A synagogue [προσευχή] and beggars and all people who ask for gifts, and as such arouse pity, and mendicants, foretell grief, anxiety

---

[152] Translated by R. Walzer in Stern, *Authors*, II, pp. 313-15.
[153] Galen, *De pulsuum* 3.3.
[154] Translated by R. Walzer in Stern, *Authors*, II, pp. 313-15.
[155] Stern, *Authors*, II, p. 330; Artemidorus, *Dreams* (tr. R.J. White), pp. 171-72; note the translation 'prayer-house' is to be preferred to 'synagogue' for προσευχή.

and heartache to both men and women. For on the one hand, no one departs for a synagogue [προσευχή] without a care, and, on the other, beggars who are very odious looking and without resources and have nothing wholesome about them are an obstacle to every plan.[156]

Interestingly, although he regards dreaming of prayer-houses as fore-telling something unpleasant, he also implies an understanding of prayer-houses as places where people might go when they had something troubling them.

Conclusions about the Jews in Graeco-Roman Writings

In this Chapter I have presented all the data I could find about the perception of Jews by Graeco-Roman authors. The inclusion of this enormous quantity of background—from the wider range of material surveyed—has been necessary to present a balanced account of what the Romans say about Jews. Some of the quotations, if taken out of context, can seem more anti-semitic that they truly are. The Graeco-Roman authors were at times hostile or inimical to Jews, but in many cases less so than they were to other races or even to other Romans.

The Jewish character, behaviour and institutions are seen quite sharply and clearly, from the outside, by acute observers who do not belong to the community of the Jews. The picture can only show Jews or Jewish meetings from the outside and can include nothing of the motives and emotions of Jews, other than what may be surmised by sensitive and sharp-eyed, though possibly mistaken, writers.

The Roman viewpoint is, in general, one of distant superiority. The only exceptions to this are Martial, whose certainty of superiority slips and reveals envy and a dread of being surpassed by a Jew, and Juvenal whose character Umbricius shares many of the snubs and humiliations felt by Jews. These writers did not attack Jews for their Jewishness, but for their presumption in equalling Romans while absolutely resisting amalgamation and assimilation. But towards the end of the second century CE the Jews and the animus towards them fade to the periphery of the Roman consciousness again.

What is known to the Romans about the sabbath? In the writings

---

[156] Stern, *Authors*, II, pp. 329-31.

of Seneca, the Jewish sabbath is known to involve the lighting of lamps, but there are no clear references to a worship service on the sabbath, though it is possible that Seneca did know and disapprove of daily services for morning prayer.[157] And he knows the practice of resting on the sabbath.

Persius describes a Jewish sabbath beginning on Friday evening with lamp-lighting and a meal which includes wine and fish.

Petronius seems to have described the sabbath in a negative way, as something that oppressed one or made one tremble at its fasting laws. But it is also possible that he describes a happy sabbath of rest which more rigorous Jews subvert with rules about fasting. But Frontinus, with less partiality, expresses a similar concept from the opposite perspective when he says that the Jews felt it was sinful to do business on the sabbath. The sabbath does not force them to inaction. They feel committed to avoiding action out of a religious obligation to obey their commandments.

Martial, though often considered to have referred to Jewish fasting on the sabbath, actually only remarks on the body odour of fasting Jewish women, without specifying when they fasted. He does, certainly, connect Jews—and notably, female Jews, who are rarely referred to in any of the texts—with fasting.

Plutarch has a confused view of the sabbath of the Jews, but he is aware that they 'keep' it, and that on that day they drink wine. Tacitus, also says nothing about sabbath worship, though he refers to sabbath rest.

Juvenal presents a much more sympathetic view of Jews than that of Martial, especially when, in my view, he tells of being mistaken for a Jew and bullied in much the same way that a Jew would have been bullied. If my understanding of that passage is correct, he also allows his readers to see Jews situated in the lower middle class group of society which is where Juvenal felt his external appearance put him in the eyes of street bullies. These were Jews who were artisans and who followed the Jewish way of life, quite well above subsistence level.

In common with Martial, Juvenal includes Jewish women in his depictions, describing an elderly, and palsied, Jewish woman who

---

[157] As revealed by his desire to 'forbid men to offer morning salutation and to throng the doors of temples' (*Moral Letters*, 95.47); see above in this Chapter.

interprets dreams for small fees and mentioning another who brings up her son in the trade of a street beggar. He says nothing pejorative about these women, especially when one makes a comparison with the attacks he delivers on Roman wives and mothers.

But Juvenal also resists the Jews' determination to preserve their way of life and their laws 'untainted', as it were from the Jewish perspective, by Roman customs. So he castigates the Jewish son of a God-fearing[158] father, who keeps the sabbath in idleness, and 'flouts the laws of Rome'. But he makes no mention of how the Jewish divinity is worshipped, only that he is.

As for the buildings in which Jews of the Graeco-Roman world may have worshipped, the references in the literature are few and far between. The building *proseucha* is depicted as a place big enough to have people gathering in it, or outside it in a courtyard, in the writings of Juvenal, Cleomedes and Artemidorus, at a time not earlier than the last years of the first century CE. This contrasts rather sharply with the fact that Philo speaks of many προσευχαί in Rome, when he writes of Rome under Tiberius in the *Embassy to Gaius* about fifty years earlier. Perhaps Philo is referring to private homes, or rooms, used as meeting-houses for prayer rather than public buildings.[159] Purpose-built προσευχαί probably appeared on the scene in Rome rather later than has been supposed by most commentators, sometime between 41 CE (the date of Philo's embassy) and the end of the century. It could be, of course, that Philo merely assumed for other cities what he knew for his own.

We should note that the only word consistently used in these texts for the meeting-house of Jews is *proseucha* (Juvenal) and προσευχή (Cleomedes and Artemidorus). The word 'synagogue' is not used at all—*pace* the English translations which give that impression. And the descriptions of the people gathered at the *proseuchae* suggest a noisy, chattering, absorbed, persistent and even obstructive group, who seem to do nothing but irritate and impede the Roman worthy going about his lawful occasions.

---

[158] I have used this word in spite of the difficulties raised about it by A.T. Kraabel, in 'Synagoga Caeca', in *'To See Ourselves as Others See Us'* (eds. J. Neusner and E.S. Frerichs: Chico, CA: Scholars Press, 1985), pp. 219-46, and in 'The Roman Diaspora: Six Questionable Assumptions', *JJS* 33 (1982), pp. 445-64, because it implies a person attracted to Judaism, but still on the fringes.

[159] Philo, *Embassy* 152-56.

The Jews are painted as a close-knit community, devoted to their god and to the interests of the family and the group. They celebrate their holy day on a Friday evening with the lighting of lamps followed by a meal including fish and wine. They have a meeting-house called a *proseucha*, large enough to warrant a courtyard, at which they can gather. No sabbath gatherings of Jews have caught the attention of any of these authors. There is nothing noticeable about the Jews' behaviour on the sabbath but their idleness.

In all these Graeco-Roman texts, I have found nothing to change my belief that Jews of the first centuries BCE and CE did not have sabbath worship services, and that when they met together, it was in buildings that were known as προσευχαί. What they did inside these buildings was a closed book to the Graeco-Roman writers. If they gathered together to discuss the law and other matters of community interest the Graeco-Roman writers apparently knew nothing about it.

CHAPTER FIVE

SABBATH IN THE SYNAGOGUES: NEW TESTAMENT SOURCES

Background to the Study of the New Testament Texts

Because the early Christian community began as an offshoot of Judaism, and because Jesus is presented as having gone to synagogues and as having taught in synagogues, the New Testament seems, at first sight, a likely source for information about Jewish sabbath practice. Most scholars assume that Jesus worshipped in the synagogue regularly on sabbath, but a close study of the New Testament literature yields no unambiguous evidence for this assumption. The activities described in the New Testament synagogue gatherings are varied: reading the Law, preaching, arguing and disciplining community members. There are no texts describing Jewish sabbath worship in synagogues.

My decision to write the chapter on the New Testaments texts following those on the works of Philo, Josephus, and the Graeco-Roman authors was taken for two reasons. First, the relative directness of the discourse in those other texts compared with the extreme complexity of the New Testament materials means that the main concepts relating to Jewish activities in sabbath gatherings have been more easily distinguished and stated before beginning the account of what the New Testament texts contribute.[1] And secondly, because

---

[1] It has not been possible to react with more than a selection of the vast amount of secondary literature generated by study of the New Testament texts. However, it is worth noting that most commentators do not address the issues raised by this study, accepting in the main the traditional view of the 'synagogues of the Jews' as religious buildings in which weekly worship services were held, following a longstanding pattern of religious observance; see especially the revised edition of E. Schürer, *The History of the Jewish People in the Age of Jesus Christ*, 3 vols. (rev. and ed. G. Vermes, F. Millar and M. Goodman; Edinburgh: T. & T. Clark, 1986), III, 1, pp. 141-49, and *The Anchor Bible Dictionary*, 6 vols. (ed. D.N. Freedman, G.A. Herion, D.F. Graf, J.D. Pleins; New York: Doubleday, 1992), articles on 'Sabbath', vol. 5, pp. 852-56, and 'Synagogue',

the time span covered by the writings explored in Chapters 3 and 4 extends, in both directions, beyond the time of Jesus to the time of the completion of the gospels, the knowledge gained creates a framework against which the New Testament data can be laid for the purposes of understanding and evaluation.[2] It is important for this study that the evidence the New Testament can supply be separated from the constructions that are often put upon the data.

Many scholars' comments on the origin of New Testament texts are imprecise. The dates of composition and editing are uncertain, and the methods used by them to arrive at datings are imprecise in their very nature.[3] The best that can be achieved is a scholarly consensus about the likely date for each text, with a wide range of perfectly possible dates before and after that estimate.[4] And a similar level of imprecision arises when efforts are made to pinpoint the place of origin of each text, the group which produced it, and the credible readerships or audiences of the early forms of the text. All these are estimates, and as such imprecise.[5]

So insights gained from the study of Jewish practice recorded outside the New Testament over a comparable time span to the New Testament texts can prove useful in understanding the depiction of the sabbath in, particularly, the gospels and Acts, and in considering whether the details of these New Testament accounts are more likely to derive from original reminiscences, or from the Christian editing of the tradition in the light of the various social and religious needs of the developing Christian community.

Sabbath observance as understood by the New Testament writers clearly involved refraining from work and other actions regarded as unnecessary on the sabbath. Sabbath rest is presupposed by several gospel healing stories and also in the Easter story, where the women

---

vol. 6, pp. 251-53, where descriptions of sabbath 'observance' become equated with the practice of 'worship' without any distinction between the two being drawn.

[2] The time portrayed in the gospel accounts is here taken to be somewhere between 23 and 36 CE, and the time of writing of the gospels between 65 and 150 CE, with preferred dates for Matthew being 80–100 CE, Mark around 80 CE, Luke–Acts post-90 CE, and John post-85 CE. In this study Markan priority will be assumed.

[3] J.C. Fenton, *The Gospel of St Matthew* (Harmondsworth, Middlesex: Penguin, 1963), p. 11.

[4] D. Hill, *The Gospel of Matthew* (New Century Bible; London: Oliphants, 1972), pp. 48-50.

[5] Hill, *Matthew*, pp. 50-55.

have to wait till the sabbath is past before they can visit the tomb. Luke specifically mentions sabbath rest as the reason for this inaction.[6] So sabbath rest, *as a general rule and principle*, is not at issue in the gospel texts—although particular forms of sabbath activity such as healing people or rescuing animals are.

Studying Jewish sabbath practice as it is presented in the gospels and Acts of necessity involves a study of 'synagogues',[7] because— apart from the synoptic story of the disciples' pulling ears of grain in a field on a sabbath, Luke's story of Jesus' dining with a Pharisee on the evening of the sabbath and John's story of the man healed beside the pool of Bethesda—all happenings that are reported as having taken place on the sabbath are set in 'synagogues'. Similarly, although it is not explicitly stated on all occasions, it appears likely that all the happenings reported in the New Testament as having taken place in 'synagogues', are envisaged as having taken place on sabbaths.

The necessity of dealing with the material on the sabbath and on the synagogues at the same juncture complicates the search for a clear understanding of sabbath practice, for the gospel accounts themselves are both scant and ambiguous; and, while there are many scholarly understandings of synagogue practice, there are no full ancient accounts of what actually happened in synagogues—the gatherings or the buildings. The gospels and Acts can yield useful evidence about synagogues, but only after a very careful teasing out of the threads of the texts.

The Sabbath and the Synagogue in the Secondary Literature

Typical of misleading claims about synagogues in textbooks is the statement that 'the synagogue was certainly a well-developed institution by the first century when they were located throughout Pales-

---

[6] Mt. 28.1; Mk 15.42; 16.1; Lk. 23.54, 56; Jn 19.31.

[7] The term 'synagogue' here translates the Greek συναγωγή, and does not necessarily mean a purpose-built religious building for Jews. The word can mean only the gathered group of people, or the gathering which is at that moment taking place. I have paid close attention to all the texts referring to synagogues to clarify, where possible, which meaning the word 'synagogue' has on each occasion it is used; but often the ambiguity cannot be resolved.

tine and the Diaspora'.[8] Such a sweeping statement cannot be supported from either literary or epigraphic evidence.[9] Nor can the description of the synagogue as providing 'the locus for the teaching of Jesus and later his apostles and so the place of recruitment of the earliest Christian converts and many aspects of the worship and organization of the early church'.[10] This superficial summary of the situation contains a miasma of misinformation, for the writer has cobbled together data from all sorts of sources, places, dates and types of literary material, giving all equal weight, and making no distinctions between all the various types of highly-coloured propagandist writings. He takes the gospel accounts and their interpretations by the evangelists as hard facts or, possibly, journalistic reporting, making no concessions to the changes in literary practice between the first century and now.[11]

A similarly uncritical re-telling of the biblical and related data can be found in Spier's appraisal of Jesus and the sabbath,[12] where he assumes that the three synoptic evangelists give severally the same account of Jesus' authentic sabbath practice. He reveals his belief in the historical exactness of the gospel accounts of Jesus' sabbath activities by devoting the next section of his chapter on the Second Temple to the Diaspora, so indicating that he believes both Philo and Josephus to be chronologically later witnesses than the gospels. He then proceeds to harmonise the evidence from Josephus and Philo into a picture of 'synagogues' in the first century, and thereafter rehearses the traditional, negative views of selected Roman writers' opinions of the sabbath.[13]

Such commentators write as if a great deal of knowledge about synagogues and sabbath worship in them may safely be assumed without argumentation.[14] Then they work with that 'knowledge' as a

---

[8] Ferguson, *Early Christianity*, pp. 456-57.

[9] See discussion in Chapter 8.

[10] Ferguson, *Early Christianity*, p. 457.

[11] See the discussion of this point in J.T. Sanders, *The Jews in Luke–Acts* (London: SCM Press, 1987), pp. 165-66.

[12] E. Spier, *Sabbat* (Das Judentum: Abhandlungen und Entwürfe für Studium und Unterricht, 1; Berlin: Institut Kirche und Judentum, 1989), pp. 25-26.

[13] Spier, *Sabbat*, pp. 27-29; these negative views attributed to Romans have already been discussed in Chapter 4.

[14] See, for example, R. Pesch, *Die Apostelgeschichte*, 2 vols. (EKK; Neukirchen–Vluyn: Benziger Verlag, 1986), II, pp. 32-34; Haenchen, *The Acts of the Apostles*, pp. 9, 407-408. R. Riesner, *Jesus als Lehrer* (Wissenschaftliche Untersuchungen zum Neuen

datum. But these over-simplifications do damage to the material surveyed and lead to misrepresentation of what these writers set out to
make clear.

Also the unqualified use of the word 'synagogue' introduces
inexactness by side-stepping the necessity of making clear what is
meant each time the word is used. For 'synagogue' could mean a
free-standing, purpose-built structure which had always been
intended for use as a religious meeting-house of Jews. Or it could
mean a room in a house set aside for this purpose on the sabbath.[15]
Or it could mean a group of people gathered in a shady spot in the
open air, or the gathering once constituted. All these possibilities
must be kept in mind by the reader, unless each scholar specifies the
meaning he or she intends in the particular instance under scrutiny.[16]

Whether a group known as a 'synagogue' would meet only in a
building called a 'synagogue', or equally in a building of another
name, for example in a προσευχή, or in a room in someone's house,
is also regarded by me as an open question.

Grandiose reconstructions of synagogues and the concomitant
descriptions of Jesus' role within them were widely accepted in the
past when 'evidence' from the Mishnah was considered relevant to
discussions about mid-first-century Palestine.[17] But, generally
speaking, evidence from the Mishnah is now regarded as having

---

Testament, II/7; Tübingen: J.C.B. Mohr, 1981), p. 223, has a particularly sentimental
view of Jesus' return to morning worship in the synagogue in his home town; see also
the assumption of B.J. Brooten, *Women Leaders in the Ancient Synagogue* (Brown
Judaic Studies, 36; Chico, CA: Scholars Press, 1982), pp. 139-40, that New Testament
texts state that women attended synagogue worship services; and even the meticulous
Sanders, *Jewish Law*, pp. 77, 78, assumes without argumentation that worship was a
recognised activity in first-century CE synagogues in Palestine.

[15] So also Riesner, *Jesus als Lehrer*, p. 136.

[16] As is the practice throughout this book, when synagogues are mentioned in texts, it
is only when there are descriptions of doorways, steps, slabs with inscriptions, seats,
threatened or actual burning to the ground, etc., that evidence of a building is recognised. Phrases such as 'entering' or 'sitting down in' or 'teaching in' a synagogue will
not be regarded as necessarily implying a building—for they may indicate a building or
a room or a meeting.

[17] See particularly the influential work of A. Edersheim, *The Life and Times of Jesus
the Messiah*, 2 vols. (London: Longmans, 1897), especially vol. 1, pp. 430-50, whose
ideas have coloured the work of many subsequent scholars; B.H. Branscomb, *The
Gospel of Mark* (The Moffatt New Testament Commentary; London: Hodder &
Stoughton, 1937), p. 29; E. Trocmé, 'The Jews as Seen by Paul and Luke', in *'To See
Ourselves As Others See Us'* (ed. J. Neusner and E.S. Frerichs: Chico, CA: Scholars
Press, 1985), pp. 145-62 (159-60), assumes the same type of service to have taken place
in the synagogues that Luke describes Paul as visiting.

been edited at a later period, and, though containing older material, also having latter-day notions retrojected into the past.[18] Thus it is usually treated more cautiously than formerly as a source for first-century CE practice.

The Approach Adopted in This Chapter

I have, therefore, decided to apply to these New Testament texts, where possible, the same methods that I have applied to the other texts being examined: to begin the study of each with what may be found in the texts themselves. Thus occurrences of the key words 'sabbath', 'synagogue' and προσευχή will be noted, what is said about them, and the types of discourse within which they arise. Differences between usages in the four gospels and Acts will be assessed for their relevance to the discussion, and where possible, deductions and inferences will be made from the differences.

As part of the basis for understanding the religious life of first-century Palestine, the pictures of the sabbath gatherings of Jews gained from Philo, Josephus and the Graeco-Roman writers will be regarded here as equally valid to those gleaned from the New Testament, and as necessary input in the search for a more detailed and accurate picture of those gatherings. Thus from Philo we learn of the Jews gathering to study, listen, learn and discuss, with one of those (males) present taking the opportunity, as it presented itself, to explain the scriptures to the others.[19] And Josephus presents a picture of violent arguments, disagreements and scuffles over matters of political and community importance, added to the same image of study that Philo depicted. The Graeco-Roman writers have contributed vignettes of Jewish behaviour, painting images of sabbath evening meals and of proseuchae and, among other characterisations, depicting Jews as persistent in persuasion, though using their own form of logic and revelling in noisy chatter which uses flowery, over-elaborate language.

---

[18] J. Neusner, *Formative Judaism: Religious, Historical, and Literary Studies* (Brown Judaic Studies, 37; Chico, CA: Scholars Press, 1982), pp. 52-53, 63, 109-10, 112-13.

[19] Philo's descriptions of buildings with slabs and inscriptions venerating the Roman rulers do not have *explicit* parallels in Josephus's descriptions and have therefore been considered as no more than *possible* for Palestine.

An appreciation that these three presentations can provide different, yet valid, perceptions of what went on in 'synagogues' (or in προσευχαί) makes a considerable difference to how one might assess and evaluate the behaviour of Jesus and of the gospel 'Pharisees' in similar situations. If the generally accepted activities of the sabbath meeting of the local community were teaching, discussing and disputing, then one can perceive in the interplay of question and riposte neither the degree of provocation often ascribed to Jesus,[20] nor the display of malice attributed to the Pharisees.[21] The opposing voices are disputing the meaning of scripture in the proper setting for such disputes. They are doing exactly what was expected of Jewish males in a sabbath gathering.

Having an appreciation of all these background data does not preclude regarding the New Testament as a separate source, distinct from the other sources. What it does imply, however, is that the number of possible meanings of the information about synagogues that can be inferred from stories in the gospels is multiplied, since the stories no longer have to be heard solely from the perspective of the gospel writers. There are now the added choices of understanding what is being said from the stance of Jews like Philo or Josephus, or of a Roman intellectual. Thus, for example, arguments in the synagogue may be perceived as ordinary rather than extraordinary events, ones which the participants could well have relished, and teaching in the synagogue can be seen as a unexceptional activity of any adult Jewish male with knowledge, wisdom and the courage to take the floor.

So I imagine that keeping the sabbath in the time of Jesus meant resting from weekday work and exercising the mind and spirit, as described by Philo and Josephus,[22] by listening, thinking, arguing and persuading in the local sabbath gathering, in ways that could

---

[20] Rordorf, *Sunday*, pp. 65-67; M.M.B. Turner, 'Sabbath', in *From Sabbath to Lord's Day: A Biblical, Historical and Theological Investigation* (ed. D.A. Carson; Grand Rapids: Zondervan, 1982), pp. 99-157 (105); R.E. Brown, *The Gospel according to John, I–XII*(The Anchor Bible, 29; Garden City, NY: Doubleday, 1966), p. 210.

[21] R.A. Edwards, *Matthew's Story of Jesus* (Philadelphia: Fortress Press, 1985), p. 42; but see the contrary view of D.J. Harrington, 'Sabbath Tensions', in *The Sabbath in Jewish and Christian Traditions* (ed. T.C. Eskenazi, D.J. Harrington and W.H. Shea; New York: Crossroad, 1991), pp. 47-56 (53), that the Pharisees were 'relatively liberal and flexible'.

[22] Philo, *Special Laws* 2.60-62; Josephus, *Antiquities* 16.42-44.

include very heated plain speaking.[23] If that were not the usual practice we would have to envisage Jesus, cast somewhat in the role of
visiting know-all, as regularly presenting himself as unwelcome
healer at village 'synagogues' and precipitating controversy over
sabbath observance.[24] It is hard to believe that such an obnoxious
visitor would get any kind of a hearing in a 'synagogue' at all. But if
all synagogues were places where disputes were argued out, then a
contentious approach would not have been considered hostile, but
could well have been welcomed as stimulating.

Synagogues, in whatever form they existed, must have operated
with restricted access and with a commonly understood purpose.
They would be quite different from a gossiping group in a market
place or at a well-head or in the public room of an inn, for there
would have been no children, possibly no women, certainly no animals present nor any non-Jewish passers-by. Strangers who would
not, or did not know how to, observe the norms would not have been
able to command the attention of the group present. None of the
accounts in Acts of non-Jews being present in synagogues envisages
them as taking the floor and enlightening the assembled company.
That freedom was reserved for Jewish males, of whom Jesus was
typical.

Some commentators believe that Jesus taught in the 'synagogues'
because he was a extraordinary teacher or preacher,[25] giving the local
synagogue a chance to hear his teaching or because he carried out a
'teaching ministry', rather like a public speaking tour given by a
famous visiting professor or evangelist.[26] But I am of the opinion that
that concept is foreign to the material we have before us and depends
on importing a twentieth-century model into our understanding of
first-century Palestine. I am convinced that teaching and 'speaking
boldly' were normal activities in all 'synagogues'. The listeners
could and would take issue with the speaker and debate with grim
determination if necessary, because it was the important matters of

---

[23] An English euphemism for telling one's opponent the most unpalatable facts and
opinions at one's disposal.

[24] As Rordorf, *Sunday*, pp. 67-68.

[25] Rordorf, *Sunday*, pp. 67-68.

[26] D.A. Carson, 'Jesus and the Sabbath in the Four Gospels', in *From Sabbath to
Lord's Day: A Biblical, Historical and Theological Investigation* (ed. D.A. Carson;
Grand Rapids: Zondervan, 1982), pp. 57-97 (71).

their common life, religion and relationship with God that were under discussion.

As I see it, Jesus would teach in the sabbath gatherings of Jews—though not necessarily in special buildings—as would Stephen, Paul, Timothy,[27] and Barnabas, because that is what adult male Jews did when they met together on the sabbath, if any among them had ideas worth sharing.

It is with this image of likely behaviour at sabbath gatherings in 'synagogues' sharply in focus that I approach the evidence about Jewish practice on the sabbath that can be culled from the New Testament, bearing in mind that in the texts 'synagogues' could mean the people at the meeting, or the building with the meeting going on within it, or the building without the people. And I shall look for any evidence of worship practices in the sabbath gatherings in these 'synagogues'.

Texts about the Sabbath in the New Testament

In this section any texts which are not germane to the ongoing discussion of the study will be discussed when they are introduced and then set on one side. Texts which contribute to the conclusions of the study will be discussed together later in the chapter.

The word 'sabbath' occurs ten times in Matthew, eleven times in Mark, eighteen times in Luke, eleven times in John and seven times in Acts—plus one reference in Acts to a sabbath's day journey.

In Matthew 'sabbath' occurs five times in the story of the disciples plucking grain on the sabbath, three times in the healing of a man with a withered hand, once in the apocalyptic section in Matthew 24, and once in the Easter story.

In Mark 'sabbath' occurs once in the story about Jesus' visit to the synagogue in Capernaum, five times in the story of the disciples plucking grain on the sabbath, twice in the healing of a man with a

---

[27] Timothy was circumcised because of the Jews' knowledge that his father was a Greek (Acts 16.3), which implies that circumcision would make him acceptable to Jews (F.F. Bruce, *Commentary on the Book of Acts* [The New London Commentary on the New Testament; London: Marshall, Morgan & Scott, 1954, pp. 322-23]). This is interpreted as authorising him to enter the synagogues (H. Conzelmann, *Acts of the Apostles* [Hermeneia; Philadelphia: Fortress Press, 1987], p. 125), or perhaps for the purpose of being allowed to speak in the synagogue.

withered hand, once in an account of Jesus teaching in a synagogue and twice in the Easter story.

In Luke 'sabbath' occurs three times in the story of the disciples plucking grain on the sabbath, which is in this gospel preceded by the stories of Jesus reading the law and expounding it in a synagogue in Nazareth on the sabbath and also in the healing in Capernaum of a man possessed by a demon. The sabbath is also referred to three times in the healing of a man with a withered hand, five times in the healing of a disabled woman, three times in the healing of a man with dropsy, and twice in the Easter story. The four extra stories account for the larger number of references to the sabbath in Luke's gospel.

In John 'sabbath' occurs four times in the story of the healing of a man by the pool of Bethesda, three times in a dispute over the rival claims to over-riding the sabbath by healing or circumcision, twice in a controversy over healing on the sabbath, and twice in the Easter story.

In Acts the word 'sabbath' is seven times associated with sabbath gatherings, of which six take place in 'synagogues', whether groups or buildings is not always apparent, and one in a προσευχή.[28]

The word 'sabbath' also occurs once in Colossians (2.16), in a sequence of holy days:

> Therefore let no one pass judgment on you in questions of food and drink or with regard to a festival or a new moon or a sabbath.[29]

This text has been described as part of a Pauline admirer's objections 'to Gentile Christians being forced to observe the Jewish calendar and its Sabbaths', and is asserting the freedom of Christians from the dominion of the Jewish law.[30]

Sabbath rest is referred to once in Hebrews (4.9), where the blessing of the original rest of one day in seven is extended into the perpetual rest of acceptance by God now available to the readers who are Christians.

---

[28] Acts 13.14; 13.27; 13.42-44; 15.25; 16.13 (προσευχή); 17.2; 18.4.
[29] This text was already referred to in Chapter 1.
[30] Harrington, 'Sabbath Tensions', p. 54.

The Lack of References to Sabbath or Synagogues in Paul's Epistles

Neither sabbath nor 'synagogues' are mentioned at all in the undisputed epistles of Paul, which would suggest that the sabbath practice of Jews was not a controversial topic between him and his addressees. This is rather surprising given the amount of discussion about the sabbath both in the gospels and in the writings of later Christian writers, such as Ignatius, Barnabas and Justin. It is difficult to suggest a reason for this discrepancy, but perhaps Paul and his correspondents simply accepted that Jews—who lived quite separate lives from them—observed the sabbath, whereas they themselves did not. They would hold their Christ-centred gatherings as the religious meeting of the week.

Supplying a plausible explanation for the seeming discrepancy is the claim of Meeks that 'the great issue in Pauline Christianity is not between "the synagogue" and the sect of the Christians, but within the Christian movement'.[31] Because, he argues, the social context of the Pauline groups was never within Judaism, and because meeting in houses arose in Paul's experience before it occurred in other Christian communities there is no need for Paul to write of any conflict with the synagogues. He contrasts this experience with that of the Johannine community, where the Christian group is constantly defining itself against the attitudes expressed by groups in the synagogues. Thus, whereas the Johannine Christians had to find for themselves a separate identity as they moved away from their origins within Judaism, there would be no occasion for discussion about the sabbath between Paul and his non-Jewish correspondents.

On the other hand, however, Paul did not interact solely with Gentiles, for, in one passage, he writes of becoming like a Jew in order to convert Jews to his beliefs:

> To the Jews I became as a Jew, in order to win Jews. To those under the law I became as one under the law (though I myself am not under the law) so that I might win those under the law. To those outside the law I became as one outside the law (though I am not free from God's law but am under Christ's law) so that I might win those outside the law (1 Cor. 9.20-21)

---

[31] W.A. Meeks, 'Breaking Away', in *'To See Ourselves As Others See Us'* (ed. J. Neusner and E.S. Frerichs: Chico, CA: Scholars Press, 1985), pp. 93-116 (106).

Commentators interpret these verses in various ways, generally on the basis of Acts. Some refer to the Jewish behaviour of Paul referred to in Acts: his having Timothy circumcised (16.3), his involvement in the Nazirite vows of four men (21.21-26), and his using 'the Jewish methods of teaching'.[32] Others read the text as implying that Paul 'lived in conformity with the Law of Moses when he was doing missionary work among the Jews'.[33] Barrett understands Paul to be quite distinct about being a Jew by choice in the matters of observance, and about being a Jew by birth and upbringing, and reads Paul's Judaism as 'a guise he could adopt or discard at will'.[34]

But reading the text on its own—without reference to Acts—I infer that Paul could if he chose observe the Law, and could attend Jewish meetings on the sabbath when it suited his purposes. To my mind, this text gives the *only* corroboration—and that by inference only—in the undisputed writings of Paul, of Luke's lengthy accounts of Paul's missionary activities in 'synagogues'.

Texts about Synagogues in the New Testament

Here, as in the section on the sabbath, any texts which are not relevant to the ongoing discussion will be dealt with immediately. Texts valuable to this study will be discussed together later in the Chapter.

The word 'synagogue' occurs nine times in Matthew, eight times in Mark, thirteen times in Luke, five times in John, fourteen times in Acts, once in James and twice in Revelation.

The English term 'ruler of the synagogue' represents ἀρχισυνάγωγος, which appears three times in Mark about Jairus and once in Luke for an unnamed ruler of the synagogue, and not at all in Matthew[35] or John,[36] and three times in Acts, for Crispus, Sosthenes

---

[32] H.A.W. Meyer, *Critical and Exegetical Handbook to the Epistles to the Corinthians* (tr. D.D. Bannerman and W.P. Dickson; Edinburgh: T. & T. Clark, 1877), p. 271; H.L. Goudge, *The First Epistle to the Corinthians* (Westminster Commentaries; London: Methuen, 1911), p. 77.

[33] J. Héring, *The First Epistle of Saint Paul to the Corinthians* (tr. A.W. Heathcote and P.J. Allcock; London: Epworth Press, 1962), p. 81.

[34] C.K. Barrett, *A Commentary on the First Epistle to the Corinthians* (London: A. & C. Black, 1968), p. 211; see also F.F. Bruce, *1 and 2 Corinthians* (New Century Bible; London: Oliphants, 1971), pp. 86-87.

[35] The word 'ruler' (ἄρχων) occurs twice for Jairus.

[36] The word 'ruler' (ἄρχων) occurs once for Nicodemus.

and a group of unnamed 'rulers of the synagogue'. Luke has a similar phrase, ἄρχων τῆς συναγωγῆς, by which he refers to Jairus.

The linking of the words 'Jew' and 'synagogue' in a phrase, 'the
synagogue/s of the Jews' (ἡ συναγωγὴ τῶν Ἰουδαίων), occurs four
times in Acts (13.5; 14.1; 17.1; 17.10).[37]

The Greek word συναγωγή appears in Jas 2.2, but is translated in
most English versions as 'assembly', and taken to mean a Christian
meeting by most interpreters. This translation depends on a belief in
the early separation or distinction of Christian and Jewish communities,[38] and also on accepting that the early Church regarded itself as
the new Israel and the inheritor of the twelve tribes.[39] This second
point certainly gives an explanation for the opening colophon of the
book, which both names the speaker as 'a servant of God and of the
Lord Jesus Christ', and names the addressees as 'the twelve tribes in
the Dispersion', which colophon would otherwise imply a Jewish
audience.

Other commentators are not certain that the two religious groups
were separated from each other so clearly, and believe that Jewish
Christians or a combination of Christians and Jews are being
addressed, in which case the designation 'synagogue' implies a place
of Jewish assembly.[40] Another interpretation reads Jas 2.3, with the
allocation of seats for the two incomers in different places in the
synagogue, as implying not a gathering for worship but a judicial
assembly, after the fashion of the 'Jewish synagogue's beth-din'.[41]
Yet others discuss the whole question without being able to draw any
firm conclusions from the data available.[42]

---

[37] I note that this expression is exactly paralleled in the writings of Josephus—from
the last decade of the first century—but nowhere else, when, in Ant. 19. 300, he refers to
the synagogue in Dora in these terms. Justin uses a similar phrase (ἐν συναγωγαῖς
Ἰουδαίων) in Dialogue, 73.

[38] As, for example, R.H. Gundry, Matthew: A Commentary on his Literary and Theological Art (Grand Rapids: Eerdmans, 1982), p. 601: 'By the time Jerusalem was
destroyed, the church had long since become a counterpart to the synagogue'.

[39] J.H. Ropes, A Critical and Exegetical Commentary on the Epistle of St James
(ICC; Edinburgh: T. & T. Clark, 1916), pp. 124-25, 188-89; P.H. Davids, The Epistle of
James (The New International Greek Testament Commentary; Exeter: Paternoster
Press, 1982), pp. 63-64; F. Vouga, L'Epître de Saint Jacques (Commentaire du Nou-
veau Testament, II/13a; Genève: Editions Labor et Fides, 1984), pp. 37, 71.

[40] R.J. Knowling, The Epistle of St James (Westminster Commentaries; London:
Methuen, 1904), pp. 4-5, 40-42.

[41] Davids, James, pp. 108-109.

[42] See, for example, J.B. Mayor, The Epistle of St James (London: Macmillan, 1897),

I believe, bearing in mind that the addressees are named as the Diaspora Jews, that the best translation of 'synagogue' in this text is a gathering of Jews, perhaps including Jewish Christians among them.

The word 'synagogue' also occurs twice in Revelation, where it means an assembly or gathering of a different religious group, variously believed by scholars to be Christians or Jewish Christians, or the local Jewish community.[43] These texts have no connection with discussions about the sabbath.

Discussion about Sabbath and Synagogue in the Gospels and Acts

Sabbath as a Day of Restricted Activity in the Gospels

The sabbath and what one could or could not do on it is an issue in the gospel texts, reflecting a similar level of interest to that which we have seen in the Dead Sea Scrolls, *Jubilees* and Maccabees.

Mark's gospel reports two controversies between Jesus and other religious spokesmen over what actions could or could not lawfully be done on the sabbath, one about plucking grain[44] and the other about healing a man with a withered hand.[45] These same two stories are paralleled in Matthew and Luke, and Luke includes three extra controversies over the legality of healing on the sabbath;[46] but while John records three disputes over the lawfulness of healing on the sabbath,[47] he nowhere records the grainfield incident.

The theological themes that underlie these controversies differ from evangelist to evangelist, as does also the amount of literary attention given to them. It is possible that the controversy stories arose out of scenes in the life of Jesus and reflect vital issues of his time, and were later modified and expanded by the early Church,[48] but it is more likely that these stories were used mainly by way of authorisation for the particular community's own behaviour in situa-

---

pp. 29-31, 79-80.

[43] See discussion in Collins, 'Insiders and Outsiders', pp. 204-207.

[44] Mk 2.23-28; Mt. 12.1-8; Lk. 6.1-5.

[45] Mk 3.1-6; Mt. 12.9-14; Lk. 6.6-11.

[46] Lk. 4.31-37 (note that the sabbath is not mentioned in the Markan parallel at Mk 1.21-28); Lk. 13.10-17; 14.1-6.

[47] Jn 5.1-18; 7.22-24; 9.1-34, esp. 13-17.

[48] Rordorf, *Sunday*, pp. 73-74.

tions parallel to those described in the controversies.[49]

One point in the argument offered by the evangelists is that Jesus was comparable to David in the providing of food to hungry followers and could similarly override the Law, and also that Jesus' supremacy over the Law was no more than the summit of his supremacy over everything.[50]

Mark's story also implies that Gentile Christians should not feel forced to keep the sabbath in the Jewish manner, although the story itself assumes that Jesus and his opponents did observe the sabbath.[51]

Matthew adds the idea that since Temple priests work on the sabbath without profaning it (12.5), and as Jesus is greater than the Temple, he can authorise his followers to do good works on the sabbath.[52] Therefore, Gentile members of Matthew's community need not feel guilty if they do not keep the sabbath.[53] This story gives more than a hint that Christian re-interpretation of what God demanded was moving away from concentration on sabbath-keeping.

In Luke's version of the story, it is only 'some of the Pharisees' who interrogate Jesus; thus Luke creates an image of two groups of Pharisees, one friendly to Jesus and the other inimical, and he verbalises a debate within the Pharisaic movement as to whether the Jesus movement was an acceptable interpretation of Judaism or not.[54] But although it is the disciples who are addressed by the Pharisees, it is Jesus who replies,[55] so the situation allows his, or the author's, less traditional views of the sabbath to be expressed.

What can be concluded from this pericope is that there was

---

[49] Harrington, 'Sabbath Tensions', pp. 49-50; Fitzmyer, *Luke*, I, pp. 606-607. Hill, *Matthew*, p. 209, takes an intermediate position.

[50] E.P. Gould, *A Critical and Exegetical Commentary on the Gospel according to Mark* (ICC; Edinburgh: T. & T. Clark, 1896), pp. 47-50.

[51] A.E.J. Rawlinson, *St Mark* (Westminster Commentaries; London: Methuen, 1925), p. 33.

[52] W.C. Allen, *A Critical and Exegetical Commentary on the Gospel according to S. Matthew* (Edinburgh: T. & T. Clark, 1907), pp. 127-28; A.W. Argyle, *The Gospel according to Matthew* (CBC; Cambridge: CUP, 1963), pp. 91-92; Fenton, *Matthew*, pp. 189-90; W.F. Albright and C.S. Mann, *Matthew* (The Anchor Bible, 26; Garden City, NY: Doubleday, 1971), pp. 149-50; E. Schweizer, *The Good News according to Matthew* (tr. D.E. Green; London: SPCK, 1975), pp. 277-79.

[53] Mt. 11.30; Fenton, *Matthew*, p. 188; Carson, 'Sabbath', p. 75; Edwards, *Matthew*, p. 42.

[54] Sanders, *Luke–Acts*, p. 172; see also pp. 88-94; Trocmé, 'Jews', pp. 157-60.

[55] I.H. Marshall, *The Gospel of Luke: A Commentary on the Greek Text* (The New International Greek Testament Commentary; Exeter: Paternoster Press, 1978), p. 231.

controversy among groups of Jews about what actions counted as 'work' on the sabbath. But there is also a very serious claim being made by the Christian writers of the gospels that Jesus in some way supersedes the old régime as it is presented in the sabbath law. Through this story, and others in the gospels, the Christians make the claim that the sabbath has been demoted as an important precept of the community. Obeying the words of the teacher Jesus has displaced it. The sabbath was no longer a key religious concept, and the commandment did not have to be followed to the extent of complete inactivity.

But nothing is said about sabbath worship. The sabbath is not the subject matter of the story; it is used in the story only to show how supremely important Jesus was to the Christians.

Sabbath, Synagogue and Healing Miracles in the Gospels
If we accept that the evangelists had theological aims when they wrote, then the story of a man with an unclean spirit in the synagogue can be seen as a negative evaluation of the state of religion in Palestine. The existing religion was so distorted that it required the ministry of Jesus to effect a cure.[56]

But, in telling the tale the way he chooses, Mark relates nothing regarding synagogue activities, and one can only infer that the situation in a synagogue, whether gathering or building, on a sabbath, was informal enough to permit an encounter between two strangers during which a healing could take place.

Matthew's way of relating the story of the healing a man with a withered hand gives his community a view of how the sabbath was to be observed.[57] Certain types of 'work' could be done because they were classed as 'doing good'.[58] And he is happy to contrast that with the picture he presents of the Pharisees 'doing evil'.[59]

But the only other details about what was happening in the synagogue that morning are of a general conversation and disagreement in the synagogue over what Jesus was doing—as he was doing it. This reminds me of the informal atmosphere of the sabbath gather-

---

[56] J. Bowman, *The Gospel of Mark: The New Christian Jewish Passover Haggadah* (Studia Post-Biblica, 8; Leiden: Brill, 1965), p. 111, on Mk 1.21-28.
[57] Mt. 12.9-14.
[58] Harrington, 'Sabbath Tensions', p. 53.
[59] Gundry, *Matthew*, p. 225.

ings described by Philo and Josephus.

In John's gospel the story of the healing of the 'dried up' man at the pool of Bethesda[60] is said by John to have taken placeon the sabbath.[61] It is possible that John has deliberately introduced the 'pallet' and the sabbath so as to involve the man in 'work' on the sabbath.[62] Then he can then make a point about Jesus' work on the sabbath, claiming that it is carried out not merely because he is greater than the sabbath and the Temple and so able to work on the sabbath, but because he is doing God's work on the sabbath and—according to John—God does not rest on the sabbath.[63]

The story effects three functions in John's theological agenda: it underlines Jesus' authority as equal with God and so above the authority of both Torah and tradition; it displays Jesus' power to 'heal' any human who is 'damaged'; and it 'authorises' Jesus' followers to tell the Jews to allow, and accept, that authority. But the story does not tell us anything about what happened in the sabbath gatherings of Jews.[64] The role played by the sabbath in the story is to provide a means by which the evangelist can put Jesus on a par with God.

Another controversy in John's gospel brings into confrontation the Jews who allow circumcision to over-ride the sabbath law but not healing, Jesus who has cured a man, and the man who has been healed.[65] By the arguments of Jesus—or the evangelist—circumcision, permitted on the sabbath by Torah, is equated with making the body whole; thus, if circumcision is to be encouraged, so healing should be encouraged, as another way of making a man whole. So healing should be permitted on the sabbath.[66] It seems to the modern

---

[60] Jn 5.2-18.
[61] B. Lindars, *The Gospel of John* (New Century Bible; London: Oliphants, 1972), pp. 213-16; Brown, *John*, p. 210.
[62] See also Meeks, 'Breaking Away', p. 98.
[63] Lindars, *John*, pp. 218-19.
[64] Carson, 'Sabbath', pp. 81-82, sees Jesus as 'precipitating a crisis over the Torah', and also implying that he is a close equal to God, since both work on the sabbath. But Carson regards this healing story as referring to a different healing from similar pericopes in the synoptics and does not regard the addition of the sabbath reference as a literary device of the evangelist, so he portrays the Pharisees holding the discussion with Jesus as actual historical opponents, rather than seeing them as characterisations of the opponents of Matthew's community.
[65] Jn 7.19-24.
[66] Lindars, *John*, pp. 290-91; Brown, *John*, pp. 311-13, 315.

mind special pleading to consider the removal of the foreskin equivalent to making someone whole—it would have to mean spiritually whole rather than physically whole—but the argument is presented as valid by the gospel writer.

And in the third story, the healing of a man born blind, the 'Pharisees' argue among themselves as to whether Jesus is 'good' and therefore able to heal or whether he is sinful because he breaks the sabbath. On the surface of the story Jesus' mode of sabbath observance is under attack,[67] but at a deeper level, the story is about Jesus' identity. So the sequence of three healing stories in John is part of 'the apologetics of Church and Synagogue in the era of spreading Christianity'.[68] Again the story is not about the sabbath but about the status of Jesus.

Luke's gospel has the greatest amount of text on the issue of healing on the sabbath, but in the first story, the exorcism of a possessed man, as in Matthew and Mark, there is no controversy over the healing,[69] and no response of Jesus about the sabbath.

The second healing story is a parallel of the healing of a man with a withered arm, but the point made by Luke here is that Jesus equates refraining from doing a possible good with doing actual harm.[70]

The third story brings in the need for watering thirsty animals as one argument for activity on the sabbath and also introduces Satan into the discussion, as a anti-type of Jesus. Satan is still working his evil on the disabled Jewish woman on this sabbath but is overcome by Jesus carrying out a good work.[71] Jesus, who works on the sabbath to counter Satan's work on that day, becomes the most powerful divine being apart from God—another theological point is being made by Luke.

In the story of the healing of the disabled woman there is no singling out of the sabbath as an especially appropriate day for healing

---

[67] Harrington, 'Sabbath Tensions', pp. 54-55.

[68] Brown, *John*, pp. 379-80.

[69] Marshall, *Luke*, p. 234, finds it necessary to explain this as being due to the general pleasurable surprise at Jesus' powers overshadowing any considerations regarding which day of the week it was, as well as the exonerating circumstance of Jesus quieting someone who was interrupting the sabbath meeting. As we can see, Marshall confines his concern to the event being described and not at all to the literary process of producing the gospel.

[70] Marshall, *Luke*, p. 235.

[71] Marshall, *Luke*, p. 559.

activities, but rather an elimination of the specialness of the sabbath from consideration when one has the choice to do a good deed or carry out a healing.[72] The story is less about healing on the sabbath than it is about how much of the Jewish religion falls under Jesus' dominion.

In the fourth incident, Jesus dines in the home of a Pharisee on the sabbath. This story might be expected to tell us more about Jewish sabbath practice, if we could determine whether the meal were on Friday evening or during Saturday. But only the doubtful practice of drawing assumptions about what time of day is meant, or whether Friday or Saturday is implied, would lead us to accept that this is 'doubtless a meal after the service in the synagogue'.[73] The text itself is silent on these matters.

In the non-biblical texts studied in Chapters 3 and 4, the sabbath meals mentioned have been a midday meal on Saturday—referred to by Josephus, and, on Friday evening, a candle-lit dinner with fish and wine—as described by Persius. This text from Luke adds nothing to the little that we already know from those two texts.

What may be concluded from the foregoing discussion on the sabbath healing incidents reported in the gospels is that the arguments over sabbath healing actions often took place in 'synagogues', and once in a home, in the presence of other Jews called by the gospel writers 'Pharisees'. The healings were not part of the 'proceedings' in the synagogue on the sabbath, nor is there any indication that they interrupted any 'proceedings'.[74] They caused comment only in terms of whether they were 'work' or not, that is, whether they constituted a breach of sabbath law. There is no reference to their suitability as a means of praising, or honouring God; in fact no religious connotation is given to the healing itself.[75]

---

[72] Turner, 'Sabbath,' pp. 107, 113.

[73] Marshall, *Luke*, p. 578.

[74] *Pace* Marshall who believes that the screams of the possessed man were causing a disturbance in the service (*Luke*, pp. 234; cf. pp. 178-81).

[75] This contrasts somewhat with the injunction of Jesus to the healed leper, reported in the synoptic gospels, that he show himself to the priest and make an offering for his cleansing and for a testimony to them; see Mt. 8.4; Mk 1.44; Lk. 5.14. In that story the healing requires a contact with official religious personnel in Jerusalem and the giving of the prescribed offering, but possibly because it was a removal of uncleanness as well as a healing; see Gould, *Mark*, pp. 32-33; Rawlinson, *Mark*, pp. 21-22; Hill, *Matthew*, pp. 156-57.

Summary

The gospel writers have used the sabbath stories to re-define the importance of both the sabbath and sabbath law in the light of the teachings and life of Jesus. They tell the stories about Jesus in such a way that they can make theological capital out of them. Indirectly, the new teacher tells the Christians what they may do on the sabbath, and how they may regard the sabbath. But neither he, nor the evangelists, have either said, or implied, anything about worship on the sabbath.

The Synagogue as Daily or Weekly Gathering Place

An issue that is often avoided when synagogue activities are being discussed in the secondary literature is whether there were meetings on weekdays as well as on the sabbath, and whether any such meetings would be solely for daily prayer sessions, or also for discussing community business.

Chapter 3 discussed Josephus's account of the business meeting in a προσευχή at Tiberias on sabbath, the daily prayer meeting on Sunday, and the supposedly religious meeting on the following Monday, called as a public fast, but in reality given over to character assassination and unsuccessful physical attack on Josephus; but I found the evidence too sparse to draw definite conclusions. Philo writes only of gatherings to study the law on the sabbath, and refers to daily prayer sessions only for the Therapeutae.[76]

The distinction between daily and weekly practice is similarly unclear in the accounts in the gospels and Acts, for the details about teaching and disputing in synagogues are presented in the gospels and Acts in a way that leaves it quite undetermined whether such activities were *always* on a sabbath. Fourteen references to the sabbath occur in eleven pericopes about sabbath in synagogues. In the seventeen remaining references to teaching in synagogues, eight in the gospels and nine in Acts, it is not clear whether this could happen only on the sabbath, or on other days too.

There are two pieces of evidence in Luke's writings that touch on this question, but unfortunately they imply opposite conclusions. First, in Luke 13.14 in the story of the healing of a disabled woman,

---

[76] See Chapter 3.

the ruler of a synagogue addresses the woman angrily: 'There are six days on which work ought to be done; come on those days and be cured, and not on the sabbath day'. This implies that she could find a healer, perhaps not necessarily Jesus, willing to cure her in the synagogue on weekdays, and that she would have the same access to the synagogue on those days as on the sabbath. But as this is the only text from which such inferences about synagogue attendance, and in particular female synagogue attendance, may be drawn, I am hesitant about accepting that it conveys a historical truth. There are enough theological reasons for the placing of the speech in the mouth of the ruler to make its historical likelihood less than determinative.

And second, in Acts 13.42, the synagogue members urge Paul and Barnabas to speak to them again on the next sabbath. This implies that no other time in the week was available for the discussion. Since Paul and Barnabas had the preaching as their main concern, it is not their freedom to talk that is the reason for waiting till the next sabbath. It is the availability of the listeners, who are assumed to be able to be there only on the sabbath.

Now it does seem likely that the sabbath would be the day when the males of the community were free from work during the daylight hours, and could turn their minds to religious matters, and the Greek of Acts 17.2 seems to agree with this idea, for the phrase about the duration of Paul's preaching in Thessalonica can be translated 'for three weeks' or 'for three sabbaths', meaning 'on three successive sabbath days'.[77] Acts 18.4 makes the point more clearly when it says that Paul argued in the synagogue every sabbath, or 'sabbath by sabbath'.[78] Turner makes the same point more firmly when he says that 'Paul met with Jews and Christians in the synagogues on Sabbath days because that was when the synagogue was convened'.[79] There would be a meeting of the 'synagogue' only when all the males came together, usually only on sabbaths.

It is similarly difficult to determine whether the gospel accounts intend to say that Jesus taught in the synagogue in Capernaum every sabbath,[80] or for a succession of sabbaths, the Greek plural (ἐν τοῖς

---

[77] Bruce, *Acts*, p. 343.
[78] Bruce, *Acts*, p. 369.
[79] Turner, 'Sabbath', p. 129.
[80] Lk. 4.31.

σάββασιν) allowing either a singular or plural translation. A singular meaning for the references in Matthew is preferred by some,[81] while others feel the issue is uncertain, yet decide for a singular meaning on grounds which do not rule out the meaning of every sabbath, or generally on the sabbath.[82] Fitzmyer is readier to accept a plural meaning, for he translates Lk. 4.31 as 'He went down to Capernaum ... where he used to teach the people on the Sabbath'.[83]

Bearing in mind the overall tenor of the references to activities in the synagogues, I believe that all the gospel references to teaching, preaching, expounding the Law, etc., in synagogues can and do refer to activity during the sabbath day gatherings, and that the gospel writers knew of such gatherings and visualised the ones familiar to them when they were writing down their accounts of Jesus' practices.

The Synagogue as a Building

In the book of Acts 'synagogue', as well as meaning a gathering of Jews, can often point definitely to a building in which Jews met together on the sabbath to read scripture and listen to teaching; but Lk. 7.1-10, as Kee points out, 'alone in the gospel tradition points unequivocally to a building',[84] for the centurion had *built* it for the Jews.

In Acts 15.21, James says, 'from early generations Moses has had in every city those who preach him, for he is read every sabbath in the synagogues'. This implies gatherings, indoors or in the open air or in someone's home or in a special building set apart for the reading sessions. This text confirms the practice of sabbath law reading which we have understood from Philo for προσευχαί and Josephus for συναγωγαί, although it leaves the precise location—for example, in a building—undefined.[85]

---

[81] W.D. Davies and D.C. Allison, *The Gospel according to Matthew*, I (ICC; Edinburgh: T. & T. Clark, 1988), pp. 413-14; *The Gospel according to Matthew*, II (ICC; Edinburgh: T. & T. Clark, 1991), p. 320.

[82] Turner, 'Sabbath', pp. 101-103; Marshall, *Luke*, p. 191.

[83] Fitzmyer, *Luke*, I, p. 541 (discussion on p. 544).

[84] Kee, 'Transformation', p. 17.

[85] Note also the references to a προσευχή in Acts 16.13-16, which do not, however, clearly indicate a building.

The Synagogue as Community Institution

Many different activities took place in the synagogues described in Acts, namely: teaching, preaching, reading, speaking, disputing, praying, sitting, scourging, beating and passing judgement on offenders.[86] The synagogue concerned itself with matters of community identity, education and solidarity. Peer group pressures were applied through the synagogue as a means of keeping the Jewish community unified.

Narrative World versus Social World of the Author

If, as I propose from my study of the extant texts relating to the sabbath, sabbath synagogue worship services were not a regular feature of Jewish religious life as it was known to Philo and Josephus, it seems probable that they could not have been known to Jesus—or Paul either. But to explain the apparent disagreement of this proposal with the gospels, one would need to acknowledge that the gospel accounts which imply or recount Jesus' attendance at sabbath worship are written with hindsight, which, in this case, makes the image of Jesus' world less clear.

Thus readers seeking a historical perspective have to work within at least two time zones: that of the events described, and that of the writers/editors.[87] The main difficulty I encounter is that, as Kee also finds, some scholars do not distinguish between 'the various strands of the New Testament, so that generalisations are made on texts from Paul and Acts, from Mark and Matthew as though these traditions were not subject to important changes within the early Christian community in the period down to the beginning of the second century'.[88] This conflation of sources means that subtlety of exegesis is diminished because items are combined that should be distinguished.[89]

And if we determine to give Matthew, Mark, Luke and John equal standing as giving historically accurate accounts of Jesus' life and

---

[86] Also almsgiving at Mt. 6.2.
[87] Harrington, 'Sabbath Tensions', p. 54, makes such a distinction for John's gospel.
[88] Kee, 'Transformation', p. 4.
[89] Sensitive commentators, for example, Brown, *John*, pp. xlvii-li, 379-80, however, do take seriously the effect of both the authors' hindsight and their present purposes on the construction of the stories within the gospels and of the gospels themselves as whole works.

teachings, then we do so in the face of the belief that Luke did not give Mark, nor possibly Matthew either, that status, for he felt free to change what had been written and did not feel bound to accept the other gospels as they stood. In Luke's gospel Luke re-modelled earlier gospel material.

The shift of perspective between different New Testament authors can be more easily detected between descriptions of Paul's preaching activities in the epistles (author Paul) and in Acts (author Luke),[90] because, in contrast to the multiplicity of descriptions of Paul's synagogue activities in Acts, there is no occurrence of the word 'synagogue' in the undisputed letters of Paul, or—for that matter— anywhere in the Pauline corpus.[91] Paul's letters refer only to visits to churches in people's houses,[92] and to lodging with friends in their homes.[93]

Admittedly, Paul's silence is not conclusive, but it is odd, for the word 'synagogue' occurs in Acts a total of nineteen times,[94] three of which refer to Paul's persecution of the Christians in synagogues, and fourteen of which report visits Paul made to synagogues while travelling in the Diaspora to proclaim Jesus as Christ.

It looks as if the writer of Acts is describing Paul's activities in terms that were intelligible to him and his readers, in what Meeks refers to as a 'later idealization',[95] and that included the synagogue building as the natural religious talking-shop in any community where Jews lived, and as the place where Christian–Jewish disagreements would take place.

Kraabel brings these issues to our attention in his somewhat ironic tribute to Luke's 'skill as a story teller', for he believes that 'Luke's "theology in historical guise" has become religious history for many historians of Judaism, both Jewish and Gentile'.[96] He is sure that Luke created much of what he wrote and so believes that there is a

---

[90] See the full discussion of this topic in A.J. Mattill, 'The Value of Acts as a Source for the Study of Paul', in *Perspectives on Luke–Acts* (ed. C.H. Talbert; Edinburgh: T. & T. Clark, 1978), pp. 76-98.

[91] This point was also made by Kraabel, 'Synagoga Caeca', p. 228.

[92] Rom. 16.5; 1 Cor. 16.19.

[93] 1 Cor. 16.6-8; the possibility of lodging in, or at, a synagogue occurs in later synagogues, as is suggested by the Theodotus inscription; see discussion in Chapter 8.

[94] Excluding the phrase 'ruler of the synagogue', which occurs three times.

[95] Meeks, 'Breaking Away', p. 105.

[96] Kraabel, 'Synagoga Caeca', p. 228; the quotation is attributed to Neusner.

character Paul, created by Luke in Acts, and a real author Paul, who
wrote the letters. But we have no way of confirming whether the
'real Paul' would have told his own story in the same terms as Luke
told it or not.

Hengel attempts to resolve the difficulty of the two pictures of
Paul by arguing that Luke became acquainted with Paul only in his
later life, long after the letters had been written, so that although
Luke knew Paul and travelled with him, he did not have access to the
letters.[97] Now, it is easy to agree with Hengel that it is not fair to
equate Luke with those ancient writers who freely invented facts as
they needed them, but it is nonetheless unfair of Hengel to suggest
that that is the only possible alternative to regarding Luke as a relatively reliable historian.[98] There is a fair spread of possibilities in
between these two positions, and I would prefer to characterise Luke
as a writer who uses and elaborates his sources to make a fresh
record of the story for his readers.[99]

The Two Attitudes of the Character Jesus to the Synagogue

What I perceive as having been one of the problems for the gospel
writers is the contrast between Jesus' willingness to enter and teach
in synagogues, and the situation the New Testament writers themselves knew—of being at loggerheads with the Jews. Thus we find in
the gospels, on the one hand, narratives of Jesus' going readily in the
company of synagogue rulers, either to a meal, or to revive a dead
daughter, and, on the other hand, warnings given in Jesus' voice to
the readers of the gospels about the violence to be undergone in synagogues. The message given by the tradition about synagogues is
inconsistent and the writers had to find some way of resolving the
tension.

Commentators vary in their degree of discomfort at recognising
and discussing these problems. Some treat the warnings as straightforward predictions in which Jesus foretells the future.[100] Others
cannot easily take this position, and so, in spite of drawing the read-

---

[97] M. Hengel, *Acts and the History of Earliest Christianity* (London: SCM Press,
1979), pp. 66-67.

[98] Hengel, *Earliest Christianity*, pp. 60-61.

[99] G. Lüdemann, *Early Christianity according to the Tradition in Acts: A Commentary* (tr. J. Bowden; London: SCM Press, 1989), esp. pp. 9-11.

[100] Fenton, *Matthew*, pp. 159-60, 376.

ers' attention to the problem, place the predictions in Jesus' own mouth, relating to Jesus' own situation—yet also having value for the early readers in their time of persecution.[101]

As I see it, the cognitive dissonance engendered in the gospel reader by being asked to assimilate both these scenarios causes gospel readers, whether modern and actual—or early Christian and ideal—discomfort as they struggle to make a coherent whole of what is being portrayed about 'synagogues'. This discomfort is eased by the evangelists' casting of Jesus' warnings in the form of predictions about the future that his followers would experience. Thus, readers can be encouraged to accept that Jesus in his own day believed in following Jewish ways but through his divine abilities he could foresee that the relationship between his followers and the 'synagogues' would be quite different. The narrative becomes coherent by this means, and the device functions as another means of underlining Jesus' special, supernatural, identity.

Discussion on Synagogues in the Gospels

I have decided to discuss the evidence from the four gospels in the order: Mark, Matthew, John and Luke, in order to work with the less complex material first and finish with what appears to me to be the most complex text.

Discussion on Synagogues in Mark

Mark's Jesus teaches three times in the synagogue in Galilee on the sabbath, three times heals in the synagogue on the sabbath, knows of rulers of the synagogue and of best seats in the synagogue, but gives a warning to his followers of the dangers of being beaten in the synagogues by the councils:

> They went to Capernaum; and when the sabbath came, he entered the synagogue and taught. They were astounded at his teaching, for he taught them as one having authority, and not as the scribes. Just then there was in their synagogue a man with an unclean spirit, and he cried out, 'What have you to do with us, Jesus of Nazareth? Have you come to destroy us? I know who you are, the Holy One of God.' But Jesus rebuked him, saying, 'Be silent, and come out of him!' (1.21-25).

---

[101] Hill, *Matthew*, pp. 188, 315-16.

Again he entered the synagogue, and a man was there who had a withered hand. They watched him to see whether he would cure him on the sabbath, so that they might accuse him (3.1-2).

Then one of the leaders of the synagogue named Jairus came and, when he saw him, fell at his feet ... (5.22).

On the sabbath he began to teach in the synagogue, and many who heard him were astounded ...(6.2a).

and to have the best seats in the synagogues ... (12.39a).

As for yourselves, beware; for they will hand you over to councils; and you will be beaten in synagogues ... (13.9a).

The synagogues warned against in Mark appear to include build-ings in which disciplinary beating takes place against Mark's com-munity. Since his readers could become Christians only after the death of Jesus, and since Jesus had been encouraging his followers to be good Jews, albeit of rather a radical stamp, this saying must refer to what will happen in Mark's day. The followers of Jesus' day would have continued to be members of a synagogue and under its authority. But, in Jesus' future—the time of Mark—the community are going to be punished in the synagogues for what would by then be classed as deviant behaviour or beliefs.

But, in contrast with this negative attitude to synagogues, the gospel also includes a picture of good relations between Jesus and the synagogue, for Jairus, described as one of the synagogue rulers (εἷς τῶν ἀρχισυναγώγων) falls at Jesus' feet and asks for his help, and Jesus makes no demur about accepting the invitation to his house.

And working from my symbolic reading of Mk 5.21-43,[102] which interrupts the story of Jairus's daughter, with the older woman repre-senting the passé and long-time ailing Jewish religion, and the young woman representing the timid, burgeoning Christian religion, I find

---

[102] The basis of this reading has been supplied by J.D.M. Derrett, 'Mark's Technique: The Haemorrhaging Woman and Jairus' Daughter', in his *Studies in the New Testament*, IV (Leiden: Brill, 1986), pp. 30-61: the older woman had been healthy up till twelve years before, the time of the birth of the younger woman, but has been ill while she has been maturing through girlhood. There is an inter-relation of their fecundities, their times of 'full life' in biblical language, for the older woman has been incapacitated while the young one becomes ready. The reader assumes the older woman to have been perfectly healthy beforehand. The younger woman is fearful of 'life' but is willing to take the risk and accept the hand of Jesus approaching her in the style of a bridegroom. In the narrative, she gets up and steps into the next phase of her life.

Jesus' words to the older woman, 'Go in shalom', suggestive of hopes of a peaceful co-existence of the two religious groups. Here, in this highly literary story, a more friendly point of view about the synagogue is apparent.

But there are no details of sabbath worship in these texts.

Discussion on Synagogues in Matthew

On the issue of synagogues, Matthew's Jesus shares many of the characteristics of Mark's, teaching and healing in synagogues in Galilee[103] and giving warnings about future maltreatment in synagogues.[104] Similar issues are raised in this gospel as those discussed for Mark above, but many are worked out in a different way by Matthew.

Some scholars, for example, Hill, believe that Matthew's use of the phrase 'their synagogues' could reflect the time, after 85 CE, when the Jews had forced the Christians from the synagogues.[105] Meeks develops this idea further, finding in Mt. 23.6-7 a fuller and more negative description of the religious accoutrements and public behaviour of the Pharisees who are Matthew's opponents than was apparent in Mark's writings.[106] Meeks sees the Pharisees' location, referred to by Matthew as 'their synagogues', as the place where their power was displayed in their ostentatious garb and actions, and their teaching function indicated by their wish to be addressed as 'rabbi'; and he concludes that Matthew's community was in the process of defining itself as different from a group of 'rabbis' who represented a merging of scribe and Pharisee, similar to the group of rabbis developing at Yavneh.[107]

Kee, with a similar understanding of the situation, reads Matthew 23 as a response by part of the early church to the growth and development of Pharisaic Judaism, and points out that this chapter, alone in the gospels, includes items that are distinctive to later Jewish synagogue practice, such as the use of Moses' seat,[108] phylacteries and

---

[103] Mt. 4.23; 9.35; 12.9-12; 13.54.

[104] Mt. 10.17; 23.34.

[105] Hill, Matthew, p. 212.

[106] Meeks, 'Breaking Away', pp. 108-14.

[107] Meeks, 'Breaking Away', p. 113.

[108] Whether this is symbolic or an actual piece of stone or wooden furniture is not made clear.

fringed garments.[109]

Taking a slightly different tack, Hare believes that the persecution of Matthew's community, by the 'Pharisees' in 'their' synagogues, while more intense than that envisaged by Mark, is over and done with by the time Matthew is writing, and was in any case applied only to Christian missionaries, and not to 'rank-and-file Christians'.[110] The Jewish Christians are no longer clearly identified *with* the synagogue, but are ostracised *from* it, and thus no longer subject to its discipline.[111]

Hare sums up his understanding of the distinction between the three synoptic gospels by saying that in contrast with Mark, who envisages all those addressed as Jews, of whom it is said that they will be beaten by their own people in their own synagogues, and with Luke, for whom 'the synagogue has always been an foreign institution', for Matthew it has *become* 'a foreign institution in which Christians of Jewish blood no longer belong'.[112]

Others believe that the phrase 'their synagogues' could indicate a distinction between 'their' Jewish synagogues and 'our' Christian ones,[113] and yet others claim that there are insufficient data about the usage of the expression to allow the matter to be resolved.[114] Hare seems to me to have presented the most convincing account of the use of the phrase.

In Matthew, Jairus is portrayed merely as a 'ruler' (ἄρχων), a person of standing in the community, and not explicitly a ruler of the synagogue. Albright and Mann claim that Matthew shortens Jairus' designation, from 'ruler of the synagogue' to 'ruler', because 'his readers were aware of what is meant' and the longer title was unnecessary, so they would still make the mental connection with the synagogue. But Gundry thinks that this change of phraseology highlights the thrust of Matthew's editing of Mark, revealing that Matthew does not want to mention the word 'synagogue' in connection with a man

---

[109] Kee, 'Transformation', p. 15.

[110] D.R.A. Hare, *The Theme of Jewish Persecution of Christians in the Gospel according to St Matthew* (SNTS Monograph Series, 6; Cambridge: CUP, 1967), pp. 88, 92, 96, 101-102, 104-106, 113-14.

[111] Hare, *Jewish Persecution*, p. 105.

[112] Hare, *Jewish Persecution*, pp. 104, 105.

[113] Harrington, 'Sabbath Tensions', p. 49.

[114] Davies and Allison, *Matthew*, I, pp. 413-14.

who 'worships' Jesus. So Matthew has removed the overt connection with Jewish religious practices by changing Jairus's specifically religious role to a more general term.[115] Gundry makes the stronger case.

Unfortunately these details about synagogues give information only about officials in later synagogue buildings where Jews showed hostility to the Christians on unspecified days; but they yield no information about sabbath gatherings at the time of Jesus.

Discussion on Synagogues in John

In John's gospel, there are only two references to Jesus' teaching in synagogues, much fewer than in the synoptics, but there are three references to the fact that those who believe in Jesus as Christ are to be expelled from the synagogue:

> He said these things while he was teaching in the synagogue at Capernaum (6.59).

> Jesus answered, 'I have spoken openly to the world; I have always taught in synagogues and in the temple, where all the Jews come together …' (18.20).

> His parents said this because they were afraid of the Jews; for the Jews had already agreed that anyone who confessed Jesus to be the Messiah would be put out of the synagogue (9.22).

> Nevertheless many, even of the authorities, believed in him. But because of the Pharisees they did not confess it, for fear they would be put out of the synagogue … (12.42).

> They will put you out of the synagogues. Indeed, an hour is coming when those who kill you think that by so doing they are offering worship to God (16.2).

These texts point to John's community knowing of a conflict with the synagogue, and John's Jesus warns his readers of this, but though the warnings are well separated in the narrative from his teaching in the synagogues, the two time zones and two attitudes to the synagogue can still be appreciated by the alert reader.

The Christians of John's community are not acceptable as members of the synagogue, no longer open to being punished in the synagogues by their peers in the hope of bringing them back to the 'proper' practice of their religion—as in Mark; but rather, they are to

---

[115] Albright and Mann, *Matthew*, p. 111; Gundry, *Matthew*, p. 172.

be excluded as no longer belonging to a group of which they were once members. They are described as 'out of the synagogue' (ἀποσυνάγωγος). They have been put out by a group of leaders of the Jews who have the power to expel them.

But John's gospel transmits also the contrasting piece of information that, even among the Jewish leaders themselves, those who believed in Jesus were fearful of being put out by 'the Pharisees' (12.42).[116] The break between the Johannine Christians and the Jewish synagogue was in the past, but Meeks believes the break had left such wounds that it is appropriate to describe the new community as '[t]raumatically divorced from the synagogues'.[117]

But in John, in contrast with the other gospels, no present-day violence is mentioned, merely exclusion from the synagogue.[118] This is a powerful insult aimed at the rival religious group. But nonetheless there is no mention of any sabbath synagogue services from which the deviants are to be excluded.

Discussion on Synagogues in Luke

Although similar to the Jesus of Matthew and Mark in the matter of his activities in synagogues, Luke's Jesus teaches in the synagogues of Judaea,[119] as well as of Galilee, reads and expounds the prophet Isaiah in the synagogue on the sabbath, and gives two warnings of danger from the synagogue authorities.[120] But in Luke the ill-treatment warned against is not so specific and direct as in Matthew and Mark, where flogging, scourging and beating are threatened; Luke's readers are being told rather that they will be taken into custody, persecuted and imprisoned. Compared with the synoptic parallels, Luke widens the possibilities of both the persecutors and the places of persecution, admitting of both Jewish and Gentile adversaries,[121] but

---

[116] Meeks, 'Breaking Away', pp. 94-99; Meeks espouses the more neutral term 'Judaeans' to avoid importing assumptions from modern conceptions of race and religion.

[117] Meeks, 'Breaking Away', p. 103.

[118] It is possible, however, that this would cause extreme social and financial difficulties and would therefore have been no trivial matter. Also there is the curious, and unintelligible, reference (16.2) to Jews in the future regarding the killing of Christians as a way of worshipping God.

[119] Lk. 4.44.

[120] Lk. 12.11; 21.12.

[121] J.A. Fitzmyer, *The Gospel according to Luke, X–XXIV* (The Anchor Bible, 28a;

softens the language of punishment. And in all Luke's writings 'the synagogue' or 'the synagogue of the Jews' is plainly characterised as a building, in which a person can move about to take up different positions for different functions. The setting is more formal than that would be usual at a group meeting in a member's home.

In Luke's account of the first time Jesus enters a synagogue, he gives a description of a reading and teaching sequence taking place there:

> When he came to Nazareth, where he had been brought up, he went to the synagogue on the sabbath day, as was his custom. He stood up to read, and the scroll of the prophet Isaiah was given to him. He unrolled the scroll and found the place where it was written: 'The Spirit of the Lord is upon me, because he has anointed me to bring good news to the poor. He has sent me to proclaim release to the captives and recovery of sight to the blind, to let the oppressed go free, to proclaim the year of the Lord's favour.' And he rolled up the scroll, gave it back to the attendant, and sat down. The eyes of all in the synagogue were fixed on him. Then he began to say to them, 'Today this scripture has been fulfilled in your hearing' (4.16-21).

> When they heard this, all in the synagogue were filled with rage. They got up, drove him out of the town to the brow of the hill on which their town was built, so that they might hurl him off the cliff (4.28-29).

So the reader of Luke learns that Jesus went to the synagogue as usual on the sabbath, he stood up to read and was given the scroll of Isaiah which he returned to the attendant after he had read, he then sat down and began to teach, or expound the scriptures to the seated group in the synagogue.[122]

Luke makes the point that Jesus is behaving according to his custom (4.16) by what he does on that sabbath, and later he uses almost the same phrase about Paul in Acts 17.2. Sanders concludes that this shows Luke highlighting the Jewish piety of Jesus and Paul as 'regular synagogue-goers', all part of the plan of the 'narrative that Luke has constructed with a purpose', namely of showing that it is God's will that salvation be taken to Gentiles and not to Jews.[123] In Sanders's understanding, Luke portrays the two men in this way in order to give them a good, sound Jewish provenance.

Garden City, NY: Doubleday, 1985), pp. 1338-41.

[122] Lk. 4.29 indicates that the group had been seated.

[123] Sanders, *Luke–Acts*, p. 164, *pace* Rordorf, *Sunday*, pp. 67-68.

Kee believes that Luke's 'greatly expanded version of the brief account of Jesus' teaching at the synagogue in Nazareth found in Mark 6.1-6' is actually a description of 'the synagogue formalization in the Diaspora', because he notes the details of highly developed ritual practices which are recorded in Luke's version alone: the standing to read, the attendant in charge of the scroll, an appointed place in the text for the reading, and the sitting down to expound the reading to the hearers.[124] But, disappointingly, his allocation of a date and place to the type of synagogue service portrayed by Luke can be no more specific than post-70 CE in the Diaspora.

Fitzmyer expresses some puzzlement at Luke's calling the character Jairus 'a leader of the synagogue' (ἄρχων τῆς συναγωγῆς), using neither Mark's nor Matthew's exact term (ἀρχισυνάγωγος) for the man's position, but he draws no conclusions from this variation.[125] It is possible that Luke's personal knowledge of synagogues intrudes here in this change from Mark's (and Matthew's) text.

Whether the reference to a centurion who had built a synagogue for the local Jews, supposedly out of love for their race (7.5), can be regarded as evidence about synagogues in the time of Jesus is called into question by Luke's technique of creating theological understandings by means of characters in stories. This centurion can be seen as the prototype of the centurion Cornelius in Acts 10, both of them, according to Sanders, playing the role of Gentiles who are willing to receive the message that the Jews refused.[126] However, it is also more likely that Luke knew of such benefactors in his own lifetime and incorporated the type into his gospel, than that he created the whole concept.

It seems to me that Luke's stories involving 'synagogues' can tell us little or nothing about synagogues in Galilee at the time of Jesus, but rather describe later synagogues elsewhere.[127] At those later synagogues, an attendant (ὑπηρέτης) brought out the scroll and handed it to the reader, who unrolled it and read aloud.[128] After reading, the

---

[124] Kee, 'Transformation', p. 18.

[125] Fitzmyer, *Luke*, I, p. 745; similar uncertainty as to why Luke imports Mark's term at other junctures but not here is displayed by Marshall, *Luke*, p. 343.

[126] Sanders, *Luke–Acts*, pp. 173-74.

[127] See discussion below on the portrayal of synagogues in Acts.

[128] Marshall, *Luke*, p. 182, believes that this service happened exactly as described by Luke and assumes that Jesus asked for the scroll he wished to read from. But the text

reader rolled up the scroll and returned it to the attendant, sat down and spoke to the seated group.

This description shows only slight developments from the reading and expounding of the scriptures described by Philo and Josephus for sabbath gatherings, namely, the addition of an attendant and a clearer statement of the standing posture of the reader, followed by the teacher seating himself to speak to the already seated listeners. There is no reference to any activities that could be classed unequivocally as worship; the situation in that respect is unchanged from that described by Philo and Josephus.

Sabbath and Synagogue in Acts

The book of Acts offers little direct evidence of sabbath observance and little more about sabbath practice,[129] but states that the law was read in the synagogues each sabbath. The texts do not make plain whether the Jews gather in groups called synagogues or in buildings called synagogues—as can be seen from the following extracts.

> But they went on from Perga and came to Antioch in Pisidia. And on the sabbath day they went into the synagogue and sat down. After the reading of the law and the prophets, the officials of the synagogue sent them a message, saying, 'Brothers, if you have a word of exhortation for the people, give it' (13.14, 15).[130]

> For in every city, for generations past, Moses has had those who proclaim him, for he has been read aloud every sabbath in the synagogues (15.21).

These texts are in harmony with the evidence of Philo and Josephus, but note that here there is no definite indication of a synagogue as building, although a building may readily be inferred.

An important fact that I noted while working with the book of Acts is that although Luke sets out there to describe the work of the apostles at a time later than the work of Jesus, and paints the picture of Paul as a later disciple of Jesus, he assumes the same picture of the synagogue in both volumes of his work, making no allowance for change or development during the time span of thirty years he him-

---

does not give any indication of such a request.

[129] Turner, 'Sabbath', p. 124.

[130] See also Acts 13.27.

self claims to be depicting.[131] This is, for me, an extra piece of evidence that the picture Luke paints of Jesus in the synagogue cannot be historically accurate, even if Luke's picture of the synagogues of Paul's day were to be taken as authentic.

It is also significant that of the three synoptists it is Luke alone who describes Jesus as 'entering the synagogue on the sabbath *in order to teach*' (6.6)[132]—presumably in contrast to a teaching situation arising while he was there as an ordinary participant in the study of Torah.[133] In the parallel accounts Jesus goes to the synagogue, his purpose unstated, and while he is there a significant event happens.[134] Luke's inclusion of the reference to a teaching motive points to the existence of a more elaborate session with an expectation of teaching—similar to those described by Philo and Josephus. Matthew and Mark describe a less formal gathering.

Thus Luke's gospel, unwittingly perhaps, shows a development of what happened in synagogues, for his depiction of the synagogue is different from that of Matthew and Mark. This is, however, apparent only if we compare his accounts of Jesus in synagogues with those of Matthew and Mark, but not if we compare his description of the synagogues of Jesus with the synagogues he describes in Acts. Between those two 'synagogues' there is no development.

These two pieces of evidence taken together indicate to me that Luke is writing about synagogues as he knew them, and painting the same picture whenever he describes a synagogue no matter what date or location he is purporting to describe. Luke's narrative depicts a later, or perhaps Diaspora, perspective on synagogues. Therefore it seems to me likely that the depiction can be faithful neither to the 'synagogues' that Jesus visited, nor to the 'synagogues' at the time of Paul that Luke purports to portray in Acts in his accounts of Paul's missions.

Discussion on Synagogues in Acts

In Acts, Luke portrays Paul and Barnabas regularly 'announcing the

---

[131] Hengel, *Earliest Christianity*, p. 35, suggests a time span of about thirty years.
[132] Ἐγένετο δὲ ἐν ἑτέρῳ σαββάτῳ εἰσελθεῖν αὐτὸν εἰς τὴν συναγωγὴν καὶ διδάσκειν.
[133] Kee, 'Transformation', p. 18 (my emphasis).
[134] Lk. 6.6; cf. Mt. 12.9 and Mk 3.1.

Christian message first of all in the Jewish synagogue or synagogues of each city they visited',[135] and many commentators infer from this text that the two apostles attended synagogue buildings where complex sabbath services were held as a regular weekly event.[136]

The more sceptical approach of Sanders sees the way Luke describes Paul's actions when he visits new places as no more than Luke's 'standard opening gambit ... first employed in the episode of Jesus' Nazareth sermon and ... utilized so frequently in his account of Paul's career'.[137] The point of this stylisation of the narrative is to show that the pattern of an initial positive Jewish response, followed by anger and rejection, is what Christian teachers, Jesus, Paul and others, can expect to receive—according to Luke.[138]

If we accept that these elaborate assemblies belong to a later period, then it is about these later assemblies that we can learn more in the book of Acts. So, Acts 13.15 tells us that the rulers of these later synagogues could invite visitors to address the company:

> And on the sabbath day they went into the synagogue and sat down. After the reading of the law and the prophets, the rulers of the synagogue sent to them, saying, 'Brethren, if you have any word of exhortation for the people, say it' (13.14-15).[139]

We also discover from Acts that there were other visiting Jews who spoke in the synagogue, as evidenced by the story of Apollos, who was well versed in the scriptures but also preached about Jesus and, possibly, John the Baptist too.

> Now there came to Ephesus a Jew named Apollos, a native of Alexandria. He was an eloquent man, well-versed in the scriptures. He had been instructed in the way of the Lord, though he knew only the baptism of John. He began to speak boldly in the synagogue; but when Priscilla and Aquila heard him, they took him aside and explained the Way of God to him more accurately. And when he wished to cross over to Achaia, the believers encouraged him and wrote to the disciples to welcome him. On his arrival he greatly helped those who through grace had become believers, for he powerfully refuted the Jews in public, showing by the scriptures that the

---

[135] Bruce, *Acts*, p. 263; Conzelmann, *Acts*, p. 134.

[136] E.g. Conzelmann, *Acts*, p. 103.

[137] Sanders, *Luke–Acts*, p. 275.

[138] Sanders, *Luke–Acts*, pp. 275-81.

[139] But whether this means that visitors could not speak without an invitation is not clear, so we cannot assume that Jesus had to be invited to speak in the synagogues of Galilee.

messiah is Jesus (18.24-28).

Apollos, a Jew from Alexandria, attends the synagogue where two Christians are also present. He is introduced into the story as a Jew, but a Jew who was ready to speak well of Jesus. Later in the account, although it is not clear that his activities in Achaia were also conducted in a synagogue, he speaks against the Jews, for if he was 'refuting Jews' they must have been present—at least in imagination if not in reality. So this story expresses some hostility to Jews—while also, *at the same time*, describing a communal gathering of Christians and Jews.

The same story also tells us that Christians attended the synagogue, namely Priscilla and Aquila. They attended to the public words of the visitor, but had private discussion with him as well. These interactions highlight the fact that the synagogue was a place where all sorts of opinions and points of view were expressed and even made welcome. In the whole story, only the phrase 'refuted the Jews' indicates any division or opposition.

In Acts 19, Paul returns to Ephesus and teaches in the synagogue for three months, presumably, although it is not stated, on every sabbath. But thereafter there was a split in the gathering and he taught his followers daily in someone else's lecture hall. Presumably these followers were city dwellers who could walk there from their workplace, perhaps in siesta time.[140]

> He entered the synagogue and for three months spoke out boldly, and argued persuasively about the kingdom of God. When some stubbornly refused to believe and spoke evil of the Way before the congregation, he left them, taking the disciples with him, and argued daily in the lecture hall of Tyrannus. This continued for two years, so that all the residents of Asia, both Jews and Greeks, heard the word of the Lord (Acts 19.8-10).

This passage is difficult to understand, for, in connection with this attendance daily at the lecture hall, it is difficult to be certain whether 'daily' means seven days a week—including the sabbath—or whether on the sabbath all were still attending the synagogue. Was Paul setting up a intensive alternative study programme to that offered in the synagogue, or was this offered in addition to syna-

---

[140] Bruce, *Acts*, pp. 388-89, suggests that Paul did this teaching during the siesta hours when the hall was free, and that the followers gave up their siesta to listen.

gogue attendance? Did Paul instigate such daily discussion meetings
or were they a familiar feature of the intellectual life of the community? The text is too brief to be more than tantalising, but it does not
state that either Paul, or his listeners, had cut themselves off from the
synagogue.

The fact that Luke's narrative changes its position on such fundamental details as whether Paul visited synagogues as a general rule
or not, and whether his listeners were Jews or non-Jews, causes readers problems. The inconsistencies can be explained on the basis of
Luke's division of the Jewish people into two sorts, 'good' Jewish
people who accept Jesus as Christ and 'bad' Jewish people who
resist and remain unconvinced.[141] This theory helps to make sense of
the variety of Jewish responses to Paul in different sections of the
narrative.

But on the matter of the function of the sabbath gatherings,
Sanders makes an important observation when he points out that, in
the New Testament accounts, 'Jesus and Paul go to synagogue not to
worship but to preach'.[142] And this particular form of activity,
described also as teaching, arguing or speaking boldly, took place on
the sabbath, following the reading of scripture. In all the references
which give the reason for attendance at synagogue on the sabbath,
there is no reference to worship as the motivation.

Sabbath in a Prayer-House in Acts

In Acts most of the references to the sabbath are in stories of visits to
synagogue, and have, therefore been included in my discussion on
synagogues, but two references describe Paul and his companion/s
trying to find a προσευχή on a sabbath,[143] and then later going to
visit it:

> On the sabbath day we went outside the gate by the river, where we
> supposed there was a place of prayer; and we sat down and spoke to
> the women who had gathered there (16.13).

> One day, as we were going to the place of prayer, we met a slave girl
> who had a spirit of divination and brought her owners a great deal of

---

[141] Sanders, *Luke–Acts*, pp. 65, 75-83, 263-66, 270-75.
[142] Sanders, *Luke–Acts*, p. 165.
[143] Haenchen, *The Acts of the Apostles*, p. 495, discussing 16.16, suggests that visiting a προσευχή 'makes sense only on the Sabbath'.

money by fortune-telling (16.16).

The text does not indicate whether or not a building is referred to, nor even indeed whether they found the προσευχή or not, but describes them sitting and discussing religious matters with women. In fact, no men are mentioned as being present, apart from Paul and his companions. But neither is the absence of other males recorded.

The setting is Philippi, a Roman colony (16.12, 21), and Paul and Silas look for a sabbath gathering to speak at—their usual practice, according to Luke. They search for a προσευχή beside the river and speak to the women gathered there.

Another day, maybe another sabbath, maybe a weekday, on the way to the προσευχή, they heal a slave-girl soothsayer, and as a result create a disturbance. After that, they are described by the Roman citizens as Jews (16.20), from knowledge gained in that brief encounter with them on their way to the προσευχή. So it appears that no matter how Christian they may be by belief, to others they appear to be Jews; possibly because of their dress, speech or by their proximity to the προσευχή.

Bruce's comments on v.13 are so influential in other scholarly discussions, but yet are full of question-begging assumptions, which must be challenged, that they merit quoting in full:

> When Paul visited a new city, it was his practice, as we have seen, to attend the local Jewish synagogue on the first sabbath after his arrival and seek an opportunity there for making the Christian message known 'to the Jew first'. At Philippi, however, there does not appear to have been a synagogue. That can only mean that there were very few Jews in the place; had there been ten Jewish men, they would have sufficed to constitute a synagogue. No number of women could compensate for the absence of even one man to complete the quorum of ten. There was, however, an unofficial meeting-place outside the city where a number of women—Jewesses and God-fearing Gentiles—came together to go through the appointed service of prayer for the sabbath day, even if they could not constitute a regular synagogue congregation. Paul and his companions found this place, by the bank of the river Gangites, and sat down with the women and told them the story of Jesus.[144]

Given my belief that Luke writes about the institutions he knows, then this story of a προσευχή in Philippi could well reflect his knowledge, either of Philippi, or of stories about Philippi. There is

---

[144] Bruce, *Acts*, p. 331.

certainly no need, with Bruce, to claim—without deciding whether a building or a gathering is implied—that there was no synagogue,[145] and therefore less than ten Jewish men, nor to hypothesise that the προσευχή was an 'unofficial meeting place outside the town'. The προσευχή that Josephus describes in Tiberias was far from unofficial.

Bruce's comments about the presence of the women also seem misjudged, for there is no suggestion in the text that they were running an 'alternative' synagogue for women, or for God-fearers, outside the town. They could very well have been present on the fringes of the gathering, or nearby, in earshot, though not in the line of vision of the speaker. That this is a possibility may be deduced from Philo's description of the women of the Therapeutae.[146] Thus these women would be able to converse with Paul as he approached to go in.

Rather than accept Bruce's convoluted explanation of why this προσευχή is not a synagogue and the meeting not a 'kosher' sabbath meeting, I conclude that the calling of the Jews' meeting-place by the name προσευχή accords well with the town being a Roman colony, for as we have seen that is the word used in both Latin and Greek by the writers we have studied in Chapter 4.[147] And it should be noted that the only two writers to use both terms—προσευχή and συναγωγή—are Josephus and Luke, both of whom are connected in some way with the cultures of both Rome and Palestine.[148]

If this text is read from the stance of awareness of the writings of Philo and Josephus, then this meeting place in Philippi is similar to sabbath gatherings described elsewhere in Luke–Acts as synagogues. And there is no need to assume the absence—or presence—of males from the mere fact that Paul is described as having spoken to the women gathered there.

---

[145] In this conclusion he is supported by Sanders, *Luke–Acts*, p. 75.

[146] See discussion in Chapter 3.

[147] See also the inscriptional evidence presented in Chapter 8.

[148] This is interesting, when considered alongside our earlier finding that only they, of all the writers studied, also use the phrase 'synagogue of the Jews'. It seems safe to conclude that Josephus and Luke have some part of their background in common.

Prayer in Synagogues—Matthew 6.5

One New Testament text that seems at first sight promising in our search for synagogue worship is Mt. 6.5, in which Matthew's Jesus gives advice about prayer:

> And when you pray, you must not be like the hypocrites; for they love to stand and pray in the synagogues and at the street corners, that they may be seen by men.

This does not make clear, as has been assumed,[149] that prayer was a commonplace action in synagogues; it may even point to the reverse conclusion, that is, that praying did not normally take place in the synagogue. For there is something to be criticised about the way the hypocrites pray.

It is presumably not their standing to pray that is remarkable, for in Mark, Jesus refers to 'whenever you stand praying';[150] rather, it is the location that draws the eye. Since the three other New Testament references to praying in a religious building describe the location as the Temple,[151] perhaps that is understood to be the place appropriate for prayer.

Opposing that understanding is Jesus' closely following recommendation to pray in private; so there must be some problem with praying in synagogues or at streetcorners that is not occasioned by praying either in the Temple, or at home, but the requirement cannot be privacy, if Temple prayer is acceptable.

Something must make synagogues and streetcorners, as locations for prayer, different from *both* the Temple and one's private room—and that can only be the factor of an audience who might marvel and gawp at one's prayers. So, it looks as if praying in a synagogue was just as ostentatious and odd as praying at a street corner, and not at all the normal practice of the true worshipper.

Jesus did not want his followers to pray like that. But as it is difficult to decide whether this is Jesus' teaching to his Jewish followers, or Matthew's teaching to his Christian ones, this saying contributes little to our knowledge of sabbath worship practices.

---

[149] E.g. P.A. Micklem, *St Matthew* (London: Methuen, 1917), p. 54; F.V. Filson, *A Commentary on the Gospel according to St Matthew* (Black's New Testament Commentaries; London: A. & C. Black, 1960), p. 94.
[150] Mk 11.25.
[151] Lk. 1.10; 18.10; Acts 22.17.

Conclusion

In this chapter we have had to confront the difficulty of dealing with the gospels and Acts as a source for Jewish behaviour and beliefs in the early stages of the Christian era, but at the same time reflecting Christian alienation from and re-working of that system of behaviour and beliefs.

We have had to hold in balance three lenses through which to read the New Testament texts: one like a jeweller's eyeglass seeking the embedded fragments of descriptions of what Jesus and his friends and opponents actually did on the sabbath, another focussing on the Christian evangelists' reaction to what they saw their Jewish leader do *with* Jews in the past and have to contend with *from* other Jews in the past, and a third, more like a mirror, reflecting for us the world of the evangelists themselves.

It has not been possible to find any reliable details of sabbath worship from the time of Jesus in any of the texts surveyed. However, Luke gives more details of the sabbath gatherings in his own, later, milieu than have been available from Philo and Josephus.

According to Luke's account of synagogues, on the occasion of the reading of the law, there is an attendant in charge of the scrolls, the reader stands while reading, but sits down with the others while he expounds the reading. Visitors may be invited to address the group. The noisy arguments and scuffles that Luke portrays in the synagogues in Acts are not very different from the accounts of angry incidents given by Philo and Josephus.

So what we learn of synagogues at the time of the writing of the Gospels and Acts, although it is from the point of view of wary and threatened Christians, exactly matches the picture already painted by Philo (for προσευχαί) and Josephus (for συναγωγαί and προσευχαί), a picture of a place where Jews met to deal with *all* matters that were of concern to them as a community.[152] They met and argued about political matters, and about innovative teaching and explanation of the Torah; they disciplined their peers for religious shortcomings, but they did not meet for communal worship on the sabbath.

---

[152] Acts 6.9; 9.2, 20; 13.5, 14, 15, 43; 14.1; 15.21; 17.1, 10, 17; 18.4, 7, 8, 17, 19, 26; 19.8; 22.19; 24.12; 26.11.

The only text which shows a definite change towards the synagogue practice of later Judaism is Luke 4.17, where Jesus is given the book of Isaiah to read, by the synagogue attendant, and stands to read, then sits down to expound the meaning of what he has read. This is the only gospel text to include scriptures other than Torah in any description of synagogue practice on the sabbath, and the only text in the gospel where Jesus is described as reading in a synagogue on the sabbath. This detail is missing from the Markan and Matthaean parallels, and the only parallel is in Acts, where the reading of the Law and the prophets is described for the synagogue in Antioch, and implied for Jerusalem, on the sabbath.[153] But there is no reference to any activities such as prayer or the singing of psalms that would indicate a service of worship.

The time between the writings of Paul and Philo, on the one hand, and the writing of the gospels and Acts, on the other, would seem to have marked a crucial stage in the development of either synagogue buildings, or of the application of that name to extant buildings—whether domestic or purpose-built; and if Luke paints a faithful picture of the synagogues of his day when writing Acts (and his gospel), he would seem also to have seen an expansion of the synagogue's religion-centred activities, over against the political ones, such as were described by Josephus.

Before that time, there is a much more equivocal picture and the clearest evidence in favour of the traditional understanding of the sabbath comes from the community at Qumrân, or from the Essenes and Therapeutae.

The development of synagogue worship seems to have been accelerated at the time of—and perhaps by the emergence of—the early Christian groups. Certainly the intensity of the descriptions of synagogues and controversy over them in the gospels would suggest that they were a great focus of attention in the community at that time.

The Christians, however, moved their attention away from the sabbath. The sabbath no longer conditioned their behaviour on Saturdays. They obeyed the words of their teacher Jesus instead and regarded the sabbath as a day on which to do good, rather than a day

---

[153] Acts 13.15, 27; 15.21.

on which to be still. Once that distinction was made the two communities no longer had cause to meet together on Saturdays.

So, while trying to assemble any evidence of sabbath worship, we must bear in mind that description of prayer in the synagogue is reserved to the gospel of Matthew, and even there it is at best ambiguous and not linked to any particular day of the week, and that descriptions of Jesus' activity in 'synagogues' are limited to healings, readings and discussions.

CHAPTER SIX

DEBATE OVER KEEPING THE SABBATH:
EARLY CHRISTIAN SOURCES

Introduction

The Christian texts studied in this chapter are those from the central and eastern Mediterranean in the first two centuries CE that refer to the sabbath of the Jews. They are the Epistles of Ignatius, the Epistle of Barnabas, Justin's *First Apology* and his *Dialogue with Trypho*,[1] along with some material from Tertullian and from Hippolytus. They will be surveyed for any information they can supply about the perceptions of these writers about the Jewish sabbath.

Sources[2]

Several epistles are attributed to Ignatius, of which those to the Magnesians and to the Philadelphians are valuable here.[3] He was bishop of Antioch in Syria, and martyred in Rome, probably in the

---

[1] Scholarly opinion is divided as to whether Trypho is a genuine Jewish acquaintance of Justin from the past re-created in this work (L.W. Barnard, *Justin Martyr: His Life and Thought* [Cambridge: CUP, 1967], pp. 39-40); a synthetic character having some of the features of Rabbi Tarphon of the second generation of Mishnah teachers (Simon, *Verus Israel*, pp. 12-13); or a totally imaginary character used as a vehicle to display the superiority of Christianity over Judaism (cf. Barnard, *Justin*, pp. 21-25, 39-40, 52).

[2] Dates and places are taken from *The Oxford Dictionary of the Christian Church* unless otherwise noted.

[3] *The Epistles of Ignatius (Shorter and Longer)*, in *The Apostolic Fathers* (tr. A. Roberts and J. Donaldson; Ante-Nicene Christian Library, 1; Edinburgh: T. & T. Clark, 1897), pp. 137-267; Ignace d'Antioche and Polycarpe de Smyrna, *Lettres. Martyre de Polycarpe* (tr. P.T. Camelot; Sources Chrétiennes; Paris: Les Editions du Cerf, 1969).

reign of Trajan, 98–117 CE,[4] though some try to pinpoint the date more closely to c. 110 CE.[5]

The Epistle of Barnabas was written, supposedly in Alexandria, at about 115–117 CE,[6] or possibly 125–50 CE,[7] or 130–38 CE.[8]

Justin's *First Apology* and his *Dialogue with Trypho* were written in Rome within the period 150–165 CE,[9] although it has been suggested that the material for the *Dialogue* had already taken shape during the Jewish war of 132–35 CE.[10]

Tertullian (c. 160–220 CE), belonging to both Carthage and Rome, wrote around the end of the second century.

Hippolytus (c. 170–236 CE) is writing at the boundary of the time limits used in this study, but his account, in his *Refutation of All Heresies*, of Callistus in a 'synagogue' in Rome is important even though it belongs to the early years of the third century—though prior to 217 CE—when Callistus was made bishop.[11]

Background

The value of these early Christian writings, for this study, lies in the fact that they supply a Christian 'anti-Jewish' perspective. In all the texts surveyed, contrasts are made or implied between Jewish practices, such as circumcision and sabbath-keeping, and Christian alternative ways of showing allegiance to God. The texts present a sharp—and ungenerous—view of Jewish beliefs and practices, and, therefore, may reasonably be expected to major on the points—such

---

[4] C.C. Richardson, *The Christianity of Ignatius of Antioch* (New York: AMS Press, 1967), p. 3.

[5] Bacchiocchi, *Sunday*, p. 186.

[6] R.S. MacLennan, *Early Christian Texts on Jews and Judaism* (Brown Judaic Studies, 194; Chico, CA: Scholars Press, 1982), pp. 21-22.

[7] P. Prigent and R.A. Kraft, *Epître de Barnabé* (Sources Chrétiennes; Paris: Les Editions du Cerf, 1971), p. 27; Simon, *Verus Israel*, pp. 68, 446, believes that *Barnabas* belongs to Hadrian's reign, more probably after 135 CE.

[8] Bacchiocchi, *Sunday*, pp. 186, 218.

[9] Barnard, *Justin*, pp. 19-23.

[10] Simon, *Verus Israel*, p. xvi.

[11] Hippolytus, *Refutation of All Heresies* in *Hippolytus, Bishop of Rome*, I (tr. J.H. MacMahon; Ante-Nicene Christian Library, 6; Edinburgh: T. & T. Clark, 1868), pp. 338-41; Hippolytus, *Refutatio*, in M. Marcovich, ed., *Hippolytus: Refutatio omnium haeresium* (Patristische Texte und Studien, 25; Berlin: de Gruyter, 1986), pp. 351-52.

as worship or sabbath practice—on which Christians were at odds with Jews.

However, this anti-Jewish stance does not mean that these texts are necessarily anti-semitic in nature—though they have been read that way. Recent studies have attempted to apply language more specific than 'anti-Jewish' or 'anti-semitic' when explaining the purpose of these texts,[12] claiming that other motives can be identified, motives such as defining *self* through the process of explaining the *other*.[13]

These writers, of whom Neusner and Frerichs are typical, take the stance that the Jews characterised in the texts are 'straw men', exhibiting few characteristics of real Jews. They are limited and uniform, having none of the diversity that characterises real human beings. They represent rather 'the pagan that lurked under the skin of every Christian convert', and their Jewishness is mere 'window-dressing' to allow the writer to re-align the new Christians more firmly in their Christian orthodoxy.[14] So, although the original motive of presenting arguments against Jewish teaching to Christian hearers may have been lost, the antithetical form of the writing persisted. This tendency is noted by Simon, who, referring to Tertullian in particular, claims that 'the anti-Jewish polemical form gradually lost the real justification with which it began; that it became no more than an academic exercise'.[15]

Therefore, alternate, and, in my view, more accurate, descriptions of this 'anti-Jewish' literature perceive the documents as pastoral letters meant to bolster the hopes and aspirations of a Christian community under threat, or as academic exercises in rhetoric whereby the authors score as many points as possible against their adversaries. So, for example, the Epistle of Barnabas has recently been characterised in several ways: as a letter, as a theological tract or as an academic treatise on the relation between Christianity and Judaism,[16] rather than simply as 'anti-Jewish' literature.

---

[12] See the collection of papers in Neusner and Frerichs, '*To See Ourselves as Others see Us*', esp. Kraabel, 'Synagoga Caeca', p. 241.

[13] Neusner and Frerichs, '*To See Ourselves*', p. xiii.

[14] Simon, *Verus Israel*, p. 137.

[15] Simon, *Verus Israel*, pp. 139-40.

[16] MacLennan, *Early Christian Texts*, p. 23.

But while Simon believes that Tertullian does not present a genuine attack on Jews, he believes that Justin does. In his view, Justin is genuinely writing against Jews in his *Dialogue*, rather than creating a discussion document for Christianity. He argues this from the fact that scriptural proofs occur more often in Justin's *Dialogue* than in his *Apology*, and he posits a Jewish audience for the former and a pagan audience for the latter.[17] He believes Justin has crafted the arguments in the *Dialogue* to convince Jewish minds, although whether to convert Jews to Christianity, or to prevent Jews converting Christians to Judaism remains unresolvable.[18]

So we may read these texts in several ways: as blatantly anti-Jewish, as drawing distinctions and boundaries between Christians and Jews, or as scoring rhetorical points against a rival group. Whichever of these readings we adopt, the texts will illustrate how Christian writers viewed their Jewish neighbours.

As the historical context of each text cannot be recovered with any certainty, any conclusions that can be drawn about the arguments against Jews, real or straw, can only be drawn from consideration of the logic of the text itself. So that will be the approach adopted here.

The Epistles of Ignatius

In *Magnesians* 9.1,[19] Ignatius states that part of the Christians' way of life was abandoning 'sabbatizing', and, instead, structuring their lives around the Lord's day, celebrated as the day of his resurrection:

> If, therefore, those who were brought up in the ancient order of things have come to the possession of a new hope, no longer observing the Sabbath, but living in the observance of the Lord's day,[20] on which also our life has sprung up again by Him and by His death—whom some deny, by which mystery we have obtained faith, and therefore

---

[17] Simon, *Verus Israel*, p. 139.

[18] Simon, *Verus Israel*, p. 144, and see also the full discussion of this theme on pp. 135-55.

[19] Full discussions of the ambiguities and complexities of the several recensions of the letters of Ignatius can be found in F. Guy, 'The Lord's Day in the Letter of Ignatius to the Magnesians', *AUSS* 2 (1964), pp. 1-17, and R.B. Lewis, 'Ignatius and the "Lord's Day"', *AUSS* 6 (1968), pp. 46-59.

[20] See Guy, 'The Lord's Day', pp. 7-17, for a discussion of the ambiguity of this text in Greek.

endure, that we may be found the disciples of Jesus Christ, our only
Master ...[21]

It has been suggested that Ignatius is referring to the 'prophets of
old', which were his subject in ch. 8, when he speaks of those who
had previously observed the sabbath.[22] But that explanation is obviously open to question, and the people referred to are more likely to
be the very early followers of Jesus who were Jews, and who had,
therefore, always observed the sabbath—as Jesus himself did.[23]
However, I, adopting yet another interpretation, believe that the
remark is addressed to the hearers of the epistle as a way of welcom-
ing, including, and reinforcing the allegiance of, Jews recently converted to Christianity.

Ignatius is convinced that Judaising has to be avoided because it
'implies the denial of Christ's death and resurrection',[24] and, according to Lieu, he continuously argues against a Judaism that he characterises in two ways, to the Magnesians as keeping the sabbath, and to
the Philadelphians as circumcision.[25]

> But if anyone expounds Judaism to you, do not listen to him; for it is
> better to hear Christianity from a man who is circumcised than
> Judaism from a man uncircumcised; both of them, if they do not
> speak of Jesus Christ, are to me tomb-stones and graves of the dead
> on which nothing but the names of men is written.[26]

Admittedly, Ignatius does say that you can more safely, in terms
of salvation, listen to a converted Jew—who is still circumcised—
but has given up sabbath-keeping, than to a Gentile convert to
Judaism,[27] who is about to be circumcised and take up sabbath-
keeping; but I cannot agree with Lieu that he is focussing upon

---

[21] Ignatius, *The Epistles of Ignatius (Shorter and Longer)*, in *The Apostolic Fathers*
(tr. A. Roberts and J. Donaldson; Ante-Nicene Christian Library, 1; Edinburgh: T. & T.
Clark, 1897), pp. 137-267 (180); see also Ignace and Polycarpe, *Lettres, Martyre de
Polycarpe* (tr. P.T. Camelot; Sources Chrétiennes; Paris: Les Editions du Cerf, 1969),
pp. 88-89.

[22] See, for example, Bacchiocchi, *Sunday*, pp. 213-18.

[23] W.R. Schoedel, *Ignatius of Antioch: A Commentary on the Letters of Ignatius of
Antioch* (ed. H. Koester; Hermeneia; Philadelphia: Fortress Press, 1985), p. 123.

[24] Schoedel, *Ignatius*, p. 124.

[25] J. Lieu, 'History and Theology in Christian Views of Judaism', in *The Jews among
Pagans and Christians* (London: Routledge, 1992), pp. 79-96 (92-94).

[26] Ignatius, *Phd.* 6.1.

[27] Schoedel, *Ignatius*, p. 202, adds the plausible interpretation that a Gentile Christian
is implied here.

circumcision at this point. Rather he is marginalising circumcision and insisting that beliefs have much more power to control one's life than physical signs. Of the two physical ways to make the distinction of faith and life between Judaism and Christianity, the physical actions of keeping one or other of the two different holy days says more about a person's commitment than the sign on the body.[28]

Ignatius urges his followers to celebrate Sunday,[29] and, by so doing, to make their reliance on Christ plain. He likewise demands that they abandon the keeping of the sabbath so that their denial of Judaism becomes plainly visible.[30] This active choice—of two quite definite courses of action—would indicate their faith publicly more than the physical sign of circumcision. Thus 'keeping' or 'not keeping' the sabbath has not only become determinative for deciding, but also for displaying, who is within the membership of each religious community.

The type of writing produced by Ignatius is as much pro-Christian as it is anti-Jewish. To be sure, Ignatius attacks the Jews, by way of contrast with the behaviour he expects from Christians, and earmarks sabbath-keeping as the defining Jewish practice; but he makes no mention of either synagogues or of any sabbath activities there in his attacks on sabbath-keeping. To him, they are not relevant to the actions required from, or to be avoided by, Christians. Those are his main concern.

More detailed information about the Jewish sabbath can be found in the longer recension of the Epistle to the Magnesians,[31] usually regarded as later than the recension of middle length quoted above.[32] In it the writer retreats from the completely anti-sabbath stance expressed in the middle recension. In it a modified form of sabbath-keeping is permitted, although it is to be as different as possible from

---

[28] It is relevant to remember that sabbath-keeping and circumcision were the two features of Jews most commented on by the writers surveyed in Chapter 4.

[29] *Pace* Guy, 'The Lord's Day', p. 17, who regards the phrase κατὰ κυριακὴν ζωὴν ζῶντες as ambiguous and just as likely to mean 'living according to the Lord's life' as 'living a life according to the Lord's day'.

[30] Ignatius, *Magn.* 10.

[31] Ignatius, *Epistles*, pp. 180-81; J.W. Hannah, The Setting of the Ignatian Long Recension', *JBL* 79 (1960), pp. 221-38 (221), dates the longer recension at 140 CE, rejecting the late fourth century date of J.B. Lightfoot, *The Apostolic Fathers: S. Ignatius, S. Polycarp* (London: Macmillan, 1889), II/1, pp. 70-134, esp. p. 125.

[32] Prigent and Kraft, *Epître de Barnabé*, pp. 14-15, and Guy, 'The Lord's Day', p. 3, suggest dates either of 140 CE, or of the 4th century.

the caricature of Jewish sabbath-keeping described in the text. It is
this somewhat polemic summary of Jewish sabbath activities that is
of most interest to us. The writer says:

> Let us therefore no longer keep the Sabbath in the Jewish manner,
> and rejoice in idleness; for 'he that does not work, let him not eat.'
> For say the [holy] oracles, 'In the sweat of thy face shalt thou eat thy
> bread.' But let everyone of you keep the Sabbath after a spiritual
> manner, rejoicing in meditation on the law, not in relaxation of the
> body, admiring the workmanship of God, and not eating things pre-
> pared the day before, nor using lukewarm drinks, and walking within
> a prescribed space, nor finding delight in dancing and plaudits which
> have no sense in them.[33] And after the observance of the Sabbath, let
> every friend of Christ keep the Lord's day as a festival, the resurrec-
> tion-day, the queen and chief of all the days [of the week].[34]

Apparently, on the sabbath Jews eat food prepared on Fridays,
drink tepid drinks and walk only short distances. The Jews portrayed
'rejoice in idleness' and enjoy 'dancing and plaudits'. The Christians
are directed to a new, 'better' form of sabbath-keeping, which for
them does include 'meditation on the law'—begging the question of
whether Jews meditate on the law on the sabbath.

Instead of following Jewish habits and practices, Christians are to
work at their normal sweat-producing labours, and should eat freshly
cooked meals and drink freshly prepared drinks, whether still piping
hot,[35] or cool and fresh from the well—not having stood in a jar
overnight. They are to celebrate the sabbath in the mind and in the
spirit, enjoying the wonders of creation and admiring God's handi-
work. And they are to follow that sabbath with a Christian day of
celebration on Sunday.

These additions to the epistle imply compromises with sabbath-
keeping—though not with its external signs. Christians who wish to

---

[33] Footnoted by the editors in Lightfoot, *Apostolic Fathers*, p. 181, as being described
in Philo for the Therapeutae. The editors claim that here the writer makes fun of Jewish
worship practices, but I disagree, for in the two places in Philo where plaudits are mentioned with respect to the sabbath-day teacher, 'exhibitions of clever rhetoric' are
specifically disclaimed, on the first occasion, and refer to an event anticipated rather
than the discourse freshly completed (*Contemplative Life* 31, 79); and the reference to
dancing describes the measured steps of a carefully executed sequence of movements as
part of the celebration of the feast of weeks (*Contemplative Life* 65), not an orgiastic
frenzy (*Contemplative Life* 80); see also Lightfoot, *Apostolic Fathers*, p. 173.

[34] Lightfoot, *Apostolic Fathers*, p. 181.

[35] Lightfoot, *Apostolic Fathers*, p. 173, believes that warmed drinks had slowly
cooled down overnight, finding here a parallel to Justin's reference in *Dialogue* 29 to
the Christians drinking hot water on the sabbath.

remember the sabbath day are free to do so, and to think holy thoughts—thus keeping the first part of the sabbath command. But what they must not do is appear to be Jews on the sabbath. So they must continue working and eating in the usual manner and confine their sabbath observance to the mental and spiritual aspects of the sabbath day. Thereafter, the group is to observe Sunday in an equally obvious and public manner.

The longer version of the epistle hints that decisions to eliminate sabbath observance among Christians were difficult to maintain, for in it we see a later writer, possibly in the middle of the second century, editing and modifying Ignatius's letters.[36] This Christian writer did not believe that Ignatius should have taken such a firmly negative line about the sabbath, and wanted to allow the group members a loophole by means of which they could obey the sabbath commandment—at least in part. But, as with the 'authentic' Ignatius, there is no reference to synagogues or to sabbath worship, and the distinction between Christians and Jews still depends on how they *spend* or whether they *keep* the sabbath, not on how or when they worship God.

The Epistle of Barnabas

Barnabas makes the general case that the former ways of worshipping, namely the sacrifices carried out by the Jews, are now abolished. Also, he claims that the fasts carried out by the Jews in the past have not been acceptable to God, and that both the Temple and circumcision have been replaced by spiritual—as opposed to physical—phenomena.[37] He claims that although Moses received the Law directly from God, his Christian community have received it afresh through Jesus.[38]

In *Barnabas* 15 the importance of the sabbath in God's intentions for the world is stressed, and the true nature of the sabbath is identified as being revealed in God's injunctions about rest on the sabbath.

---

[36] Lightfoot makes no comment about the origin and purpose of the longer recension. To him the material is not genuine Ignatius, and therefore of little interest.

[37] *Barn.* 2, 3, 9 and 16, in *The Epistle of Barnabas*, in *The Apostolic Fathers* (tr. A. Roberts and J. Donaldson; Ante-Nicene Christian Library, 1; Edinburgh: T. & T. Clark, 1867), pp. 97-135.

[38] *Barn.* 6, 9, 10 and especially 14 and 16.

The sabbath should celebrate the completeness of creation by means of rest both human and divine. But Barnabas believes that because of human failings God cannot rest and can only look forward to having true rest after the second coming of Christ when the created world will be perfected.

He argues this from the scriptures and from his beliefs about Jesus as Christ. From the scriptures Barnabas finds that to sanctify the sabbath one must have pure hands and a clean heart (Ps. 24.4) and he combines this with his belief that only Jesus, his Lord, possesses those qualifications. So, in order to have even 'one [person] properly resting' on the sabbath, humankind has to wait for Jesus to return.

> Behold, therefore: certainly then one properly resting sanctifies it, when we ourselves, having received the promise, wickedness no longer existing, and all things having been made new by the Lord, shall be able to work righteousness. Then we shall be able to sanctify it, having been first sanctified ourselves.[39]

Therefore, he argues, any sabbaths supposedly 'kept' by Jews at the present time cannot be adequately 'kept', nor can any human 'keep' the sabbath properly, until the time after the second coming, when the Christians will be able to 'keep' the sabbath properly. He concludes that the Christians do much better to celebrate the day of Jesus' resurrection every week since that was the day that heralded the future possibility that the sabbath could one day be properly kept.[40]

In *Barnabas* 16 he speaks of the Temple, and of how Jews believed that that was the one place where God could properly be worshipped—though he does not say on which days he believes that God was worshipped in the Temple. He likens Jewish worship in the Temple to the worship of other races in the temples of idols, and thus dismisses its validity with God who, he believes, rejects such ritualised worship. God has abolished the Temple, for—as Barnabas explains matters—heaven is God's throne and the earth is his footstool, and so God has no need of an earthly temple. He interprets the destruction of the Temple by the Jews' enemies in wartime as such

---

[39] *Barn.* 15.
[40] See also the alternative, but similar, exposition of the same material in Bacchiocchi, *Sunday*, pp. 221-22.

abolition, thus linking the recent actual destruction of the Temple with Isa. 49.17 (LXX).[41]

He himself regards the temple of God as presently existing. By that he does not mean the Jerusalem Temple, made of stone and housing priests and sacrifices, but a spiritual temple. This was created by Christ's death and resurrection, regarded by Barnabas as fulfilling the gospel saying about the destruction of the Temple followed by its rebuilding in three days. Because this salvific concept is accepted by Christians, but not by Jews, the Christians can regard God as satisfied with the spiritual temple, and as no longer requiring a physical one.

Shea decides that Barnabas is thoroughly anti-Jewish and believes that Barnabas opposes everything that is characteristic of the Jewish faith as he knew it.[42] But this seems a rather ferocious condemnation of a rather generally exhortatory and encouraging letter to a Christian group, typical of paraenetic material.

What in particular causes me to disagree with Shea is that much of the tenor of anti-Jewish feeling in the epistle is generated by the chapter headings found in translations of the text—which headings are not present in the Greek text.[43] Reading the text without them makes the material much more bland in its demands and claims. There appear to be no slighting references clearly addressed to the Jews of Barnabas's day, and all the denigrations can be interpreted as referring to groups castigated by the prophets in the Hebrew Bible, or to erstwhile Jews, even, perhaps, to some who are now within the company addressed.

In similar vein MacLennan reads Barnabas's rhetorical use of 'synagogue' as anti-Jewish. He does not accept that the LXX quotations which include the Greek word συναγωγή are referring to 'assemblies' in times gone by. He claims that Barnabas 'is telling his readers that the synagogue is a place of the wicked (5.13; 6.6; 11.2) and those who are in the synagogue are unable to understand clearly

---

[41] 'And thou shalt soon be built by those by whom thou wert destroyed, and they that made thee desolate shall go forth of thee.'

[42] W.H. Shea, 'The Sabbath in the Epistle of Barnabas', *AUSS* 4 (1966), pp. 149-75 (168).

[43] For example, the heading of chapter 3, which contains no more than an exegesis of Isa. 58.3-4, is 'The Fasts of the Jews are not true fasts, nor acceptable to God'.

the covenant (10.12), or correctly interpret its meaning'.[44] But a plain reading of the text of *Barnabas* shows that the harangue is aimed at the 'bad old ways' of the Jews in their distant past.

If MacLennan wishes to argue that Barnabas has introduced these particular biblical quotations[45] as *doubles entendres*, carrying a reference to the local synagogues of Barnabas's day, then he should point out that not only does Barnabas make theological mileage out of prophetic complaints against Jews of the past, he also makes subtle jibes at the Jews of his day. MacLennan must make the case that the words of the quotations can also be heard with a meaning for Barnabas's own time as well as the past.

I disagree with MacLennan, gaining my understanding of Barnabas's tactics from the use he makes of the clause 'the assembly (συναγωγή) of the wicked have risen up against me'.[46] These words are taken by Barnabas as proof that 'the prophet' was predicting Jesus' sufferings. The overt use Barnabas makes of the phrase is to align his voice with that of the righteous innocence of the prophet, and the covert use he makes of the phrase is to suggest that Jesus was the supreme righteous and suffering innocent one, who is now vindicated. But that Barnabas makes a more secret and polemic attack on Jews in his local community by these words is something that needs to be proved and not merely stated.

So, although it is possible that the use of the word συναγωγή in the letter could signal to Barnabas's readers that the Jews were still as wrong as they had always been, it does not seem likely that this flood of rhetoric couched in biblical language was working on that other level where the obvious functions as a code for the subtle. To be convinced of that I would need to see other clear examples of the same activity elsewhere in the epistle or in other writings of a similar provenance. I do not find in these misquotations of the LXX any attacks on local Jews.

---

[44] MacLennan, *Early Christian Texts*, pp. 24, 44 (the references correspond to the numbering in the Greek–French text of Prigent and Kraft, *Epître de Barnabé*).

[45] 5.13 and 6.6 correspond to Ps. 22.21, 17 and Ps. 119.120 (11.2 seems to be on totally unrelated matters); 10.12 does not refer to the synagogue, but indicates Jews by a reference to circumcision.

[46] This pseudo-quotation, used in 5.13 and 6.6 and attributed to 'the prophet', is a conflation of clauses from Psalms 22 and 119; see Barnabas, *Epistle*, pp. 109-10.

Addressing the matter of sabbath observance, Shea notes that Barnabas has made only two points against sabbath-keeping, namely the belief that the true sabbath will come at the eschaton, and that only pure persons can keep the sabbath properly. In response to this—as he sees it—neglected opportunity, he lists the less exotic reasons that he would have expected to see given for the abandonment of sabbath-keeping: that there was a teaching of Christ about discontinuing sabbath-keeping, a command from, or the example of, the apostles, an abolition of the sabbath law, or a replacement of the sabbath by some aspect of Jesus' life and death.[47]

If Shea's approach has value, and the Christian community had evolved different reasons for giving up sabbath-keeping, then it is even more remarkable that Barnabas makes no mention of synagogues,[48] for when Jewish worship is criticised, only the Temple, already destroyed, is denigrated. It appears that Barnabas had no complaint to make about synagogues in his general survey of Jewish ways of going 'utterly astray'; meeting in synagogues is not linked with sabbath-keeping in his rhetoric.

But in my view, more justice is done to the text by ignoring the chapter headings which condition particular, and anti-Jewish, interpretations of the sections which follow.[49] Barnabas was evidently opposed to a group of sabbath-keepers, but their identity remains mysterious. Whether they were Jews pursuing their ancestral religion, or whether they were Christians wishing to keep the laws of Judaism cannot be resolved from this evidence alone.

Barnabas's opposition to sabbath-keeping was firm in spite of consisting mainly of special pleading, in that he defines a sabbath kept by anyone other than Christ as improperly kept, and then defines the end of creation when God will be able to rest as the time after the second coming when Christ will have vanquished evil and set the world to rights. And it is clear that Barnabas makes these Christian conclusions about the inability of humans to keep the sabbath in the face of the injunctions in the Hebrew Bible scriptures

---

[47] Shea, 'Sabbath in Barnabas', pp. 170-71.

[48] There are no references to synagogues in *Barnabas* apart from the quotations from the LXX.

[49] The heading of chapter 4, which quotes Daniel as an exhortation to Barnabas's readers, is 'Anti-Christ is at hand: let us therefore avoid Jewish errors'. Note that the words 'Anti-Christ' and 'Jews' are not included in the chapter.

towards sabbath-keeping as a way of showing a positive response to God.

The thrust of the Epistle of Barnabas seems to be towards raising the consciousness of his readers about the ways in which they differed and should differ from Jews. But he does not include any specific references as to how the two groups should *behave* differently on the sabbath, or advocate *worshipping* differently on different days of the week. Any remarks about the sabbath are confined to *sabbath-keeping*. Barnabas plainly believes that the true nature of the sabbath is for rest and as 'proper' rest cannot happen until the end of time, Christians should not make fruitless attempts to keep the sabbath. They should distance themselves from the futile sabbath observance of Jews—their 'resting'—which cannot possibly please God.

Justin's First Apology

In ch. 67 of his *First Apology*, Justin describes the coming together of the Christians on Sunday.[50]

Τὴν δὲ τοῦ ἡλίου ἡμέραν κοινῇ πάντες τὴν συνέλευσιν ποιούμεθα...[51]

Thereafter he gives two reasons for the choice of Sunday, the second of which is the same as that used by Barnabas—that Sunday was the day of the resurrection of Jesus. But the first reason, based on the creation account of Genesis 1, is that Sunday is 'the first day[,] on which God, having wrought a change in the darkness and matter, made the world'.

This is a very interesting contrast to the sabbath commandment in Exodus 20, which instructs the Israelites to imitate the rest of God at the end of the creation sequence, for Justin asks Christians to celebrate, in their Sunday observances, both the beginning of creation, God's first action, and the beginning of the new creation, initiated by the resurrection. Thus he gives verbal form to a Christian belief in a parallelism between God's actions at the beginning of time and at the

---

[50] Justin, *The First Apology*, in *The Writings of Justin Martyr and Athenagoras* (tr. M. Dods; Ante-Nicene Christian Library, 2; Edinburgh: T. & T. Clark, 1897), pp. 7-69.
[51] 'And on the day of the Sun, we all come together communally ...'

resurrection. God is equally involved in and committed to the two actions.

It should be noted that, in this piece of apologetic, Justin turns on its head the Jewish view of creation as a sequential act with rest as its completion. The Jewish sabbath is, of course, not mentioned by name—it is only present by analogy, contrast and allusion—and could only be present in the minds of those of Justin's hearers familiar with the ten commandments.

Justin supplies different reasons for re-interpreting the plain meaning of the fourth commandment from those offered by Barnabas, although both his reasons seem to be developments of the ideas expressed by Barnabas. He endorses the fact that Christians celebrate the first day of the week, as commemorating the beginning of creation, and implies the rejection of sabbath rest which commemorated the completion of creation. He wants his readers to regard the second coming as exemplifying the new creation rather than—as Barnabas claimed—providing the situation where true sabbath rest can begin.

Justin does not speak, in this work, of the sabbath gatherings of Jews but his description of Christian Sunday meetings closely parallels what is known about Jewish sabbath gatherings from Philo, Josephus and Luke, although the Christian meeting in Justin incorporates also a reading from the memoirs of the Apostles.[52] The believers gather together, they listen to readings from the prophets and memoirs of the Apostles, and then the president instructs them and exhorts them to imitate the good things they have heard. The subsequent detail, that they stand together and pray, has not been attested for Jewish meetings in any of the texts surveyed so far, but has parallels in the New Testament.[53] Thus it can be seen that Justin writes of gatherings of Christians similar to the Jewish gatherings known from other sources, and, we should note, Justin does not describe these

---

[52] As also the description of Christian worship given by Pliny the Younger in *The Letters of Pliny the Younger* (tr. B. Radice; Harmondsworth, Middlesex: Penguin, 1963), pp. 18-19, 292-95; and in *C. Plinii Caecilii secundi: Epistulae ad Traianum imperatorem cum eiusdem responsis* (tr. E.G. Hardy; London: Macmillan, 1889), pp. 210-16.

[53] Mk 11.25; Lk. 18.10-13.

gatherings as worship. That conclusion is presented by the chapter heading in the English translation only.[54]

Justin's Dialogue with Trypho

Early in the *Dialogue*, Trypho lists the basic requirements for becoming a Jew: circumcision, observance of the sabbath, the feasts and the new moon, and obedience to the law.[55] Almost these same requirements are reiterated by Justin in ch. 10 when he asks Trypho whether his case against the Christians is based on their non-obedience to the law, with respect to circumcision and observance of the sabbath. He selects these as the distinguishing features of Judaism, and comes back to these two features over and over again,[56] although on several occasions the requirement of keeping the feasts is also included.[57]

Justin rejects the requirement of circumcision for Christians, referring to Abraham's lack of circumcision as a way of showing that the Christians' lack of circumcision cannot make them unacceptable to God.[58] Throughout the *Dialogue*, Justin reveals a deep knowledge of Judaism and uses that knowledge to make telling or witty points against his supposed interlocutor.[59]

Justin highlights the failures of Judaism in keeping the laws of Moses by explaining that the new law, given by the new lawgiver, demands that there be a perpetual sabbath. The Jews' weekly sabbath is paltry compared with that requirement, because a day's rest is easy to do, but giving up perjury, theft and adultery and becoming totally pure is necessary to keep 'the sweet and true sabbaths of God'.[60]

---

[54] Justin, *Apology*, 1.67, is headed 'Weekly worship of the Christians', and what Justin describes as 'our common assembly' includes reading of the memoirs of the apostles or the prophets, instruction and exhortation to good works, prayer and thanksgivings and a sharing out of charity.

[55] Justin, *The Dialogue with Trypho, a Jew*, in *The Writings of Justin Martyr and Athenagoras* (tr. G. Reith; Ante-Nicene Christian Library, 2; Edinburgh: T. & T. Clark, 1897), pp. 85-278; in *Dialogue* 8 Justin referes to the new moon; in *Dialogue* 46, seemingly a parallel in English, the reference to months corresponds to observing the law of the niddah, the ritual abstention of Jewish women from marital relations for the first fifteen days or so of every month in which they menstruate.

[56] *Dialogue* 19, 27, 92.

[57] *Dialogue* 18, 23, 26, 46, 92.

[58] *Dialogue* 11.

[59] See the comment of Simon above about the supposed audience of Justin's *Dialogue*.

[60] *Dialogue* 12.

Thus, in this text, he, possibly following Barnabas, implies that the Jews are not able to keep the sabbath truly. And he reveals that what he identifies as the Jews' response to God on the sabbath is nothing other than their idleness. In his view Jews do nothing for God on the sabbath, nothing active, that is.

Justin takes Trypho, and Jews in general, to task for the practice of 'cursing in your synagogues those that believe on Christ', which is an activity he refers to several times in the *Dialogue*.[61] This is taken by many scholars to be a reference to the cursing of heretics as part of the Benedictions of Jewish daily prayers.[62] And although the texts referring to synagogues give no definite indication of buildings, that meaning seems a likely inference.[63]

But in the references to the animosity expressed in synagogues, there are no details of anything else that happened in the synagogues. It is also not indicated whether this cursing took place on the sabbath, most commentators regarding it as part of the daily prayers. Also in *Dialogue* 137, although it is not clear, it seems likely that daily prayers are being spoken of, when Justin exhorts the Jews to refuse to excoriate Jesus at the end of their prayers.

Chapters 18, 19 and 21 of the *Dialogue* present Justin's reason for saying that sabbath-keeping is not required of Christians, namely that it was laid upon the Jews by God as a punishment for their shortcomings, because, as he points out, the Hebrews before Moses lived godly lives without the sabbath, and before Abraham without circumcision. In this way he gives the Christians a good reason not to feel obliged to keep the sabbath commandment—the Christians are not inheritors of this punishment of God

In *Dialogue* 24 Justin expounds on the superiority of the Christians' *eighth day* compared with both the seventh day of the Jews and with Jewish circumcision;[64] the blood of circumcision is

---

[61] *Dialogue* 16, 96; also the reference to cursing is repeated at 93, 95, 103, 133.

[62] See the comprehensive survey by W. Horbury, 'The Benediction of the Minim', in *JTS* n.s. 33 (1982), pp. 19-61.

[63] It appears that Justin uses συναγωγή for the Jews' meeting-house instead of προσευχή which occurred in the works of Roman authors surveyed in Chapter 5. The word 'synagogue' seems to mean a building by the time Justin was writing in Rome; see discussion in Chapter 8.

[64] This circumlocution, of calling Sunday the eighth day, draws attention to the fact that the first day of the week *follows* the sabbath, and also carries an allusion to the Easter narratives in the gospel.

obsolete, being replaced by the blood of salvation. He appears to be indulging in a word play at his supposed opponents' expense, since male Jewish babies are circumcised on the eighth day of their lives.[65]

Chapter 27 of the *Dialogue* develops two arguments, originally propounded by the evangelists, that show the absurdity of having an absolute law about sabbath rest and then having exceptions. The first is that used also in Mark and Matthew about the actions of priests on the sabbath. Not only do they continue with their daily practice uninterrupted, but they actually carry out extra tasks in terms of increased sacrifices. And the second, put forward also in Luke's gospel by Jesus, points out the fact that sabbath rest can be laid aside if the day is the eighth day after the birth of a male child and circumcision is carried out. So, another argument has been employed to bring the sabbath commandment into disrepute with the Christians and obviate the need to obey it.

Justin adds two more stages in the argument against sabbath-keeping.[66] One is that the elements do not rest one day in seven,[67] and moreover that God continues to direct and control the universe on the sabbath.[68] Here Justin develops the argument about God's continued working on the sabbath, earlier expressed in John's gospel and uses them to support Christians in working on the sabbath.

The discussion in *Dialogue 29* seemingly centres on quotations from the Hebrew Bible which show that God visits all nations—including Gentiles, but quickly moves off that point to make another, namely that Christians do not need to be circumcised since they have been baptised with the Holy Ghost. The fact that humans are created uncircumcised is also recalled and the point is made that uncircumcised Christians should not be regarded as lesser in any way. Apparently as an aside, Justin then says that the Jews should not look askance at Christians for drinking hot water on sabbath since God still directs the universe on the sabbath and priests were under the obligation of offering sacrifices on the sabbath.

There is no obvious reason for the inclusion of the clause about hot water along with the other arguments—but it is interesting for it

---

[65] This material would only convey wit or irony to Jewish readers, so perhaps Simon is right to suggest a Jewish audience for the *Dialogue*.

[66] Bacchiocchi, *Sunday*, pp. 226-27.

[67] *Dialogue* 23.

[68] *Dialogue* 29.

provides a distinguishing feature in sabbath behaviour between Christians and Jews.

In *Dialogue* 134 the two rival groups, the church and the synagogue, are contrasted as a matched pair with reference to Laban's daughters, Leah and Rachel. Readers familiar with Genesis would know what the difference between Leah and Rachel was, and how age and priority were overturned when it came to finding success and favour. To Christians who knew those stories the meaning of calling the synagogue, Leah, and the church, Rachel, is transparent. Christ will love and favour the church out of delight in her. The synagogue will be treated fairly as an obligation or duty. But everyone knows which of the two had weak eyes and was handicapped in her vision. However, there is no reference in the chapter as to how the two daughters or, by analogy, the two institutions, worship God.

What Justin strives to achieve is a way of defining the Christians over against the Jews. He makes distinctions between the requirement to keep the sabbath physically and keeping the perpetual sabbath spiritually, and between the requirement to circumcise male children and the circumcision of the heart or spirit carried out for all by Jesus' death and resurrection. And by calling Sunday the eighth day he can link the two topics rather neatly.

But in all his arguments and rhetoric, and although he contrasts church and synagogue, old law from the old lawgiver with new law from the new lawgiver, physical circumcision with the circumcision of the Lord's (eighth) day, he never contrasts the worship of the Jews with the worship of the Christians; in fact he says nothing at all about any current Jewish form of worship. There is no attack on the 'inferiority' of Jewish meetings as there is about former Jewish fasts. Any arguments about the sabbath, and there are many, are centred on whether or not the Christians are required to observe it as a sabbath of 'idleness' or rest.

The Writings of Tertullian

The ideas and arguments gained from a study of the writings of Tertullian show little advance on what has been argued by Justin. The same ideas are worked to their threadbare limits.

Tertullian does not present his arguments as clearly as Justin, tending towards a heavily rhetorical and even florid style. This makes it difficult to follow the point of some of the contrasts and comparisons he seems to be drawing. The reader can readily endorse the gentle reproof of Strand, that Tertullian weaves his apologetic web by 'the use of puns, irony, satirisation, quick turns of thought, and other devices which at times complicate for us the meaning of his language'.[69]

In *Apology* 21, Tertullian writes 'we neither accord with the Jews in their peculiarities in regard to food, nor in their sacred days, nor even in their well-known bodily sign, nor in the possession of a common name, which surely behoved to be the case if we did homage to the same God as they'. Here he stresses the distinctiveness of the two religious groups and includes in his catalogue of characteristics the disagreement as to their sacred days.[70]

In *On Idolatry* 14 Tertullian writes against keeping the sabbath and festivals like the Jews, quoting Isa. 1.14 as the words of the Holy Spirit upbraiding the Jews for their failures in offering acceptable worship to God. He sees the result of this rejection of Temple worship as the development of a situation whereby to the Christians 'Sabbaths are strange, and the new moons and festivals formerly beloved by God'.[71] He distances the Christians from the observance of festivals once favoured but now displeasing to God.

Writing on the subjects of circumcision and sabbath-keeping, Tertullian expounds at length essentially the same arguments that Justin used against the necessity of circumcision and sabbath-keeping as a way of living righteously before God.[72] He adduces the cases of

---

[69] K.A. Strand, 'Tertullian and the Sabbath', *AUSS* 9 (1971), pp. 129-46 (129).

[70] Tertullian, *Apology*, in *The Writings of Tertullian*, I (tr. A. Roberts and J. Donaldson; Ante-Nicene Christian Library, 11; Edinburgh: T. & T. Clark, 1869), pp. 53-140 (91).

[71] Tertullian, *On Idolatry*, in *The Writings of Tertullian*, I (tr. S. Thelwall; Ante-Nicene Christian Library, 11; Edinburgh: T. & T. Clark, 1869), pp. 141-77 (161-63); see also a similar list of festivals in Tertullian, *To the Nations (To the Heathen)* 13, in *The Writings of Tertullian*, I (tr. P. Holmes; Ante-Nicene Christian Library, 11 Edinburgh: T. & T. Clark, 1869), pp. 416-506 (450): 'For the Jewish feasts are the Sabbath and "the Purification," and the ceremonies of the lamps and the fasts of unleavened bread, and the "littoral prayers"'.

[72] Tertullian, *An Answer to the Jews*, in *The Writings of Tertullian*, III (tr. S. Thelwall; Ante-Nicene Christian Library, 18; Edinburgh: T. & T. Clark, 1897), pp. 201-58 (203-13).

Adam, Enoch, Melchizedek and Lot, who were not circumcised and yet were in full receipt of God's approval. Then in chs. 5–6, the same contrasting arguments about the former, unacceptable Jewish sacrifices and laws show how the Christian sacrifices of praise and new laws are much superior as offerings to God. His peroration comes to a crescendo in the following rhetorical climax which encapsulates the contrasts he wishes to draw between Judaism and Christianity:

> And, indeed, first we must inquire whether there be expected a giver of the new law, and an heir of the new testament, and a priest of the new sacrifices, and a purger of the new circumcision, and an observer of the eternal sabbath, to suppress the old law, and institute the new testament, and offer the new sacrifices, and repress the ancient ceremonies, and suppress the old circumcision together with its own sabbath, and announce the new kingdom which is not corruptible.[73]

He points to a new law-giving with Jesus as law-giver replacing Moses, a new covenant with God with Jesus replacing Abraham, a spiritual circumcision replacing the physical sign, the 'eternal' sabbath replacing the Saturday sabbath, the Christian rites of eucharist and prayers replacing the Jewish rites of sacrifice and festivals. But the only reference to a contrast in worship between the two groups is the phrase 'repress the ancient ceremonies', an indication that Christians should no longer observe the Jewish festivals. This list of definitive distinctions between Christians and Jews—which specifically contrasts the worship of the two groups—makes no reference to Jewish sabbath worship.

In both *An Answer to the Jews*,[74] and *Against Marcion*,[75] Tertullian points out that the walking round Jericho on the sabbath by Joshua and his followers was not a violation of the commandment for it was not a matter of doing one's own work. Those Jews were doing God's work on that occasion, not their everyday labours, so they were not flouting God's commandments to Jews.

In the same chapter Tertullian reiterates all the gospel arguments about the disciples' eating corn plucked from the field on the sabbath, climaxing with the view that now, in the Christian dispensation,

---

[73] Tertullian, *An Answer to the Jews* 5–6, in *The Writings of Tertullian*, III, p. 216.
[74] Tertullian, *An Answer to the Jews* 4, in *The Writings of Tertullian*, III, p. 212.
[75] Tertullian, *Against Marcion* 2.21, in *Tertullianus against Marcion* (tr. P. Holmes; Ante-Nicene Christian Library, 7; Edinburgh: T. & T. Clark, 1868), p. 101.

certain kinds of work, such as eating and doing good, are excepted
from the sabbath command.[76]

In *Against Marcion* 5.4 he uses again the oft-repeated accusations
of Isaiah, Amos and Hosea against feasts and sabbath, which were
also used by Justin. Strand summarises Tertullian's arguments very
succinctly:

> On the one hand, *Christ's example* demonstrates true Sabbath-keep-
> ing as it was intended from the beginning; on the other hand, *Paul's
> discussion in Galatians* deprecates a ceremonialism which God in the
> OT deprecated and whose cessation he had even there predicted.[77]

The Christians are being told by Tertullian to do good on the
sabbath, rather than do nothing at all, and they are to worship God in
ways that eschew ceremony.

Tertullian uses arguments almost identical with Justin's for not
keeping the sabbath, though more lengthily expressed, namely that
the sabbath was given to the Jews because of their failings. But he
adds another stage in the argument by treating the ten commandments, not as God's own words quoted by Moses, but as being
Moses' own, human, words. He can, therefore, claim that there is not
the same requirement on Christians to obey Moses' words for they
are merely the words of—as he would imply—an erring Jew.

But in all his contrasts between Christians and Jews, and in all his
discussions of the sabbath, he never refers to what Jews do on the
sabbath or to how Jews worship God in their assemblies.

At one point, in the middle of an extremely complex piece of
rhetoric, Tertullian does refer to Diaspora synagogues. But the text
does not make clear whether to him synagogues are enclaves or
buildings:

> He says, 'they have quite forsaken the fount of water of life, and they
> have digged for themselves worn-out tanks which will not be able to
> contain water.' Undoubtedly, by not receiving Christ, the 'fount of
> water of life', they have begun to have 'worn-out tanks', that is, syn-
> agogues for the use of the 'dispersions of the Gentiles'.[78]

Lieu believes that Tertullian is here dating the beginnings of synagogue buildings in the Diaspora to the time when the message of

---

[76] Also Tertullian, *Against Marcion* 4.30, pp. 307-10; the arguments for healing on
the sabbath found in Lk. 13.15 are re-expressed by Tertullian.

[77] Strand, 'Tertullian and the Sabbath', p. 141.

[78] Tertullian, *An Answer to the Jews* 13, in *The Writings of Tertullian*, III, p. 249.

the Christians was being spread.[79] She, therefore, discounts his 'historical integrity' and feels secure in overturning his supposed claim.

But it is not clear to me that that is what Tertullian implies; rather he says that the synagogues, whether buildings or groups, have become 'worn-out', which is a fair comment from his Christian point of view. He treats the synagogues as places of value in the past, but now superseded. But unfortunately, because he does not give details of what he regards as having taken over the synagogues' role, there is no way of discovering what he thought the role of the synagogue was in his day.

The Refutation of Hippolytus

In his *Refutation of All Heresies*, Hippolytus tells the sardonically humorous narrative of Callistus and his erstwhile bogus assumption of Christianity when it suited his needs. In the middle of the story, Hippolytus describes an incident in which Callistus obtrudes himself into a sabbath synagogue gathering of Jews in Rome.[80]

Callistus has been incarcerated by his Christian master Carpophorus for defrauding people of their savings in the guise of banking them. But he has persuaded some of his creditors that he has the money working at interest on their behalf, and that if they can have him released he will try to recover it.

He implies that the money is in the hands of Jews and so 'pretending that he was repairing as it were to his creditors, he hurried on their Sabbath-day to the synagogue' where the Jews were gathered,[81] presumably expecting to be able to transact financial business of some sort with them—even if only as a 'cover' story. He 'took his stand, and created a disturbance among them. They, however, being disturbed by him, offered him insult, and inflicted blows upon him, and dragged him before the city prefect'.[82]

---

[79] Lieu, 'Christian Views of Judaism', p. 84.
[80] Leon, *Ancient Rome*, p. 42, dates the Callistus story between 180 and 192 CE; Smallwood, *Roman Rule*, p. 524, suggests 185–190 CE.
[81] Hippolytus, *Refutation* 9.7.
[82] Hippolytus, *Refutation* 9.7.

The Jews were questioned by the prefect and answered as follows: 'Romans have conceded to us the privilege of publicly reading those laws of ours that have been handed down from our fathers'. They continue by explaining that Callistus prevented this by creating a disturbance, claiming to be a Christian.

Leon concludes that Callistus 'broke into a synagogue in Rome and disrupted the Sabbath service'.[83] He infers two things that are not explicit in the Greek: first, that the synagogue was a building—or meeting—closed to Callistus, making his entry somehow illicit, and secondly, that there was a sabbath service in progress which could be disrupted by his behaviour.

Because Smallwood makes similar assumptions and imagines a sedate service of sabbath worship taking place in a synagogue building, she also believes that total disruption of that service resulted from Callistus's declarations that he was a Christian.[84]

These commentators, and also the translators,[85] regard the synagogue as a building, but the Greek does not demand that interpretation. The 'synagogue of the Jews' means the group of Jews who had gathered together to read the law as a group. This is a description of a sabbath gathering of Jews reading the law together.

Callistus rushed into the synagogue of the Jews that had gathered (ἐπὶ τὴν συναγωγὴν τῶν Ἰουδαίων συνηγμένην); he rushed in to a group of people, not into a building. The Jews report that they were reading their laws communally (δημοσίᾳ) not *publicly* as it is translated, and he 'surprised' them (ἐπεισελθών).[86] The people were surprised and disturbed, the group was disrupted. But no service of worship in a building is referred to or implied.

We can have little clarification on these difficulties from the author, for Hippolytus alleges that this intrusion into the group of Jews was a stratagem on Callistus's part so that he might be put to death—the logic of which is difficult to follow—possibly in preference to his actual punishment of being sent to a mine in Sardinia

---

[83] Leon, *Ancient Rome*, pp. 42-43.

[84] Smallwood, *Roman Rule*, pp. 523-25.

[85] See the insertion in brackets by the translator of 'our place of worship' as an explanation of what it was Callistus had entered on the sabbath (Hippolytus, *Refutation*, p. 340).

[86] See the parallel use of this verb in 1 Macc. 16.16, where Simon and his sons were 'surprised' and killed by Ptolemy.

once convicted of fraud. The narration of the piece is very complex as Hippolytus reports the words, actions and explanations of others from different settings and times. So, it is difficult to determine how much of the account has been hypothesised by him, rather than reported to him.

However this story increases our knowledge of sabbath gatherings in synagogues a little more, by relating that in the gathering the Jews were standing and that their hearing of the law being read aloud was prevented by the scuffles and disturbance caused by Callistus. There may have been a service of worship in a synagogue building, but there is no evidence of it in the text, and there are no details of any acts of worship.

Conclusion

In the eyes of these early Christian writers, Jews are characterised mainly by sabbath observance and by circumcision, and to a lesser extent by fasting and keeping festivals. The Christian readers of the tracts are to take pains to avoid being like Jews, in terms of these characteristics, particularly sabbath-keeping.

Throughout these documents, all activities of Jews are contrasted with the 'proper' and Christian way to live and to show obedience to God. Christians are to behave actively on the sabbath in ways that will show others that they are not Jews.

These distinctions reach their peak in the longer version of Ignatius's letter to the Magnesians. Now, while it is important to remember that while the longer recension of Ignatius's letter to the Magnesians may not be authentic Ignatius, it does give an authentic *account* of the Christian view of Jewish sabbath practice when it was written. And that is described as being idle and relaxing the body, consuming food and drink prepared in advance on Friday and restricting the distance walked. There seems to be an implication of dancing and mutual praise taking place on the sabbath as well. This is difficult to grasp fully, and possibly signifies Jewish practice at festivals, but as it is so non-specific it could refer to nothing more elaborate than a convivial Friday evening.

Christians are therefore expected to do the opposite, to work visibly on the sabbath, to cook and eat hot meals, to prepare fresh drinks—whether hot or cold—to walk further than the sabbath limits imposed on Jews. They are free to meditate on the law, but notably, the Jews' commitment to that activity is ignored for the purposes of this argument. In the mental aspect of their sabbath religious life the Christians may behave in the same way as the Jews. They may think thoughts about the majesty of God on the sabbath, and meditate on the law on the sabbath.

But in spite of all the contrasts made between Jews and Christians, none refers to any difference or contrast between the sabbath gatherings of Jews and the Sunday gatherings of Christians. All that is addressed is the reason for the change of day. There is silence about what happens in the sabbath gatherings of the Jews—apart from Hippolytus's understanding of the sabbath as a time of communal reading of the law. There are no Jewish activities on the sabbath that Christians must avoid, and certainly no sabbath worship.

CHAPTER SEVEN

SABBATH AS DAY OF REST AND READING THE TORAH:
THE MISHNAH

Introduction

There are various theories about, and explanations of, the origin of
the Mishnah. They are usually coloured by legend and tradition and
attribute only the highest of motives to those untraceable authors
who compiled the volume.

One explanation of the origin of the Mishnah claims that in the
last centuries before the turn of the era, midrashim were prepared to
explain the unclear sections of the teachings in the Torah.[1] In time,
the quantity of such midrashim was such that a method of organising
the material was required, and so, during the first two centuries CE,
the code of oral law, the Mishnah, was prepared. And in order to
make clear that the oral law was not monolithic, the disputes and disagreements that were included in the formation of the final opinion
were gathered together in the Mishnah. Tradition states that the bulk
of the organisation of the laws and their sub-divisions was carried
out by R. Akiba,[2] and that the compilation was completed near the
beginning of the third century CE.

Neusner sees the organising principle of the compilers as being
neither abstract nor theological, but grounded in the needs of everyday life. These needs, he believes, have been organised in six sections: agriculture (including blessings and prayers), festivals,

---

[1] S.A. Handelman, *The Slayers of Moses: The Emergence of Rabbinic Interpretation
in Modern Literary Theory* (Albany: State University of New York Press, 1982), pp. 42-
46, explains briefly the processes which led to the creation of the Mishnah. A more
detailed outline is given in S. Safrai, ed., *The Literature of the Sages*, I (Assen: van
Gorcum, 1987), pp. 227-35.
[2] R. Akiba died in 132 CE.

women, damages, sacred things and purifications.[3] And, although he
notes that the Mishnah portrays an orderly world revolving harmo-
niously round the Temple,[4] he concedes that the bulk of it represents
the views of rabbis active between 135 CE and 200 CE, long after the
Temple had been destroyed.[5] He explains this apparent contradiction
by claiming that those later rabbis wished to incorporate what they
regarded as really important in their writings and to build a Jewish
future based on the most excellent parts of their past.

Sanders takes issue with Neusner's conclusions about the content
and purpose of the Mishnah and believes that a more measured
approach to evaluating the Mishnah would begin with a consideration of the genre of the work.[6] He regards as unwarranted the claim
of Neusner that the Mishnah couched its philosophical writings in
the guise of 'legal discussion about everyday activities'.[7] The
Mishnah—according to Sanders—is no more than it appears to be, 'a
collection of legal debates and opinions', and is likened, by Sanders,
to a highway code.[8]

An important part of Jewish worship is religious devotion in the
home, but of that little is said in the Mishnah. As Sanders comments,
'[c]ommon piety is difficult to discover in the Mishnah'; only rules
about the sabbath and the synagogue are recorded there.[9]

Such details as are given about the sabbath are found in the tractate of that name (Shabbat), and details of Jewish worship in the synagogues are found within the tractates on festivals (Mo'ed) and on
sacred things (Hodashim), but there is no section that deals directly
and specifically with sabbath worship either in the synagogue or in
the home.

The Sabbath in the Mishnah

There are many texts about the sabbath in the Mishnah, but most of
the references are to a person's culpability or blamelessness with

---

[3] Neusner, *Formative Judaism*, p. 112.
[4] Neusner, *Formative Judaism*, p. 25.
[5] Neusner, *Formative Judaism*, pp. 113-14.
[6] Sanders, *Jewish Law*, pp. 309-31.
[7] Sanders, *Jewish Law*, pp. 311-12.
[8] Sanders, *Jewish Law*, pp. 314-16.
[9] Sanders, *Jewish Law*, p. 331.

respect to infringements of the sabbath commandment. Jews were expected to be scrupulous in their observance of sabbath rest, so Mishnah elaborates rules that obviate any need for personal interpretation of the sabbath command.

At first sight the list of thirty-nine activities forbidden on the sabbath seems to include all sorts of unrelated tasks:

> sowing, ploughing, reaping, binding sheaves, threshing, winnowing, cleansing crops, grinding, sifting, kneading, baking, shearing wool, washing or beating or dyeing it, spinning, weaving, making two loops, weaving two threads, separating two threads, tying (a knot), loosening (a knot), sewing two stitches, tearing in order to sew two stitches, hunting a gazelle, slaughtering or flaying or salting it or curing its skin, scraping it or cutting it up, writing two letters, erasing in order to write two letters, building, pulling down, putting out a fire, lighting a fire, striking with a hammer and taking out aught from one domain to another[10] (*Sab.* 7.2).

However, these tasks have been organised, by Goldenberg, into groups of activities necessary for the provision of food, clothing, writing and shelter, and representing 'the indispensable foundations of civilised life as the early rabbis understood' it.[11]

The lighting of the sabbath lamp by the woman of the house before sunset on Friday is often considered to be a worship activity special to the beginning of the sabbath—though in the Mishnah it is contained within the category of preparing shelter. The action is specifically required of the woman of the house, if she is to be an observant Jewish woman, and also if she wishes to take all possible steps to avoid dying in childbirth:[12]

> For three transgressions do women die in childbirth: for heedlessness of the laws of the menstruant, the Dough-offering, and the lighting of the [Sabbath] lamp (*Sab.* 2.6).

The man of the home has a different responsibility at the beginning of the sabbath, but among the requirements the fulfilment of which he has to verify is the lighting of the lamp[s].

> Three things must a man say within his house when darkness is falling on the eve of Sabbath: Have ye tithed? Have ye prepared the *Erub*? and, Light the lamp ... (*Sab.* 2.7)

---

[10] Quotations from the Mishnah are from H. Danby, *The Mishnah* (Oxford: OUP, 1933).

[11] Goldenberg, 'Rabbinic Judaism', pp. 33-35.

[12] Goldenberg, 'Rabbinic Judaism', p. 35.

These three requirements had to be met before dusk—before sabbath began. So the lighting of the lamps is not precisely a sabbath action.

Some might consider the reciting of the blessing over the Kiddush cup of wine on Friday evening to be a sabbath ritual. However, this prayer is not strictly speaking a prayer special to the sabbath, because it is recited on every occasion when wine is drunk—only the addition of words about the sabbath in the prayer itself identifies the blessing with the sabbath.[13]

Others texts deal with the overriding of the sabbath by actions required for the proper observance of festivals. Thus slaughtering the passover lamb, scraping its entrails and burning its fat pieces are all permissible on a sabbath if necessary, but roasting the lamb and rinsing its entrails are not (*Pes.* 6.1). Only those actions are permitted that cannot be performed before or after the sabbath in question, and there are similar exemptions for the feasts of weeks (*Hag.* 2.4), and booths (*Men.* 10.3, 9), and for former activities in the Temple (*Men.* 11.2, 3, 6, 8, 9).

The Mishnah itself states that the scriptural teaching about the sabbath is slight:

> (The rules about) release from vows hover in the air and have nought to support them; the rules about the Sabbath, Festal-offerings, and Sacrilege are as mountains hanging by a hair, for (teaching of) Scripture (thereon) is scanty and the rules many ... (*Hag.* 1.8).

The only action positively required on the sabbath by the Mishnah is the lighting of the sabbath lamp by the woman of the home—but in that action she is creating fire for the last time just before the sabbath begins. The prayer in which the woman welcomes the sabbath is a domestic act of worship on the sabbath.

Synagogues as Buildings

In most references to synagogues (הכנסת or בית הכנסת) a building is implied. It is a shared possession of the members of the community, as are also the public place, the bath-house, the Ark [of the Law] and the Books [of Scripture] (*Ned.* 5.5).

---

[13] Goldenberg, 'Rabbinic Judaism', p. 39.

References to the synagogue are in the main in connection with happenings or actions in synagogues for which actions—if carried out elsewhere—the legislation has already been given. The occurrence of the event in the synagogue is merely a special case of the regular happening. So, for example, the synagogue is one place where the consumption of unclean heave offering oil in lamps is permitted. Similarly, synagogues are among the places a priest might enter—along with: houses of study, dark alleyways, rooms of sick people, the house of a priest's wife's father, a house with a wedding, but not a house of mourning (*Ter.* 11.10).

Little is said that clearly links the synagogue with the sabbath. One possible reference—although the sabbath is not mentioned directly—is the provision of a cubicle in the synagogue for the use of lepers.

> When he[14] enters a synagogue they must make for him a partition ten handbreadths high and four cubits wide. He must enter in first and come forth last ... (*Neg.* 13.12).[15]

That other people would also be there, suggesting to me days on which meetings took place, is implied by the proviso about his entering first and leaving last, but daily gatherings could be the correct inference.

The holiness of the synagogue building is attested by the fact that a synagogue can be sold only on condition that it may be at a later date re-purchased (*Meg.* 3.1-2).[16] There are also lists of possible uses a former synagogue may or may not be put to, if it is sold, It may not be used as a bath-house, tannery, ritual bath or urinal, but it can be used as a courtyard. Resting quietly in the ex-synagogue and chatting will not be considered defiling, though pollution by unclean fluids will (*Meg.* 3.2).

Even for derelict synagogues certain activities are forbidden. Thus twisting ropes and spreading out produce or nets is banned, as are delivering funeral orations or making use of the building as a short-cut (*Meg.* 3.3). So, work, remembrances of grief and trivial activities are not allowed to take place in the ruins of a synagogue building.

---

[14] A leper.

[15] Only male lepers are referred to.

[16] Safrai, *Literature*, p. 230; P. Blackman, *Mishnayoth.* II. *Order Mo'ed* (New York: The Judaica Press, 1963), pp. 450-51.

Synagogues as Groups of Jews

The only reference in the Mishnah that portrays the synagogue as a group of people is one in which the transfer of impurity due to a person having a flux is being discussed:

> ... If they[17] were weaving together, whether standing or sitting, or grinding wheat together, in every case R. Simeon declares clean [him that was before clean], save only when they were grinding with a handmill. ... But in every like case they are clean for [ordinary] members of the congregation, and unclean only for [them that eat of] Heave-offering (*Neg.* 13.12).[18]

The rule seems to be considering the relative closeness of contact between people, and the reference to forms of association in the congregation—or synagogue, לבני הכנסת—is a particular example of that. Therefore, those with the enteric disorder are considered clean for being ordinary members of the synagogue, but unclean in the matter of eating the heave-offering.[19] The people as a group is meant by לבני הכנסת—not the building or the benches; the people would become unclean—not the building or the benches.

Prayer in Synagogues

The Mishnah lacks any description of communal prayers to be carried out in the synagogue, and a recent survey confirms the lack of references to group prayer in synagogues in rabbinic literature as a whole.[20] There are many references to individual prayer, even coordinated individual prayer,[21] but a group of people each engaged in private prayer is different from a group of people engaged in communal prayer. And, in many cases, the prayers are prescribed for the home, for example, grace before meals. So, although it was customary for pious Jews to pray twice daily, these prayers are not described as a group activity associated with the local synagogue. Individual prayer is the dominant perception of prayer in the

---

[17] Sc. one who was ill and one who was healthy.
[18] Only male lepers are referred to.
[19] A. Oppenheimer, *The 'Am Ha-Aretz* (Arbeiten zur Literatur und Geschichte des hellenistischen Judentums, 8; Leiden: Brill, 1977), p. 137.
[20] Sanders, *Jewish Law*, pp. 73-74, considers Talmudic texts as well as the Mishnah.
[21] Throughout *Berakoth*.

Mishnah, and communal prayer can be inferred only from later practice.

Reading Scriptures in Synagogues

Synagogue behaviour associated with the reading of scrolls, either of Esther at Purim or of Torah on other occasions, is described in chapter 4 of the tractate *Megillah,* so that is where the details of synagogue practice on Mondays, Thursdays and sabbaths are given (*Meg.* 4.1-6.).

Particular passages from the Torah are specified for reading on sabbaths throughout the year, and for festivals. During the preceding week parts of the lection for the following sabbath are read at afternoon services:[22]

> ... and on Monday and on Thursday and on the Sabbath at the *After-noon Service* they read in the regular order, but it is not taken into account ... (*Meg.* 3.6).

However, although the section of Torah had been read—on a weekday—in its proper sequence from the cycle of readings, it had to be repeated on the following sabbath.[23] This means that the sequence of sabbath readings is the important sequence, in spite of the same lections having been read and heard by some members of the group on the intervening Monday and Thursday. This rule indicates a priority given to readings that took place on the sabbath.

The Mishnah also lists the number and stance of the readers at afternoon services on Mondays, Thursdays and sabbaths:

> He who reads the *Scroll* may stand or sit; if one read it, or if two read it, they have fulfilled their duty. In the place where the custom is to recite a Benediction one should recite it, but where it is not customary to recite a Benediction he does not recite it. On Monday, and on Thursday, and on Sabbath at the *Afternoon Service* three persons read; they must not reduce the number nor add to it; nor do they conclude with a reading from the Prophets. He that begins the reading from the *Law* and he that concludes it recites a benediction, the one at the start and the other at the conclusion (*Meg.* 4.1).

---

[22] Blackman, *Mishnayoth*, II, pp. 453-54.
[23] Blackman, *Mishnayoth*, II, p. 454.

Blackman's notes clarify the rather compressed prose of this paragraph: there is a freedom to stand or sit if one reads from the scroll of Esther, but for Torah readings the reader must stand, the Torah may not be read by voices in unison, but only by a single voice.[24]

Thereafter details of numbers of readers for festivals and on the sabbath are given:

> ... any day when there is [an] *Additional Service* but is not a Holyday, four read; on a Holyday, five; on the Day of Atonement, six; on the Sabbath, seven. They must not reduce the number but they may increase it, and they conclude with a reading from the Prophets. He who commences and he that concludes recites a Benediction, the one before it and the other at the completion (*Meg.* 4.2).

The sabbath is different from the other days only in having more readers—the number of the readers being seven. Readings of Torah on the sabbath must be read by one male, who must stand. The sabbath Torah readings must follow the programme of readings for the year in an unbroken order. But there are no details given of any other activities in the synagogue special to the sabbath.

Conclusions

The Mishnah portrays the same picture of sabbath activities in the gatherings of Jews that has been noted in the other literary sources. There is a concentration on meeting, on study and on reading the Law. But no other activity has the same unchallenged place in the meetings. There are no descriptions of psalm singing or of the saying of communal prayers. The communal activity described is a combination of male reading and communal listening to Torah.

---

[24] Blackman, *Mishnayoth*, II, p. 454.

CHAPTER EIGHT

THE UNOBTRUSIVE SABBATH: ARCHAEOLOGICAL DATA, INSCRIPTIONS AND PAPYRI

Introduction

As all the previous chapters of this book have dealt with the literary evidence about sabbath practice available from the religious, apologetic and polemic documents of the time, it is important to cross-reference that material with concrete evidence from the material deposits of everyday life and its transactions. Thus the evidence from inscriptions, papyri, and archaeological discoveries that relates to the sabbath, προσευχαί or synagogues will be reviewed in this Chapter.

The materials of ancient buildings still exist, whether in their original location or moved elsewhere for various purposes. Occasionally these remains give evidence of the activities that took place in the buildings. For instance, many dedicatory or memorial slabs from Jewish buildings have been found which reveal the public and private thoughts of the owners,[1] builders or restorers of the original structures. Papyri from Egypt bring the legal and commercial life of the ancient towns to life. Added to that is the evidence from bills and letters that indicates the power of individuals and groups to make transactions in goods and services. An awareness of the civic life of these ancient communities can be recovered from the data provided by the artefacts. And in this record of civic life some indications of the religious practice of Jews is preserved.

---

[1] The distinction between *public* and *private* inscriptions is made by A.G. Woodhead, *The Study of Greek Inscriptions* (Cambridge: CUP, 1981), pp. 35-36, the former referring to official decrees and transactions and the latter to matters of family or community concern.

Methodological Considerations for Epigraphic Material

One of the problems with archaeological evidence is that it is often fragmentary. Parts of buildings, mosaics or frescoes are often broken, missing or misplaced. Inscriptions are damaged or eroded, papyri are torn or incomplete.

Another problem is that buildings, architectural features, artefacts, inscriptions and written texts are difficult to date. Unless an actual dating reference occurs on the artefact, which happens only rarely, datings have to be arrived at by involving the methods of other disciplines. Thus error or uncertainty is multiplied.

Out of the many archaeological items found, only a few contain enough information in themselves to give an incontrovertible set of data. Usually items are identified by means of their position and location, using estimates of the date of the style of any writing on them, or from coins found around them or at different levels in the same site. This leads to all such datings having margins of error.[2]

And even if one could find a clear example of an early Jewish building, with a sure date and with self-evident furnishings, the building itself would not be able to supply details of what happened in the building. There would need to be illustrations showing typical cult objects or typical activities and celebrations to give an indication of the worship practices contemporary with the building. Ideally a dated inscription as part of the same decoration would indicate the nouns and verbs associated with the activities portrayed, and allow comparison with literary materials. But there have been no such finds for synagogues before the third century CE.

Even with perfectly clear inscriptions there are also problems. The stones may have been moved far from their original site before being studied by an expert, who is therefore handicapped by lack of context for the stone on which the inscription has been incised. Without the location and the evidence from the surrounding artefacts, making judgements about any inscription is much more difficult.

Reconstructions for missing sections of the material often depend on the existence, in a better state of preservation, of parallel material. But the judgement as to what can be considered parallel material depends on many factors. Thus fragmentary inscriptions always

---

[2] For a full treatment of these and related issues see Woodhead, *Greek Inscriptions.*

remain fragmentary and have to be made use of in that state, even if read alongside their reconstructed selves.

The modern language into which the inscription is first translated can also affect its perceived meaning, partly because of the range of meaning in the second language, and partly because of the cultural and educational background of scholars speaking that particular language. For this and all the other reasons cited above, I have always used two or more editions for each inscription.

However, on the positive side, it can be said that inscriptions 'are almost always contemporary with the people and events mentioned', and often give both historical and linguistic data which bring 'insights into the life of individuals and groups'.[3] This highlights the value of inscriptions and papyri and must be set against the drawbacks to their use.

The epigraphic material provides both the public and the private expression of the views of persons who paid for the inscriptions or documents to be prepared. Thus it may be possible to discover from them the views that widely separated groups of Jews held about their communal religious life, including those about the sabbath, and whether these expressed views included, or could include, the practice of worship.

A substantial difficulty encountered in working with the papyrus material is that the editors of the *Corpus papyrorum judaicarum* assume that any reference to a synagogue, apparently also including honorific titles which include the term synagogue, will indicate the existence of an organised Jewish community with a communal building called a synagogue.[4] They infer the existence of these synagogues and refer to them as places for meetings, deliberations, prayer, study and hospitality for strangers. They further assert that in 'Egypt a synagogue was called a *proseuche* (προσευχή), a place of prayer'.[5] An unfortunate side effect of this way of dealing with the

---

[3] Thus F.V. Filson, 'Ancient Greek Synagogue Inscriptions', *The Biblical Archaeologist* 32 (1969), pp. 41-46 (41), prefaces his summary of B. Lifshitz, *Donateurs et fondateurs dans les synagogues juives: Répertoire des dédicaces grecques relatives à la construction et à la réfection des synagogues* (Cahiers de la Revue Biblique, 7; Paris: Gabalda, 1967).

[4] V.A. Tcherikover and A. Fuks, *Corpus papyrorum judaicarum*, I (Cambridge, MA: Harvard University Press, 1957), pp. 7-8.

[5] Tcherikover and Fuks, *Corpus papyrorum judaicarum*, I, p. 8.

terms προσευχή and 'synagogue' is that no distinction is made between the usages of the two terms, and so any nuances of meaning, in particular of the word 'synagogue', are lost both in the translations supplied and in the discussion about the inscriptions.

I, on the other hand, believe that the phrases 'synagogue of the Jews' and 'leader of the synagogue', when employed in inscriptions, always relate to the congregation in question but do not refer to a building nor necessarily imply the existence of a building.

Therefore, I have read all the papyri and inscriptions primarily from the standpoint that προσευχή means a public or civic building associated with a community of Jews and συναγωγή means a group of Jews who made community decisions. Thus architectural or epigraphic evidence for the existence of προσευχαί is not here regarded as evidence for the existence of synagogue buildings. Any instances of synagogue buildings will be authenticated by archaeological material that indicates that those buildings were known as synagogues. As a result of taking this position I will not say, for example, that Jews dedicated their synagogue to a ruler,[6] but that a synagogue of Jews dedicated their προσευχή to a ruler.

The work of Leon raises another methodological point, for as he deals only with the epitaphs of the Jewish catacombs in Rome, his evidence cannot be archaeological data about synagogues or *proseuchae*, because in order for an inscription to be archaeological evidence it would have to be on a stone that was part of the structure of the building it described.

The numbers in brackets for each inscription are those assigned by Frey, and are used when, as far as can be determined, the inscription was originally displayed on a structural part of a building where Jews congregated. The language of the inscriptions will be specified only if it is other than Greek.

The relevant inscriptions and papyri will be presented and explained, then the discussion which follows will homologate what may be known from other archaeological features with what may be known from the written material.

---

[6] Out of all the evidence surveyed, only the building used by Jews in first-century Berenice was unambiguously called a synagogue.

Locations

In the first century CE, large Jewish communities were flourishing in cities of the central and eastern Mediterranean, Jerusalem, Alexandria, Rome, Antioch and Caesarea having the largest numbers,[7] and there seems to be enough similarity in what has been found in the different communities settled round the Mediterranean area from Rome to Palestine to Cyrenaica to permit us to make comparisons across the region.[8]

Inscriptions and Papyri

Rome

The epigraphic evidence from Rome is from sepulchral inscriptions from the catacombs only. Five inscriptions referring to an archisynagogos (one in Latin), of which two specify the name of the synagogue the person belonged to;[9] and seven epitaphs, referring to persons as 'father of the synagogue',[10] and two as 'mother of the synagogue' (one in Latin),[11] and many epitaphs to ordinary members of 'synagogues' give confirmation of many different congregations of Jews in Rome. Altogether the inscriptions indicate that there were sixteen synagogues in Rome,[12] but none of these inscriptions indicates definitely the presence of a building—even though the dates of the catacomb inscriptions span the period from the first century BCE to the third century CE.[13]

---

[7] L.I. Levine, *Caesarea under Roman Rule* (Studies in Judaism in Late Antiquity, 7; Leiden: Brill, 1975), p. 22.

[8] W. Horbury, 'The Benediction of the Minim', *JTS* n.s. 33 (1982), pp. 19-61 (48-49), speaking of the second century CE, says that such comparisons are valuable because of 'the degree of solidarity between Jewry in Dispersion and in the Land assumed in the ancient sources' and adds that 'Roman legislation presupposes a scattered but unified Jewish ethnos'; Leon, *Ancient Rome*, pp. 173-74, speaking of the occurrence of the word ἄρχων in inscriptions, finds a similarity of occurrence from various 'parts of the Jewish world, not only from Italy, but also from the eastern and western Mediterranean areas and from Egypt and North Africa'.

[9] Leon, *Ancient Rome*, pp. 171, 303, 306, 314, 322, 339.

[10] Leon, *Ancient Rome*, pp. 186-88.

[11] B.J. Brooten, *Women Leaders in the Ancient Synagogue* (Brown Judaic Studies, 36; Chico, CA: Scholars Press, 1982), pp. 57-72; Leon, *Ancient Rome*, pp. 188-89.

[12] Leon, *Ancient Rome*, pp. 139-40.

[13] Leon, *Ancient Rome*, pp. 65-66.

Throughout his book Leon maintains the distinction between the groups, or congregations—the 'synagogues'— and the buildings Jews met in—the *proseuchae*. He finds that the sepulchral inscriptions never refer to the building, *proseucha* or προσευχή, in connection with groups of Jews or their gatherings, the sole occurrence of a building called a *proseucha* being in the business address, 'at the wall by the synagogue' [*sic*],[14] given in the epitaph of a deceased non-Jewish Roman fruit vendor.

DIS M
P CORFIDIO SIGNINO
POMARIO
DE AGGERE
A PROSEUCHA
Q SALLUSTIUS HERMES
AMICO BENEMERENTI
ET NUMERUM OLLARUM DECEM[15]

To the divine shades—Publius Corfidius, of Segni, fruit vendor at the rampart by the prayer-house, Quintus Sallustius Hermes to his worthy friend and the number of urns is ten.[16]

This inscription has to be treated as a literary text about *proseuchae*, since it is not a tablet or slab from the structure of a *proseucha*. Thus it adds to the literary evidence of Juvenal and Philo as to the existence of *proseuchae* in Rome.

There are no inscriptions on structural stonework from any *proseuchae* or synagogue buildings in Rome from the period of this study.

Elsewhere in Italy

There are two Latin inscriptions to 'mothers of the synagogue', indicating Jewish groups in Venosa and Venetia,[17] but, *pace* Brooten, not necessarily indicating the existence of synagogue buildings there.[18]

---

[14] Leon, *Ancient Rome*, p. 139, here contradicts his own avowed distinction.

[15] Leon, *Ancient Rome*, p. 139; J.-B. Frey, *Corpus inscriptionum judaicarum*. I. *Europe* (rev. B. Lifshitz; New York: Ktav, 1975), p. 391.

[16] Unless there is a reference to the contrary, I have supplied my own translation of the inscriptions.

[17] Brooten, *Women Leaders*, pp. 60-61.

[18] Brooten, *Women Leaders*, pp. 28-29, assumes that the existence of an official called an archisynagogus implies a synagogue *building*.

Greece

Corinth
An inscription (718), roughly incised in sloping, uneven characters on a marble lintel, dated between 100 BCE and 200 CE, has been restored to read 'the synagogue of the Hebrews':[19]

[Συνα]γωγὴ Ἐβρ[αίων]

This indicates that the building was used by, or owned by, or, possibly, known as—the synagogue of Hebrews.

Aegina
Two undated inscriptions (722, 723) from a mosaic floor, must, sadly—for they give the most helpful details about the building they decorated—be ruled out from this study on account of their likely (late) date. Both are complete, but with some letters eroded, and report the deeds of an archisynagogos who re-built a synagogue building from the foundations, and of someone of the same name, but younger, who, using the revenues of the synagogue, completed the mosaics.[20] The second of the two does not refer to the synagogue building directly, but 722 does.

Θεόδωρος ἀρχισυν[άγωγος φ]ροντίσας ἔτη τέσσερα [φθαρεῖσαν?]
ἐκ θεμελίων τὴν συναγ[ωγὴν] οἰκοδόμησα. Προσοδευ[θησαν]
χρύσιν[ο]ι [ρ]ε′ καὶ ἐκ τῶν τοῦ Θε(οῦ) δωρεῶν χρύσινοι ρο′ ...[21]

I, Theodorus, the Archisynagogos, who functioned for four years, built this synagogue from its foundations. Revenues amounted to 85 pieces of gold (i.e. gold dinars), and offerings unto God to 105 pieces of gold.[22]

The lack of any definite date for either of the inscriptions makes the information they give quite tantalising, since the first is one of the few clear pieces of evidence for the word 'synagogue' meaning unequivocally a building.

However, an attempt at dating can be made using two approaches. First, because early synagogues had floors paved with flagstones,

---

[19] Frey, *Corpus*, I, p. 518.
[20] Frey, *Corpus*, I, p. 522; Lifshitz, *Donateurs et fondateurs*, pp. 13-14; E.L. Sukenik, *Ancient Synagogues in Palestine and Greece* (The Schweich Lectures of the British Academy; London: British Academy, OUP, 1934), p. 44, pl. XI.
[21] Inscription 722, as photographed in 1928, retains only the first letter of the word συναγωγή, but Frey gives the first five letters of the word as extant.
[22] Sukenik, *Ancient Synagogues*, p. 44.

which were usually overlaid with mosaic floors, the fact that the whole floor of this synagogue was covered by a complete mosaic with a central design and complex border is evidence that this building is from a later period.[23] Then, from the late date of the secondary usage of the stones from this synagogue in buildings close at hand, the original building appears to have remained standing until the seventh century CE. So, on the basis of these two pieces of evidence I accept a fourth-century CE origin for the mosaic inscriptions,[24] and therefore exclude them as evidence in this study.

Delos

A brief inscription (726), dated to the second century BCE, indicates a donation or contribution to the προσευχή by persons named Agathocles and Lysimachos.[25]

Ἀγαθοκλῆς	Agathocles
καὶ Λυσίμα	and Lysima-
χος ἐπὶ	chos for the
προσευχῆι	prayer-house

Pannonia

Mursa

A marble slab has been found with a fragmentary Latin inscription (678a), dating from around the close of the second century CE or the beginning of the third, indicating the existence of a *proseucha* building in Mursa.[26]

The inscription highlights the extent of the geographical range of occurrences of the word *proseucha* used to mean a civic building, although there are no details in the inscription that specifically indicate a Jewish community building. The restored opening section shows that addressing the Roman ruler in an conciliatory manner was a possible opening for an inscription.

---

[23] So Sukenik, *Ancient Synagogues*, pp. 27-28, although the clearest sign of fourth-century CE provenance—depictions of animals in the design—is not present.

[24] Cf. the inscription (720) of a donation of a vestibule to a synagogue, which similarly implies a building, and is similarly dated to the fourth century CE (Frey, *Corpus*, I, p. 520; Lifshitz, *Donateurs et fondateurs*, pp. 16-17).

[25] Frey, *Corpus*, I, p. 525; Lifshitz, *Donateurs et fondateurs*, pp. 14-15; Sukenik, *Ancient Synagogues*, pp. 37-40, pl. X.

[26] Frey, *Corpus*, I, pp. 60-61, reconstruction of Comfort supplied by Lifshitz.

PP	[Pro salute im]p(eratorum)
RTINACIS	[L(ucii) Sept(imii) Severi Pe]rtinacis
AUGG	[et M(arci) Aur(elii) Antonini] Aug(ustoruni)
RORUM	[et Iuliae Aug(ustae) matris cast]rorum
NDUS	........................[Secu]ndus
SEUCHAM	[...........................pro]seucham
STATE	[......................vetu] state
LO	[conlapsam a so]lo
	[restituit].

For the safety of the emperors Lucius Septimius Severus Pertinax and Marcus Aurelius Antoninus, the Augusti and Iulia Augusta mother of the camps, Secundus has restored from the foundations the synagogue [*sic*] fallen from age [translation: Lifshitz].

The Northern Shores of the Black Sea

Olbia

A marble plaque, now apparently lost, bears an inscription (682) about a group of named men who restored the προσευχή there.[27] There is no date for the inscription, and there are disagreements as to the restoration of the end of the inscription, but the relevant section reads:

... ἄρχ[οντες] τὴν προσευχὴν ἐ[πε]σκεύασαν τῇ ἑαυ[τῶν] προνοίᾳ στεγάσα[ντες] ...

... rulers repaired the προσευχή by their own forethought, having covered ...

The Jewish provenance of this inscription is disputed, partly because of the names of the men: Satyros, son and grandson of Artemidoros; Achilles, son of Demetrios; Dionysiodorus, son of Eros, and Zobeis, son of Zobeis. These names are more typically Greek than Jewish.The other strand of uncertainty is caused by the restoration of the last line to read ἀπὸ τοῦ θεοῦ μέχρι [...], which can be considered to be addressed to a pagan god.[28] Liddell and Scott regard this inscription as evidence of a pagan προσευχή,[29] but since

---

[27] B. Latyschev, ed., *Inscriptiones antiquae orae septentrionalis ponti Euxini graecae et latinae*. I. *Inscriptiones Tyrae, Olbiae, Chersonesi Tauricae aliorum locorum a Danubio usque ad regnum Bosporanum* (2nd edn; Petersburg, 1916; r.p. Hildesheim: Georg Olms Verlagsbuchhandlung, 1965), pp. 189-91; Frey, *Corpus*, I, pp. 493-94; Lifshitz, *Donateurs et fondateurs*, pp. 19-20.

[28] Lifshitz reads the word as θεμελίου, so 'from the foundation'.

[29]*Greek–English Lexicon*, p. 1151, *s.v.* προσευχή.

no other evidence supports that view, I accept, following Frey, the Jewish origin of the inscription. The prayer-house is clearly a building, since it is described as having been restored.

Panticape (Kertsch)

1 A well-preserved inscription of nineteen lines on a marble slab (683) links the προσευχή with the local Jewish community.[30]

> Βασιλεύοντος Βασιλέως Τιβε
> ρίου Ἰουλίου Ῥησκουπόριδος φιλο
> καίσαρος καὶ φιλορωμαίου, εὐσε
> βοῦς, ἔτους ζοτ´ μηνὸς Περει[τί]
> 5 ου ιβ´, Χρήστη γυνὴ πρότε
> ρον Δρούσου ἀφείημι ἐπὶ τῆς [προ]
> σευχῆς θρεπτόν μου Ἡρακλᾶν
> ἐλεύθερον καθάπαξ κατὰ εὐχή[ν]
> μου ἀνεπίλεπτον καὶ ἀπα[ρ]ενό
> 10 χλητον ἀπὸ παντὸς κληρονόμ[ου]
> τ]ρέπεσ(θ)αι αὐτὸν ὅπου ἂν βού
> λ[ητ]αι ἀνεπικωλύτως καθὼς ε[ὐ]
> ξάμην, χωρὶς ἰς τ[ὴ]ν προ[σ]ευ
> χὴν θωπείας τε καὶ προσκα[ρτε
> 15 ρ]ήσεω[ς], συνεπινευσάντων δὲ
> καὶ τῶν κληρ(ο)νόμων μου Ἡρα
> κλεί[δο]υ καὶ Ἑλικωνιάδος,
> συνε[πιτ]ροπεούσης δὲ καὶ τῆ[ς]
> συναγωγῆ[ς] τῶν Ἰουδαίων.

In the reign of King Tiberius, Julius Rescuporis, friend of Caesar and friend of the Romans, and pious, in the year 377 [80 CE], on the twelfth of the month Peritios, I, Chreste, former wife of Drousos, release, in the προσευχή, my home-reared slave Heraclas, free, once and for all, according to my vow, irrevocable and unable to be altered by any of my heirs, to go wherever he wishes, unhindered, according as I have vowed, except towards the προσευχή devotion and assiduity, with the agreement both of my heirs Heraclides and Heliconias and under the joint guardianship also of the synagogue of the Jews.

Dating from approximately 80 CE, the inscription describes a manumission. Chreste, a widow, frees one of her household slaves at the προσευχή in order to fulfil a vow she has made. She gives him

---

[30] B. Latyschev, ed., *Inscriptiones antiquae orae septentrionalis ponti Euxini graecae et latinae. II: Inscriptiones regni Bosporani graecae et latinae* (2nd edn; Petersburg, 1916; r.p. Hildesheim: Georg Olms Verlagsbuchhandlung, 1965), pp. 49-51; Frey, *Corpus*, I, pp. 495-96.

total liberty, apart from his obligations to the προσευχή. The inscription states that this manumission has the agreement both of her heirs, who bear Greek names, and of the Jewish synagogue, obviously a group of people and not a building, who will act as joint guarantors of the slave's continuing freedom.

The sole commitment the slave has to keep is the mysterious reference to showing attention or 'flattery' (θωπεία strictly means that) and perseverance towards the προσευχή. There is no means by which to decide if this is a commitment to work of a menial sort, or a religious commitment to be given by the freed slave, either voluntarily or under duress.

2   The other, less well-preserved, but similar, inscription (684) from the same place is undated.[31] It also names the προσευχή as the place where an enfranchisement took place, and similarly names the synagogue of the Jews as co-guarantors of the slaves' freedom, and makes the previously noted enigmatic requirement of 'flattery and perseverance' towards the προσευχή. And the reading of this closely parallel text does not depend on the text of 683 for decipherment.

3   Inscription 683a, also similar, is dated to the second century CE.[32] The author of the inscription releases, in the προσευχή, his home-reared slave, to be totally free of disturbance by the author's heirs, and liable only to be constantly at hand in (or regularly attend) the προσευχή, the conditions to be under the joint guardianship of the author and the synagogue of the Jews and the God-fearers.[33]

In all three inscriptions the synagogue of the Jews is referred to only in its civic function as a group with memory, voice and power in the community. The buildings associated with these synagogues of Jews are called προσευχαί.

Gorgippia
Another similar inscription (690), addressed to the Most High God, and internally dated to 41 CE, describes the dedication by one Pothos of a female slave, in a προσευχή, according to a vow.[34] She is to be

---

[31] Latyschev, *Inscriptiones*, II, pp. 51-53; Frey, *Corpus*, I, pp. 496-97.
[32] Frey, *Corpus*, I, pp. 65-66.
[33] See also the much more fragmentary, but similar, inscription 683b in Frey, *Corpus*, I, p. 66, also dated to the second century CE.
[34] Latyschev, *Inscriptiones*, II, pp. 208-209; Frey, *Corpus*, I, pp. 500-501.

undisturbed and unmolested by his heirs. The main difference between this and the previous inscriptions is that the new status of the slave, which is not clearly described as freedom, is to be guaranteed by the heirs through Zeus, Ge and Helios.

It appears that the προσευχή of Gorgippia was the setting for manumissions without the involvement of the Jewish synagogue being stated, but whether they were involved on that occasion is undiscoverable. This inscription may be regarded as having belonged to a pagan προσευχή, or as coming from a Jewish community which was tolerant of names of alien deities being used in formulaic expressions.

I incline to the view that the προσευχή had a civic function in Gorgippia and that manumissions by non-Jews could be published there.

Asia Minor

Phocaea
An inscription (738), possibly from the third century CE, describes the honouring of a woman benefactor by the synagogue of the Jews:[35] Tation built extensive premises and then donated them to the synagogue.

> Τάτιον Στράτωνος τοῦ Ἐν
> πέδωνος τὸν οἶκον καὶ τὸν πε
> ρίβολον τοῦ ὑπαίθρου κατασκευ
> άσασα ἐκ τῶ[ν ἰδ]ίων
> ἐχαρίσατο τ[οῖς Ἰο]υδαίοις.
> Ἡ συναγωγὴ ἐ[τείμη]σεν τῶν Ἰουδαί
> ων Τάτιον Σ[τράτ]ωνος τοῦ Ἐνπέ
> δωνος χρυσῷ στεφάνῳ
> καὶ προεδρίᾳ

Tation, daughter of Straton, son of E(m)pedon, having built the house and the wall of the courtyard out of her own funds, gifted it to the Jews. The synagogue of the Jews honoured Tation, daughter of Straton, son of Empedon, by means of a golden crown and the privilege of sitting at the front.[36]

---

[35] Frey, *Corpus*, II, p. 8; Lifshitz, *Donateurs et fondateurs*, pp. 21-22; P.R. Trebilco, *Jewish Communities in Asia Minor* (SNTS Monograph Series, 69; Cambridge: CUP, 1991), pp. 110-11.

[36] Lifshitz, *Donateurs et fondateurs*, p. 22, implies that equipping the precinct could

The name given for the building is οἶκος rather than the more familiar word προσευχή, but it is again clear from the inscription that the synagogue of the Jews is not a building, but is a body which could award favours and privileges. And, despite the lack of clear date, the value of this inscription is its witness that the forms used in inscriptions were similar in different regions.

The giving of a golden crown is reminiscent of items of a similar sort reported by Philo for προσευχαί in Alexandria.[37]

Smyrna

One tomb inscription (741), undated, indicates that a Jewish woman called Rufina was archisynagogos there.[38] A dating of the second or third century CE has been proposed. This indicates the presence of a group of Jews in Smyrna.

Synnada

A marble fragment from the first or second century CE refers to an archisynagogos.[39] The existence of a group of Jews in Synnada may be inferred from this inscription.

Acmonia

Inscription 766 describes a building (literally a house: οἶκος) founded or built by Julia Severa,[40] a Roman citizen, around the time of Nero in the middle of the first century CE, and later restored by Jewish dignitaries of the town, named as the ἀρχισυνάγωγος and ἄρχων. The synagogue honoured them for this work in ways suggestive of Philo's description of the commemorative slabs in προσευχαί in Alexandria.[41]

> Τὸν κατασκευασθέντα οἶκον ὑπὸ
> Ἰουλίας Σεουήρας Π. Τυρρώνιος Κλά
> δος, ὁ διὰ βίου ἀρχισυνάγωγος καὶ
> Λούκιος Λουκίου ἀρχισυνάγωγος

---

include enclosing the courtyard and installing a fountain with basin therein.

[37] See data and discussion below on inscriptions from Acmonia and Berenice.

[38] Frey, *Corpus*, II, pp. 10-11; Brooten, *Women Leaders*, pp. 5-11, notes pp. 223-25; Trebilco, *Jewish Communities*, pp. 104-106, 125.

[39] Frey, *Corpus*, II, p. 23.

[40] Frey, *Corpus*, II, pp. 27-28, but note that this reading has been superseded by that of Robert quoted by the other sources; Lifshitz, *Donateurs et fondateurs*, pp. 34-36; Trebilco, *Jewish Communities*, pp. 58-60.

[41] See discussion below on Phocaea, Acmonia and Berenice.

5 καὶ Ποπίλιος Ζωτικὸς ἄρχων ἐπεσ
κεύασαν ἔκ τε τῶν ἰδίων καὶ τῶν συν
καταθεμένων καὶ ἔγραψαν τοὺς τοί
χους καὶ τὴν ὀροφὴν καὶ ἐποίησαν
τὴν τῶν θυρίδων ἀσφάλειαν καὶ τὸν
10 λυπὸν πάντα κόσμου, οὕστινας καὶ
ἡ συναγωγὴ ἐτείμησεν ὅπλῳ ἐπιχρύ
σῳ διὰ τὴν ἐνάρετον αὐτῶν δ[ι]άθ[ε]
σιν καὶ τὴν πρὸς τὴν συναγωγὴν εὔνοιάν
τε καὶ σπουδήν

The building constructed by Julia Severa, Publius Tyrronios Klados,
archisynagogos for life, and Lucius, son of Lucius, archisynagogos,
and Popilios Zotikos, restored both out of their own funds and from
the deposited sums, and they inscribed the walls and the ceilings,
made secure the windows and made all the rest of the ornamentation,
whom also the synagogue honoured with a gilded shield because of
their virtuous disposition and both their good will and enthusiasm
towards the synagogue.

In line 11 of the inscription the 'synagogue' which honours its
two officials is clearly the group of Jews, but in the last line of the
inscription it is possible to understand that the building is named as a
'synagogue' at the unstated time of its restoration. However, the
closing phrase is ambiguous, since people can show good will to a
community by their actions in enhancing the community building.[42]

Palestine

Jerusalem

A well-preserved inscription from Jerusalem is the Theodotus
inscription (1404) which describes the building of a synagogue.[43]
The author of the inscription built a synagogue on the foundations
laid by his forebears. The synagogue included a hostel, chambers and
water fittings, and had as its stated purposes the reading of the law

---

[42] This is the understanding of Lifshitz for he translates συναγωγή as *communauté*
both times it occurs in the inscription, which is surprising on two counts. First that in so
doing he departs from the translation of Frey, and second in that he often refers to a
building as a *synagogue* when the Greek has προσευχή. In a similar way it is surprising
that Frey, who usually translates συναγωγή as *communauté*, has in this case *synagogue*,
indicating a building.

[43] Frey, *Corpus*, II, pp. 332-35; Lifshitz, *Donateurs et fondateurs*, pp. 70-71; M.
Chiat, *Handbook of Synagogue Architecture* (Brown Judaic Studies, 29; Chico, CA:
Scholars Press, 1982), pp. 201-202.

and the teaching of the commandments.

Θ[ε]όδοτος Οὐεττήνου, ἱερεὺς καὶ
ἀ[ρ]χισυνάγωγος, υἱὸς ἀρχισυν[αγώ]
γ[ο]υ, υἱωνὸς ἀρχισυν[α]γώγου, ᾠκο
δόμησε τὴν συναγωγὴν εἰς ἀν[άγν]ω
5   σ[ιν] νόμου καὶ εἰς [δ]ιδαχ[ὴ]ν ἐντολῶν, καὶ
τ[ὸ]ν ξενῶνα, κα[ὶ τὰ] δώματα καὶ τὰ χρη
σ[τ]ήρια τῶν ὑδάτων, εἰς κατάλυμα τοῖ
ς [χ]ρήζουσιν ἀπὸ τῆς ξέ[ν]ης, ἣν ἔθεμε
λ[ίω]σαν οἱ πατέρες [α]ὐτοῦ καὶ οἱ πρε
10 σ[β]ύτεροι καὶ Σιμων[ί]δης

Theodotus, son of Quettenos (Vettenos), priest and
archisynagogus, son of an archisynagogus,
grandson of an archisynagogus, built
this synagogue for the reading
5   of the Law and for the teaching of the Commandments, and the
hostel and the chambers and
water fittings for the accommodation of those
who [coming] from abroad have need of it, of which
[synagogue] the foundations
were laid by his fathers and by the
10 Elders and Simonides [translation: Chiat].

This text is clear evidence of a synagogue building in Jerusalem, possibly with an early date, since some scholars give a date in the first century CE, perhaps pre-70 CE.[44] But this date is disputed, the original discovers dating the inscription to the second century CE. This important text will be discussed later in the Chapter.

Egypt

Alexandria
A badly damaged inscription from the Gabbary quarter in the south-west of Alexandria (1432), dated to c. 37 BCE, refers to a προσ-ευχή.[45] Only the bottom left-hand corner of the slab remains.

---

[44] The original dating is palaeographic; see further in discussion later in the Chapter.
[45] Frey, *Corpus*, II, p. 360; Lifshitz, *Donateurs et fondateurs*, p. 76; Lewis, 'Jewish Inscriptions', in V.A. Tcherikover, A. Fuks and M. Stern, eds., with an Epigraphical Contribution by D.M. Lewis, *Corpus papyrorum judaicarum*, III (Cambridge, MA: Harvard University Press, 1964), p. 139; note that Lewis gives ἐπόει for ἐπο(ί)ει, corrected to normal Greek orthography by Frey.

['Υπὲρ]⁴⁶ βασ[ιλίσση]ς καὶ β[ασιλ]έως θεῶι [με]γάλω[ι] ἐ[πηκό]ωι, "Αλυπ[ος τὴν] προσε[υχὴν] ἐπο(ί)ει (ἔτους) ιε΄ Με[χείρ ...].

For the queen and the king, to the great god who listens, Alypos made the προσευχή in the 15th year, (in the month) Mecheir ...

Schedia

A limestone slab from Schedia bears an inscription (1440) about the foundation or building by the Jews of a προσευχή for Ptolemy III Euergetes (246–221 BCE) and his wife Berenice.⁴⁷

['Υ]πὲρ βασιλέως Πτολεμαίου καὶ βασιλίσσης Βερενίκης ἀδελφῆς καὶ γυναικὸς καὶ τῶν τέκνων, τὴν προσευχὴν οἱ Ἰουδα(ῖ)οι.

For King Ptolemy and Queen Berenice, sister and wife, and their children, the Jews [? built] the προσευχή.

Xenephyris

A marble block bears an inscription (1441) in good condition about the addition of a vestibule to a προσευχή, by the Jews of Xenephyris between 143 and 115 BCE.⁴⁸

Ὑπὲρ βασιλέως Πτολεμαίου καὶ βασιλίσσης Κλεοπάτρας τῆς ἀδελφῆς καὶ βασιλίσσης Κλεοπάτρας τῆς γυναικὸς οἱ ἀπὸ Ξενεφύρεος Ἰουδαῖοι τὸν πυλῶνα τῆς προσευχῆς προστάντων Θεοδώρου καὶ Ἀχιλλίωνος.

For King Ptolemy and Queen Cleopatra, his sister, and Queen Cleopatra his wife, the Jews from Xenephyris, [? built] the vestibule of the προσευχή, Theodoros and Achillion being presidents.

Nitriai

A similar inscription (1442), with a similar date, points to the exis-

---

⁴⁶ ὑπέρ 'for', Frey and Lifshitz give en l'honneur de, 'in honour of', which in my view overlays the phrase with a meaning of subservient veneration not warranted by the Greek preposition.

⁴⁷ J.G. Griffiths, 'Egypt and the Rise of the Synagogue', JTS n.s. 38 (1987), pp. 1-15 (2-3); Lewis, 'Jewish Inscriptions', p. 141; Lifshitz, Donateurs et fondateurs, p. 78; Frey, Corpus, II, pp. 366-67; E. Breccia, Inscriptiones graecae Aegypti. II. Inscriptiones nunc Alexandriae in museo (Chicago: Ares Publishers, 1978), p. 6; no verb is supplied in the Greek.

⁴⁸ Frey, Corpus, II, pp. 367-68; Lewis, 'Jewish Inscriptions', pp. 141-42; Lifshitz, Donateurs et fondateurs, pp. 78-79. Ptolemy VII Euergetes II Physicon (145–117 BCE) was married to both his sister Cleopatra and his niece Cleopatra between 143 BCE, when he married his niece, and 115 BCE, when his sister died.

tence of a προσευχή with outbuildings or appurtenances.[49] This indicates that a προσευχή could consist of a complex of chambers rather than only a single hall.

Ὑπὲρ βασιλέως Πτολεμαίου καὶ βασιλίσσης Κλεοπάτρας τῆς ἀδελφῆς καὶ βασιλίσσης Κλεοπάτρας τῆς γυναικὸς Εὐεργετῶν, οἱ ἐν Νιτρίαις Ἰουδαῖοι τὴν προσευχὴν καὶ τὰ συγκύροντα.

For King Ptolemy and Queen Cleopatra, his sister, and Queen Cleopatra his wife, the Jews of Nitriai [? built] the προσευχή, and the outbuildings.

Athribis

1 An inscription (1443) from the first or second century BCE, it being difficult to date since five Ptolemies had wives named Cleopatra, shows a named person joining with the Jews of the community to build the προσευχή:[50] It is not clear from this inscription whether the chief of police was Jewish, or merely associated with the Jews in this matter.

Ὑπὲρ βασιλέως Πτολεμαίου καὶ βασιλίσσης Κλεοπάτρας Πτολεμαῖος Ἐπικύδου ὁ ἐπιστάτης τῶν φυλακιτῶν καὶ οἱ ἐν Ἀθρίβει Ἰουδαῖοι τὴν προσευχὴν Θεῶι ὑψίστωι.

For King Ptolemy and Queen Cleopatra, Ptolemy, son of Epikydos chief of police and the Jews of Athribis [? built] the προσευχή to the Most High God.

2 Inscription (1444) describes an addition to the προσευχή:[51]

Ὑπὲρ βασιλέως Πτολεμαίου καὶ βασιλίσσης Κλεοπάτρας καὶ τῶν τέκνων Ἑρμίας καὶ Φιλ(ω)τέρα ἡ γυνὴ καὶ τὰ παιδία τήνδε ἐξέδραν τῆι προσευχ(ῆι).

For King Ptolemy and Queen Cleopatra, and the[ir] children, Hermes and Philotera his wife and their children [built?] the portico on the προσευχή.

Here, as in 1443, it is not clear that the donors are definitely Jews.

---

[49] Frey, *Corpus*, II, p. 369; Lewis, 'Jewish Inscriptions', p. 142; Lifshitz, *Donateurs et fondateurs*, p. 79.
[50] Frey, *Corpus*, II, pp. 370-71; Lewis, 'Jewish Inscriptions', p. 142; Lifshitz, *Donateurs et fondateurs*, p. 79.
[51] Frey, *Corpus*, II, pp. 370-71; Lewis, 'Jewish Inscriptions', p. 143; Lifshitz, *Donateurs et fondateurs*, pp. 79-80.

Arsinoë-Crocodilopolis

1   A inscription for a προσευχή (1532a) from the middle of the third
century BCE, similar to the one found in Schedia (1440):[52]

> Ὑπὲρ βασιλέως Πτολεμαίου τοῦ Πτολεμαίου καὶ βασιλίσσης
> Βερενίκης τῆς γυναικὸς καὶ ἀδελφῆς καὶ τῶν τέκνων οἱ ἐν
> Κροκ[ο]δίλων πόλει Ἰουδ[αῖ]οι τὴν προ[σ]ε[υχὴν] ...

> For King Ptolemy and Queen Berenice, his wife and sister, and the[ir]
> children, the Jews in Crocodilopolis [? built] the προσευχή ...

Here also a verb relating the Jews to the προσευχή and indicating
the nature of their actions is lacking.

2   A papyrus recording a land survey in the late second century BCE
indicates the existence of a Jewish προσευχή on the outskirts of the
town. The relevant pieces are quoted below.

> Col. II
> 16   ... βο(ρρᾶ)
> προσευ(χή),   λι(βὸς)   περίστασις   πό(λεως),   ἀπη(λιώτου)
> Ἀργα(ίτιδος) διῶρυ(ξ)
> βο(ρρᾶ) [ἐ]χ[ο(μένης)] προσευχῆς Ἰουδαίων διὰ Περτόλλου ...

> ... to the north, a synagogue [*sic*]; to the west the city boundary; to
> the east the canal of Argaitis.
>   Situated to the north, a Jewish synagogue [*sic*] represented by
> Pertollos ...

> Col. III
> 29 γεί(τονες) νό(του) προσευχῆς Ἰουδαίων, βο(ρρᾶ) [καὶ λι(βὸς)]
> περίστα(σις) πόλεως ...

> ... Neighbours: to the south a Jewish synagogue [*sic*]; to the north
> and west the city boundary ...[53]

The papyrus indicates that the προσευχή was a considered to
belong to the same category as a consecrated garden, a store house,
an empty dove cote, other sacred land and houses.

3   Another papyrus from Arsinoë-Crocodilopolis, dated to 113 CE,
gives an account of the water supply in the municipality, including
details of payments to be made by certain bodies.

---

[52] Griffiths, 'Egypt and the Synagogue', pp. 3-4; Lewis, 'Jewish Inscriptions', p. 164;
Lifshitz, *Donateurs et fondateurs*, pp. 80-81.
[53] Tcherikover and Fuks, *Corpus papyrorum judaicarum*, I, pp. 247-49.

Col. III
57 ἀρχόντων Ἰ[ου]δαίων προσευχῆς Θηβαίων μηιναίω(ν) (δρ.) ρκη·
58 Παχὼν (δρ.) ρκ[η], Παῦνι (δρ.) ρκη, Ἐπεὶφ(δρ.) ρκη, Μεσορὴ (δρ.) ρκη,
59 ιζ (ἔτους) Θὼθ (δρ.) ρκη, Φαῶφι (δρ.) ρκη (γίνονται) (δρ.) ψ[ξη].
60 εὐχείου ὁμοίως Παχὼν (δρ.) ρκη, Παῦνι (δρ.) ρκη, Ἐπεὶφ (δρ.) ρκη, Μεσο(ρὴ)(δρ.) [ρκη] …

From the *archontes* of the synagogue [*sic*] of the Theban Jews 128 dr. monthly: Pachon, Payni, Epeiph, Mesore, 17th year, Thoth and Phaophi. Total 768 dr. From the *eucheion* likewise 128 dr. monthly: Pachon 128 dr., Payni 128 dr., Epeiph 128 dr., Mesore 128 dr., …[54]

Two Jewish prayer-houses are included in the list of customers, one referred to as a προσευχή and the other as a εὐχεῖον. The 'rulers of the προσευχή' of Theban Jews make the payment for water. This is the sole occurrence of that phrase used to describe Jews with responsibility and executive powers.

Also of interest is the fact that the monthly charge for the prayer-houses, both 128 drachma,[55] corresponding to 31 obols daily, is far greater than the charge of 18 obols made to a bath-house, or 13 obols for a brewery and 9 obols for a fountain. As the editors remark, 'the use of water in a Jewish synagogue [*sic*] might be extensive'.[56]

Philadelphia
A papyrus from the middle of the third century BCE suggests that the sabbath was observed by someone engaged in the building trade, since in the tally of bricks for each day of the week there is no entry for the seventh day, sabbath, the name of the day being written in place of a total of bricks.[57]

Col. I	Ἐπεὶφ		Col. I	Epeiph	
	ε	ἔχω πλίνθον		5th	I have on hand bricks
		τῆς παρὰ Φιλέα			from Phileas
		Τκ		920	
5	ς	Ἀ		6th	1000
	ζ	Σάββατα		7th	Sabbath
	η	Ἀ		8th	1000

---

[54] Tcherikover and Fuks, *Corpus papyrorum judaicarum*, II, pp. 220-24.
[55] Since 1 drachma = 7.25 obols, the monthly charge of 128 dr. per month of 30 days represents a daily charge of 31 obols.
[56] Tcherikover and Fuks, *Corpus papyrorum judaicarum*, II, p. 221.
[57] Tcherikover and Fuks, *Corpus papyrorum judaicarum*, I, pp. 136-37.

Alexandrou-Nesos

Only the right half remains of a papyrus that tells the story of a woman's complaint to King Ptolemy about a stolen mantle.[58] It indicates that there was a προσευχή of the Jews[59] there in 218 BCE, for the cloak is taken by a third party to the attendant (νακόρος) of the προσευχή to hold until the dispute can be tried. The relevant section, lines 4-7, reads:[60]

>] ... αἰσθομένης δέ μου κατε
> τὸ ἱμ]άτιον ἐν τῆι προσευχῆι τῶν Ἰουδαίων ἐπιλα
>]ωπους. ἐπιπαραγίνετα[ι] δὲ Λήζελμις (ἑκατοντάρουρος)
> το ἱμά]τιον Νικομάχωι τῶι νακόρωι ἕως κρίσεως

>] ... When I saw him, (?)
> the cl]oak in the prayer-house of the Jews (?)
>] (?). Lezelmis, a holder of 100 arourai, comes up to help
> the clo]ak to Nikomachos the attendant (to keep) until the case

As it is not clear whether any or all of the people concerned were Jews, less can be made of this text than would at first appear, but the προσευχή, as well as its attendant, had apparently quite definite civic standing and power in this village.

Oxyrhynchus

Two scraps of papyrus from Oxyrhynchus, one dated 7 BCE, and the other, in Latin, dated to the second century CE, mention the sabbath by name as a dating reference for the matter discussed in the missing parts of the documents.[61]

The first has only the partial phrase:

> ἕως Σαμβ[

till Sabbath.

The second is a fragment of a business letter in Latin; it indicates that the sabbath was known as a day that had an effect on some people's business transactions.

---

[58] Tcherikover and Fuks, *Corpus papyrorum judaicarum*, I, pp. 239-41.

[59] ἐν τῆι προσευχῆι τῶν Ἰουδαίων, with no reconstruction of the phrase.

[60] I have re-arranged the text as supplied by the editors to show more clearly that the right half of each line remains. I have also removed hyphens from the ends of the lines of the Greek text, and inserted square brackets at appropriate places in words in my English translation.

[61] Tcherikover and Fuks, *Corpus papyrorum judaicarum*, III, pp. 14-16.

d[.]i[..].[.]r
mandas
se·propter
sambatha
fac·itaque
emas·et
tradas
suimer[o]ti

. . .

... to have consigned (?) because of the Sabbath. Therefore be sure to buy and hand over to ...

Of unknown provenance, but acquired in Egypt

1 A badly preserved papyrus, possibly from the second half of the first century BCE in the reign of Cleopatra, seems to refer to a meeting of Jews in a προσευχή to discuss some business in the community.[62] The opening line of the text reads:

...] ἐπὶ τῆς γενηθείσης συναγωγῆς ἐν τῆι προσευχῆι

... At the session held in the proseuche

or, my translation:
... at the meeting of the synagogue in the προσευχή

The editors' translation seems to me to depend on an unwillingness to distinguish between προσευχή and συναγωγή, but this text seems to do that most effectively. In the προσευχή building the entity called the συναγωγή came into being in order to discuss common business. This agrees exactly with the model I have for the functioning of the synagogues of the Jews.

2 A broken slab of white marble, of which only the bottom right-hand corner survives, bears a dedication inscription (1433) for the sacred precinct, the προσευχή and its subsidiary buildings.[63] Lewis gives the provenance of the slab as Hadra.

[... θε]ῶι ὑψίστωι [ἐπηκόωι, τ]ὸν ἱερὸν [περίβολον καὶ] τὴν προσ[ευχὴν καὶ τὰ συγ]κύροντα.

---

[62] Tcherikover and Fuks, *Corpus papyrorum judaicarum*, I, pp. 252-54.

[63] Frey, *Corpus*, II, pp. 360-61; Lifshitz, *Donateurs et fondateurs*, p. 76 (the phrase 'la proseuque' is omitted from the translation); Lewis, 'Jewish Inscriptions', in Tcherikover and Fuks, *Corpus papyrorum judaicarum*, III, pp. 139-40.

... to the Most High God ... the sacred precinct and the προσευχή, and the outbuildings.

As can be seen, the reconstruction supplies a large proportion of the text, but it can be accepted on the basis of its similarity with the inscription from Nitriai (1442 above).

3 An inscription (1447) on the base of a statue in black granite, with a possible Alexandrian provenance, refers to a man who was the προστάτης of the synagogue. No date can be assigned to it.

Ἀρτέμον Νίκωνος πρ(οστατήσας)[64] τὸ ια' (ἔτος) τῇ συναγωγῇ...

Artemon, (son) of Nikon, having been προστάτης of the synagogue ... the eleventh year ...

The meaning of the reference to the eleventh year is not clear, but the position of προστάτης as an office within the synagogue is attested in the inscription from Xenephyris (1441 above).

4 A well-preserved inscription (1449) on a rectangular slab, found in Cairo, but of unknown original provenance, is written in Greek with a Latin coda.[65] The date is uncertain, but 270 CE, in the reign of Queen Zenobia and her son, has been suggested as a better estimate than the earlier suggestion of 44-30 BCE.

Βασιλίσσης καὶ βασιλέως προσταξάντων ἀντὶ τῆς
προανακειμένης περὶ τῆς ἀναθέσεως τῆς προσευχῆς ἡ
ὑπογεγραμμένη ἐπιγραφήτω. Βασιλεὺς Πτολεμαῖος Εὐεργέτης
τὴν προσευχὴν ἄσυλον.
REGINA ET REX IUSSER(UN)T.

On the orders of the queen and king, in place of the previous plaque about the dedication of the προσευχή let what is written below be written up. King Ptolemy Euergetes [proclaimed] the προσευχή inviolate.
The queen and king gave the order.

No reason has been discovered, or suggested, as to why a second inscription was necessary, or why the first one might have needed to have been renewed,[66] and as the inscription is likely to be late third century CE, it has only been included for comparison purposes, since

---

[64] The inscription has a symbol made of the two letters Π and P with Π superimposed on P.
[65] Frey, *Corpus*, II, pp. 374-76; Lewis, 'Jewish Inscriptions', p. 144.
[66] Tcherikover and Fuks, *Corpus papyrorum judaicarum*, I, p. 94.

it shows a late usage of the word προσευχή for a communal build-ing, and in that regard agrees with the Latin inscription from Mursa.

Cyrenaica

Berenice
Two inscriptions from Berenice provide important background to understanding the religious life of the Jewish community there.[67] One is well preserved, but the other is badly mutilated and depends on the first for decipherment. Both report the honouring of important public figures in exactly the same way by the local Jews, referred to here not as a synagogue, but as a πολίτευμα; it is the ἄρχοντες (rulers) and the πολίτευμα (ethnic group) who make the decision.

The honours conferred and the notification of them by means of an inscription are reminiscent of items with similar purposes reported by Philo for προσευχαί in Alexandria, when he refers to decorated slabs on the interior walls.[68] These inscriptions thus add to our knowledge of how Jews honoured Romans in ways that were accept-able to both groups.

The inscriptions also name some of the religious festivals of the Jews, but do not directly refer to the sabbath.

The first inscription honouring Decimus Valerius, who refur-bished the amphitheatre in Berenice, is damaged, and has date letters which are somewhat obliterated. It could be from 8–6 BCE, but Roux and Roux recommend a latitude in the dating of between 30 BCE and 100 CE.

The inscription to Decimus Valerius shows that the Jews decided to exonerate him from any public charges in return for his refurbish-ment of the amphitheatre, as well as honouring him at the assemblies and new moons and making the details of the honouring public by means of an inscribed stone stele in the amphitheatre.

The clearer inscription, honouring Marcus Tittius for his honest

---

[67] J. Roux and G. Roux, 'Un décret du politeuma des juifs de Bérénikè en Cyrénaïque', *Revue des études grecques* 62 (1949), pp. 281-96 (283-96); S. Applebaum, *Jews and Greeks in Ancient Cyrene* (Studies in Judaism in Late Antiquity, 28; Leiden: Brill, 1979), pp. 160-65, 192-93, but note that what Roux and Roux call the first inscription Applebaum generally calls the second, although in one paragraph on p. 161 he uses the opposite nomenclature, thus implying that both inscriptions refer to re-furbishing the amphitheatre.

[68] See discussion below.

and kind dealings with both the Jews and the Greek citizens of Berenice, is from 25 CE. There the Jews resolved, at the Feast of Tabernacles, to honour Marcus Tittius whenever they met together for assemblies and new moons. And they similarly decided to place the inscribed stele in the most publicly obvious place in the amphitheatre. But neither inscription refers to where the Jews met for these assemblies, indicating only the public place in which they put the commemorative stele.

These inscriptions show that first century Jews in Berenice celebrated assemblies (including the Feast of Tabernacles) and new moons. But there is no indication of where or how they celebrated them, and their communal building is not named.

21 ὧν χάριν ἔδοξε τοῖς ἄρχουσι καὶ τῶι πολιτεύ
    ματι τῶν ἐν Βερενίκῃ Ἰουδαίων ἐπαινέσαι τε αὐ
    τὸν καὶ στεφανοῦν ὀνομαστὶ καθ' ἑκάστην
    σύνοδον καὶ νουμηνίαν στεφάνωι ἐλαίνωι καὶ
25 λημνίσκωι· τοὺς δὲ ἄρχοντας ἀναγράψαι τὸ
    ψήφισμα εἰς στήλην λίθου παρίου καὶ θεῖναι εἰς
    τὸν ἐπισημότατον τόπον τοῦ ἀμφιθεάτρου
    Λευ   καὶ   πᾶ   σαι

On account of these things, it seemed good to the rulers and to the ethnic group of the Jews in Berenice both to honour him and crown him by name at every assembly and new moon with a crown of olive leaves and chaplet, and that the rulers should record the vote on a stele of Parian stone and place it in the most visible place in the amphitheatre.
All   votes   white.

The inscriptions share a common piece of text which deals with the nature of the honours accorded and with the involvement of the Jews in publicising that honour. This is presented here from the clearer of the two inscriptions, but the texts are identical, barring a few verbal flourishes.

However, although unfortunately another inscription from Berenice is available now only as a photograph,[69] it does refer to a synagogue building. This clear inscription, of twenty lines dating from the middle of the first century CE, is about the restoration of a

---

[69] ש. אפלבאום, כתובת יהודית חדשה מברניקי שבקירינאיקה [S. Applebaum. 'A New Jewish Inscription from Berenice in Cyrenaica'], *BIES* 25 (1961), pp. 167-74.

synagogue building and lists the names of the contributors.[70] The photograph of the slab shows that it was found as part of the wall of a building, and also shows that the language and lettering of this inscription are less precise than those on the two inscriptions on the Parian marble steles.[71]

("Ετει) β' Νέρωνος Κλαυδίου Καίσαρος Δρούσου
Γερμανικοῦ Αὐτοκράτορος χοϊάχ ισ'
ἐφάνη τῇ συναγωγῇ τῶν ἐν Βερενεικίδι
'Ιουδαίων τοὺς ἐπιδιδόντες εἰς ἐπισκευ
ἠν τῆς συναγωγῆς ἀναγράψαι αὐτοὺς εἰς στ
ήλην λίθου Παρίου vacat

In the second year of the rule of Nero Claudius Caesar Drusus Germanicus, Emperor, on the sixteenth of Khoïakh, it appeared [sic] to the synagogue of the Jews in Berenice to inscribe on a stele made of marble from Paros [the names of] those who had contributed to the restoration of the synagogue.

This inscription from Berenice in 56 CE is of vital interest for it provides the earliest, unequivocal, and dated, use of the word συναγωγή meaning a building. Both the Jewish community and their building are referred to independently in the text by the word 'synagogue' in this inscription.

Discussion of the Data about the Sabbath

The three epigraphical texts that refer to the sabbath occur in papyri found in Egypt. All three use the sabbath as a dating reference, and two indicate that the sabbath was somehow different from other days, the clearest indicating that the sabbath was a day on which no bricks were delivered. But there are no further details about the sabbath in any inscriptions from any of the locations surveyed here.

Applebaum, however, regards the assemblies of the Jews mentioned in the two inscriptions honouring Marcus Tittius and Decimus Valerius as referring to *sabbath* assemblies, as well as monthly gatherings and the New Year.[72] But this is not a faithful rendering of the

---

[70] Lifshitz, *Donateurs et fondateurs*, pp. 81-83.
[71] Applebaum, *Ancient Cyrene*, pp. 161-63; J. Robert and L. Robert, 'Bulletin Epigraphique: 514. Berenikè', *Revue des études grecques* 72 (1959), pp. 275-76.
[72] Applebaum, *Ancient Cyrene*, pp. 160-65, 193.

Greek texts on two counts: first, there is no way of identifying which
assemblies are meant, and second, the monthly gatherings when Jews
met were the new moons and not gatherings at any other recurring
monthly date. There is no clear allusion to either the sabbath or the
New Year as is implied by Applebaum.

It has to be concluded that whatever Jews did on the sabbath in all
the places surveyed here over the period prior to 200 CE, no details
or indications have survived on stone or papyrus.

Archaeological Data about Synagogues

There are no undisputed remains of synagogue buildings from the
first two centuries of the common era. What have been found do not
bear any written or pictorial details which would allow definite
identification of the buildings as synagogue buildings. Similarly
there are no inscriptions identifying those buildings as προσευχαί.
So because of the necessity of interpreting the evidence in order to
understand it, it must be presented alongside the discussion about its
meaning and implications.

Discussion of Synagogue Remains

That previously long-held beliefs about synagogues have been
recently opened to question can be seen in the critical re-assessment
of the evidence for early synagogues by several scholars.[73]

Grabbe is convinced of the existence of synagogues in the Diaspora from the second century BCE, accepting an equation of the

---

[73] J. Gutmann, 'Synagogue Origins: Theories and Facts', in *Ancient Synagogues: The
State of Research* (ed. J. Gutmann; Missoula: Scholars Press, 1981), pp. 1-6; J. Gut-
mann, 'The Origin of the Synagogue: The Current State of Research', in *The Syna-
gogue: Studies in Origins, Archaeology and Architecture* (ed. J. Gutmann; The Library
of Biblical Studies, ed. H.M. Orlinsky; New York: Ktav, 1975), pp. 72-76; E.M.
Meyers and J.F. Strange, *Archaeology, the Rabbis and Early Christianity* (London:
SCM Press, 1981), pp. 141-46; M. Chiat, 'First-Century Synagogue Architecture:
Methodological Problems', in *Ancient Synagogues: The State of Research* (ed. J.
Gutmann; Missoula: Scholars Press, 1981), pp. 49-60; A.R. Seager, 'Ancient
Synagogue Architecture: An Overview', in *Ancient Synagogues: The State of Research*
(ed. J. Gutmann; Missoula: Scholars Press, 1981), pp. 39-48 (43); L.L. Grabbe,
'Synagogues in Pre-70 Palestine: A Re-Assessment', *JTS* n.s. 39 (1988), pp. 401-10;
S.B. Hoenig, 'Temple-Synagogue' in *The Synagogue: Studies in Origins, Archaeology
and Architecture* (ed. J. Gutmann; The Library of Biblical Studies, ed. H.M. Orlinsky;
New York: Ktav, 1975), pp. 55-71

terms προσευχή and συναγωγή,[74] but he finds the archaeological evidence for synagogue buildings in Palestine to be slender before the first century of the Common Era. Meyers and Strange see a burgeoning of the synagogue as a fully fitted and decorated building in the third century CE, but not before then. Gutmann, Seager, and Chiat take the stance that there are no certain first-century synagogue remains in Palestine, and Gutmann's criteria for identifying the building at Gamla as a (later) synagogue are: the seating, the two entrances, the heart-sectioned corner columns and a carving of a rosette.[75]

Others believe that there were synagogue buildings in Palestine before the destruction of the Temple.[76] Yadin claims that the finding of portions of a scroll below the floor of a chamber at Masada is certain proof of a synagogue there before 74 CE.[77] Foerster accepts first-century dates for the buildings identified as synagogues at Masada, Herodium, Chorazin, Migdal and Gamla, using as criteria similarities with other types of securely dated buildings, such as temples at Dura-Europos,[78]

Sharing the view that there were first century synagogue buildings, Ma'oz gives the latest possible date for the building at Gamla as 67 CE, for it was then that the Romans destroyed the city, and then he modifies the views of Gutmann as to its date of building.[79] He concludes that the Gamla building was erected between 23 BCE and 41 CE, using both literary evidence from Josephus, and stratigraphic evidence of coins and pottery to make this judgement. He also remarks on the rosette motif as being a design found on Jewish tombs, but he does not give the criteria by which he decided that the building was a synagogue.

Chiat takes these authors to task on methodological grounds. She first objects to the lack of evidence or argumentation to show that buildings in Palestine took buildings from Dura-Europos as their model, and that they can be validly identified as religious buildings

---

[74] Grabbe, 'Synagogues', pp. 402-403.

[75] Levine, *Ancient Synagogues*, p. 34.

[76] L.I. Levine, ed., *Ancient Synagogues Revealed* (Jerusalem: The Israel Exploration Society, 1981), pp. 11-12 and *passim*.

[77] Levine, *Ancient Synagogues*, pp. 21-22.

[78] Levine, *Ancient Synagogues*, pp. 24-29.

[79] Levine, *Ancient Synagogues*, pp. 35-36.

by means of similarities with temples found there. Then she resists
the assumption that there was 'a uniform widespread Jewish religious ceremony during the era of the Second Temple that would
require a particular type of building', and refuses to accept that
premise since no evidence has been provided for it.[80] She sees
assumptions being used to interpret archaeological data, and is
adamant against the acceptance of any conclusions arrived at by such
methods.

Thereafter she demolishes the claims made by Foerster about the
similarity of the buildings he calls first-century Palestine synagogues,
by presenting the data in numerical and tabular form so that
differences become apparent. Her judgement is that the two buildings built by Herod at Masada and Herodium were chambers, in the
style of *triclinia*, for the use of Herod's entourage, and that the
buildings at Gamla, Migdal, and Chorazin were village assembly
halls. She does not dispute the first-century origin of these five
buildings, but resists the claim that they were built specifically to suit
Jewish religious requirements.

The archaeological remains of buildings cannot lie about the
functions of the buildings, but the scholarly 'readers' of such remains
may bring assumptions to bear that allow them to see in the stones
what others do not see. Until all scholars can find the evidence
unequivocal, the existence of first-century synagogue buildings in
Palestine remains, in my estimation, unproven.

Discussion on Inscriptions about Prayer-Houses and Synagogues

Prayer-House Buildings

Greek inscriptions from the third century BCE in Arsinoë-
Crocodilopolis, from the second century BCE in Delos, Xenephyris
and Nitriai, from the first or second century BCE in Athribis (2), from
the first century BCE in Alexandria, Berenice (2), from the first
century CE in Gorgippia, Panticape, and from the second century CE
in Panticape, along with undated ones from Olbia, Panticape,
Schedia and three of unknown provenance and date all point to the
existence of prayer-house buildings known as προσευχαί in all the
provinces of the central and eastern Mediterranean.

---

[80] Chiat, 'Methodological Problems', p. 51.

Latin inscriptions from Rome and from the late second century CE in Mursa show that similar buildings were known by the Latin name *proseucha*. And papyri from Egypt, from Alexandrou-Nesos in the third century BCE and from Arsinoë-Crocodilopolis in the late second century BCE, confirm the inscriptional evidence.

That these prayer-houses were controlled by Jews is indicated by three inscriptions from Panticape and one from Olbia on the northern shores of the Black Sea and also by seven inscriptions from five places in Egypt. There are also papyri from three Egyptian sites, two of which coincide with the sources of the inscriptions, confirming this connection.

An interesting feature of the papyrus from Arsinoë-Crocodilopolis detailing the accounts of the water department there is the fact that the 'rulers' are referred to as 'rulers of the προσευχή', an expression equivalent to the later title 'ruler of the synagogue' or indicative of a role with respect to the community building; in either sense there is a possible bridge between the concept of 'ruler of the synagogue' as leader in a community, and the later usage of 'ruler of the syna-gogue' to mean a person with responsibility for a synagogue building.

Seven dedication slabs from προσευχαί in Egypt have as their opening a reference to the ruling king and queen. The French trans-lations of the inscription render ὑπέρ as 'in honour of', but that shows more veneration than is warranted, and I have rejected that translation as being too strong. But it should be noted that the very first line of all such inscriptions is given to this naming of the rulers. And there is a similar first section in the Latin inscription from Mursa, indicating that the practice was not confined to Egyptian Jewry addressing Egyptian rulers.

Perhaps these inscriptions, and these translations, have con-tributed to the views of Rivkin, referred to in Chapter 3, that Jews built προσευχαί and dedicated them to their ruler in order to avoid having to introduce statues of the rulers. Such statues would have to be worshipped, or addressed in some way, in their meeting-houses,[81] and that would be anathema to the Jews. By dedicating the whole building to the rulers, the problem could be side-stepped, for in some

---

[81] Rivkin, 'Ben Sira', pp. 350-51.

sense the building dedicated to the ruler could be thought of as an offering to the glory of the ruler, and in that guise might satisfy the ruler's expectations of loyalty. Jews wishing to live peaceably under their rulers could make such non-idolatrous dedications without feeling compromised.

However, none of the inscriptions or papyri links the Jews and the προσευχή with any kind of Jewish worship, or with any Jewish assembly whatsoever, apart from, apparently, those involved in the enfranchisement of slaves and in hearings about petty thefts.

Synagogues as Groups of Jews

Many of the inscriptions refer to the role of archisynagogos, ruler of a synagogue. This is a person who rules over others and has been chosen by them to do so. Other inscriptions record that the 'synagogue of the Jews' made a decision, or conferred honours or privileges. In these usages 'synagogue' clearly means the group of people and cannot mean a building.

The catacomb inscriptions provide a reliable literary witness to the existence of sixteen Jewish groups or 'synagogues'—most of which had officials with distinct titles—in Rome around the turn of the era, and Latin inscriptions in two other sites in Italy indicate Jewish groups there also.

An Egyptian papyrus of the first century BCE, and an undated inscription, both of unknown provenance, indicate that there were groups of Jews known as 'synagogues'.

A door lintel from Corinth inscribed with the words 'the synagogue of the Hebrews' points to the existence of a Jewish group using that building there at the time. While this could be evidence of a building known as a synagogue, the inscription on the lintel is not, *per se*, necessarily evidence that the building was known by the name synagogue. What is certain is that *either* there was a building used by a group of people known by that name *or* there was a building known by that name. The value of this inscription is that it shows a possible means by which the name 'synagogue' could become transferred from the group to the building.

In Asia Minor the synagogues of the Jews had an important role to play in the community, and they exercised some sort of civic power. At Panticape in the first and second centuries CE, the synagogue of the Jews was involved in guaranteeing the continuing

freedom of enfranchised slaves. At Phocaea the synagogue honoured
a woman benefactor in the third century CE, as did the synagogue of
Acmonia in the first, or possibly second, century CE. At both Smyrna
and Synnada inscriptions record the existence of a person acting as
archisynagogos around the second century CE.

The importance of the first Panticape inscription (683) to this discussion is that it employs the two words συναγωγή and προσευχή in
ways which clearly confirm the distinction between them, namely
that the building associated with the community life of the Jews is
the προσευχή, whereas the community itself is described as the
synagogue.

Also clear from this and the other two inscriptions from Panticape[82] is the fact that the Jewish synagogue was in some sense a
civic body which had been accorded responsibility and authority in
the town, whether officially or unofficially. The public ceremony of
the freeing of slaves took place in the προσευχή and under the aus-
pices of the synagogue of the Jews.

Other civic functions of the synagogue of the Jews included honouring citizens with inscriptions and privileges. Thus Tation, a
woman of Phocaea, was given a golden crown and seating privileges
as a result of building work donated to the οἶκος there. And although
the similar inscription from Acmonia can be dated no more exactly
than to some time after the reign of Nero, it is similar, and honours
Lucius and Popilios Zotikos with a gilded shield for their restoration
of a building, an οἶκος otherwise described as 'their goodwill and
enthusiasm towards the synagogue'.

The translation of the last phrase of the inscription is not straightforward, and depends on one's understanding of grammar and syntax. As 'synagogue' is definite in the last line it should refer back to
the previous usage of the word, where it meant 'the community', and
that is the reading I have followed. Also the building under discussion is referred to at the beginning of the inscription by the word
οἶκος so it is not likely that another word, particularly one already
used to mean the community, would be employed to indicate the
building at the end of the inscription. So, in my judgement,
'synagogue' means the group of Jews in both places where it occurs

---

[82] Cf. also the undated inscription from Gorgippia.

in this inscription, but it has been taken by others to mean a synagogue building.

It is not clear from the inscriptions from Acmonia whether the crowns and shield were objects given to the benefactors, or placed in the προσευχαί as decorations near the inscription, or whether they were carved parts of the framework of the inscription. It is therefore tempting, although there are not exact verbal parallels, to assimilate the reference to the golden crown given to Tation at Phocaea, and the gilded shields awarded to the benefactors at Acmonia, with Philo's references to the presence in προσευχαί of 'shields and gilded crowns and the slabs and inscriptions'.[83] The two practices seem similar and appear to be designed to allow quasi-public recognition of the goodwill expressed to Jews by other Jews or by Romans without breaking the second commandment.

Also similar is the practice recorded twice for Berenice, in Cyrenaica. The 'synagogue' of the Jews honoured Marcus Tittius and Decimus Valerius, both in the same way by inscribing on a marble stele, placed in a most conspicuous spot, their decision to honour these men with a crown of olives at every assembly. This is in harmony with the avowals of both Philo and Josephus that the Jews gave honour, though not worship, to people who deserved it. Here, in Berenice as elsewhere, the synagogue of the Jews had civic power, for they could place inscribed steles in the public amphitheatre.

But although both inscriptions refer to the holding of regular Jewish assemblies, they do not state the names of the Jewish assemblies, other than new moons and the Feast of Tabernacles, nor give the name of the Jews' communal building.[84]

In Jerusalem, near Mount Ophel, a representative from each of three generations of the one family served as archisynagogos of a Jewish community there, some time in the first two centuries CE. The Theodotus inscription shows the existence of the group 'the synagogue' preceding the existence of the synagogue building by some fifty or so years.

This survey of inscriptions and papyri shows that the use of the

---

[83] Philo, *Embassy* 133, has ἀσπίδων καὶ στεφάνων ἐπιχρύσων καὶ στηλῶν καὶ ἐπιγραφῶν (shields and gilded crowns and stelae and inscriptions); and the inscriptions have the phrases χρυσῷ στεφάνῳ (gilded crown), and ὅπλῳ ἐπιχρύσῳ (gilded shield).

[84] See discussion on the synagogue building in Berenice below.

word 'synagogue' or the phrase 'synagogue of the Jews' to mean the group of Jews who made decisions and carried them out is widespread in all the regions studied here. The only variant is at Olbia where the phrase 'rulers of the προσευχή' occurs in situations where a corporate act is envisaged.[85]

The inscriptions indicate the existence of Jewish groups called 'synagogues', which had appreciable civic power. But the only religious function ascribed to these groups, and that at Berenice only, is their commitment to holding assemblies and new moon festivities.

Synagogues as Buildings
Inscriptions which refer to restoration of a synagogue, or the addition of a portico or water fittings, clearly speak of buildings and not people.

Two undated mosaics from Aegina (772, 723) refer to the restoration of synagogue buildings, but such evidence as there is suggests that they are later than the second century CE.

The undated inscription (738) in which the Jews of Phocaea honour Tation on account of her extension and refurbishment of the building there does not add anything to our information about Jewish synagogues as buildings, for the word used for the building is οἶκος.

The Julia Severa inscription (766) from, perhaps, the end of the first century CE, also refers to a building called an οἶκος, and to later officials who expressed their regard for the synagogue by building works. Some scholars believe that this refers to a synagogue building but the grammar of the inscription makes that at least suspect and in my view unlikely. The synagogue here is the Jewish group of which these enthusiasts were members.

The most certain reference to a synagogue building from the first century CE is now available only as a photograph of an inscription found at Berenice.[86] The fact that names of contributors to the restoration of the synagogue are inscribed on a stele indicates that there was a building in Berenice called a synagogue. Of interest is the fact that the lettering and grammar of the inscription are not up to the standard of the two inscriptions placed in the amphitheatre. Pos-

---

[85] At Arsinoë-Crocodilopolis, the phrase 'rulers' is used on its own. Another variant occurs in the papyrus from Alexandrou-Nesos where the phrase 'the prayer-house of the Jews' (ἡ προσευχὴ τῶν Ἰουδαίων) occurs in reference to the building.
[86] *BIES* 25 (1961), pp. 167-74 (photograph on p. 170).

sibly this indicates a Jewish stone-cutter working on the slab in the synagogue building, certainly someone less expert than the carver of the inscriptions to Marcus Tittius and Decimus Valerius.

But the most problematic of the inscriptions—as far as interpretation is concerned—is the Theodotus inscription (1404) from Mount Ophel in Jerusalem which is usually regarded as providing proof of the existence of a synagogue in Jerusalem in the first century CE. This 'existence' of a synagogue is then taken to be 'proof' of weekly worship services close to the temple. But a closer reading shows that several assumptions have to be made to reach that conclusion. Reading the text of the inscription without assumptions points to rather a different conclusion.

The ten lines of inscription commemorate a man who ruled the synagogue after his father and grandfather (3 lines), and who had built this synagogue, a building in which the reading of the Law took place and the teaching of the Commandments (2 lines). Also important enough to merit space in the inscription is the hospitality suite, with 'water fittings' for the accommodation of travellers (2.5 lines). The inscription closes with another reference to the building process and the Elders (2.5 lines).

The inscription commemorates three generations of a Jewish family, and, in particular, the man who ruled the synagogue—succeeding his father and grandfather in that office—and who built the synagogue, a building in which the reading of the law took place and the teaching of the commandments.[87] The first two generations in the family did not 'build' this synagogue, although they 'ruled' it. They were responsible for the foundations, but they could hardly rule over those. So they were rulers of the *gathering*, and their grandson was the one who provided or completed the *building*.[88]

We should note that the building was not one room only, designed for study, for important enough to merit space in the inscription is the hospitality suite, with 'water fittings', for the accommodation of travellers. The stone which bears the inscription was obviously part of a building which acted as a place for withdrawal from daily life, to

---

[87] No mention is made of the day or days on which the law would be read or on which teaching took place; daily could be just as likely as weekly if this were our only indication of the practice.

[88] Cf. Lk. 7.5 for a literary reference to someone building a synagogue, in this case a Roman centurion, apparently not a member of the synagogue.

read and study Torah, and no doubt Jews who were travelling needed a place with guest chambers in which to rest—perhaps during a sabbath break in a journey.[89]

This picture, of the synagogue as a vital community centre as well as a place for withdrawal from daily life, is in complete accord with the picture we find in the works of Josephus, Philo and the New Testament, but with the addition of the idea of hostel as well. However, in common with the other sources studied, there is no mention of any communal practices—other than reading and teaching—being carried out in the synagogue. And the sabbath is not referred to at all.

If this stone could be accurately dated, it would give some idea of when Jews built synagogues in Jerusalem. But unfortunately one of the methods for dating this stone, palaeography, suggests quite widely differing results.

The discussion in the scholarly literature, dating from the first quarter of the present century, is dominated by the views and conclusions of Clermont-Ganneau to such an extent that neither the article by Reinach,[90] who obsequiously agrees with Clermont-Ganneau, nor that of Vincent,[91] who attempts, timorously, to present an alternate dating and provenance, give the exact reference to his first, I think, oral presentation.[92] The inscription was kept secret at first for fear of 'foreign' scholars outstripping the results of the French archaeological team.

It is difficult to pinpoint the arguments of Clermont-Ganneau, even using his article,[93] largely because he supports his conclusions—in the main—by means of speculation and bombast.

Vincent's views are referred to by Reinach as an 'ingénieux petit roman', and are refuted by that means alone. Vincent, while taking the trouble to flatter Clermont-Ganneau in his article,[94] also tries to

---

[89] Filson, 'Synagogue Inscriptions', p. 45, assumes that the inscription was set up where it could be seen by local or visiting Jews, but he does not state whether he means by that that it was on the outside or inside wall of the synagogue.

[90] T. Reinach, 'L'inscription de Théodotus', *Revue des études juives* 71 (1920), pp. 46-56.

[91] L.L. Vincent, 'Découverte de la "Synagogue des affranchis" à Jérusalem', *RB* 30 (1921), pp. 247-77.

[92] Reinach, 'L'inscription de Théodotus', p. 52; Vincent, 'Découverte', pp. 256-57.

[93] C. Clermont-Ganneau, 'Découverte à Jérusalem d'une synagogue de l'époque hérodienne', *Syrie* 1 (1920), pp. 190-97.

[94] Vincent, 'Découverte', p. 256.

present a case for a date in the first third of the second century.[95]
However his arguments comparing the inscription with inscriptions
from the reigns of Augustus and Nerva—though based on palaeo-
graphic arguments that I find at least as convincing as those of
Clermont-Ganneau that compare the script with the inscription from
Herod's Temple—seem to have been ignored or by-passed by the
scholarly world. Yet his dating—by palaeography—to the reign of
Hadrian seems every bit as plausible as the earlier dating of
Clermont-Ganneau.

But after all their palaeographic arguments have been deployed,
both come to their conclusions by means of their separate ideas of
the identities of the persons named in the inscription. Thus, as far as
they were concerned, the dating was not made on palaeographic
grounds. The palaeography merely supported the other, equally
imprecise, arguments.

Vincent's extension of the possible dating obtained by palaeographic means down to the time of Hadrian makes a dating of post-
135 CE also a possibility, but he, finally, moves away from that position by various arguments based on conflating references to the
proper names of the inscription in other classical sources with references in Acts and finally declares that the synagogue housing the
inscription fell in 70 CE.[96]

The whole discussion is fraught with circumlocutions hinting at
the strain of preserving professional etiquette in situations where
scholarship and personalities are at odds. As a result I find it impossible to agree with any of the proposals of these arguing scholars and
conclude that neither the palaeographic method, nor the investiga-
tions as to likely bearers of the proper names, can give an precise
date for the Theodotus inscription.

These same scholars also try the approach of historical reconstruction and suggest that because, as they see it—in my opinion
erroneously—three generations of one family knew the synagogue
'building', it 'must have' stood on Mount Ophel for 70 years or so.
Therefore, because it 'must either have been built before the Temple
was destroyed in 70 CE, or after 135 CE'—since it was 'unlikely' that
the Romans would have sanctioned such building between those

---

[95] Vincent, 'Découverte', pp. 263-71.
[96] Vincent, 'Découverte', p. 277.

years—the synagogue must have been built by about the turn of the era. But, as this argument depends on the premise of a religious function for the building, it is not clear to me that the Romans would have had to sanction the building of a study hall with guest chambers—whether Jewish or not.

As a result of the consensus of this enclave of scholars, many modern scholars accept a pre-70 CE date for the Theodotus inscription, without realising how fragile is its basis, and go on from that to make generalised statements about synagogues and Judaism in first-century Palestine, including such inferences as the ritual use of water.[97]

In short the Theodotus inscription is not certain evidence of the existence of a pre-70 CE synagogue in Jerusalem; it may well belong to a much later building. And any constructions built on the evidence of the stone are not data in themselves.

Conclusions from the Archaeological and Epigraphic Evidence

There are a few conclusions which can be made with complete certainty.

1 Jews in many parts of the Greek-speaking Diaspora[98] maintained communal buildings called προσευχαί in which they exercised civic functions for the community and venerated their rulers by dedicatory inscriptions. In Latin-speaking regions the buildings were called *proseuchae*, and one inscription, from Mursa, carries an expression of loyalty to the Emperor similar to Greek inscriptions.

2 Jews in Palestine did not as a rule call their communal buildings προσευχαί.[99]

3 In Asia Minor the Jews made use of a building called an οἶκος, and there are no inscriptions referring to προσευχαί in Asia Minor.

4 In Berenice the Jews met together to celebrate assemblies, new

---

[97] Brooten, *Women Leaders*, pp. 24-26; M. Goodman, *State and Society in Roman Galilee AD 132–212* (Oxford Centre for Postgraduate Hebrew Studies; Totowa, NJ: Rowman & Allanheld, 1983), p. 86.

[98] Delos, Olbia, Panticape, Gorgippia, and many sites in Egypt.

[99] Apart from Josephus's description of the προσευχή at Tiberias, and the reference to a προσευχή at Philippi in Acts 16.13, 16.

moons and the feast of booths, and their building was called a 'synagogue' in the first century CE.

5 Jews had communal buildings in Palestine in the first century CE, but there is no clear evidence that they were built for a specifically religious function, nor that they were known by a specific name. In later centuries there were similar or more elaborate buildings called 'synagogues' in which Jewish religious and educational gatherings were held.

6 The Jews of a town or village were known communally as the 'synagogue of the Jews' in Egypt, Asia Minor and in towns on the northern shores of the Black Sea. The 'synagogues of the Jews' had a public voice and a public memory. They had standing in the community and could mediate in disputes and give honours to local citizens of worth.

7 There was in Jerusalem—in the first or second century CE—a synagogue in which the teaching of the law and the reading of the commandments took place, and hospitality was given to travellers.

from the literary texts already studied. There is no indication of gatherings for worship on the sabbath.

CHAPTER NINE

CONCLUSIONS

Introduction

This study has presented what may be known about the sabbath
worship activities of non-priestly Jews in the cities and towns of the
eastern Mediterranean, through the period up to 200 CE. The results
are mainly negative. If collective sabbath worship, or even daily
worship offered also on the seventh day, took place in those Jewish
communities few descriptions of it have survived, and those relate to
the priests of the Jerusalem Temple and to members of particularly
religious groups of Jews. Communal sabbath religious rituals and
practices for non-priestly Jews are not described in any of the
surviving texts.

The Evidence from the Texts

For non-priestly Jews what the Hebrew Bible prescribes is rest on the
sabbath. They have no religious duties peculiar to the sabbath. Some
texts indicate that special sabbath activities were required from the
priests in the Jerusalem Temple. The priests had to work on the
sabbath, as on other days, and in some texts (Num. 28–29; Ezek. 45–
46) they are instructed to offer extra sacrifices on each sabbath day.

The early post-biblical Jewish writings provide a variety of views
about the importance of the sabbath in the lives of their authors.
Some texts ignore the sabbath completely—even where mention of it
might be expected, as in the description of the religiously observant
life led by Tobit. Other texts, for example the Dead Sea Scrolls,
require a strong commitment to the sabbath from the membership of
the Qumrân group. They provide many strict rules curbing both
behaviour and thought on the sabbath and they also provide an
inventory of liturgical texts that suggests that the Qumrân community

had a regular practice of singing a particular psalm on the numbered sabbaths throughout the year.

The Apocryphal and Deutero-Canonical works do not present a unified picture of the sabbath—many books make no reference to sabbath at all. The few texts that do refer to the sabbath portray it as a highly significant day. In Judith and in the Books of the Maccabees the sabbath is regarded as a holy entity with some kind of existence in its own right. The sabbath day is to be protected, or shown respect, and it can influence one's behaviour on the day before as well.

The book of *Jubilees* conveys an attitude to the sabbath that has much of the strictness shown by the texts from the Dead Sea community. Many actions are there prohibited which are not forbidden in the Hebrew Bible or in the Apocryphal and Deutero-Canonical works. Punishment is harsher, including the death penalty for sabbath-breaking. But also in this book—alone among those studied—is an injunction to positive action on the sabbath, namely, that the readers are to eat, drink, be content and bless God.

In brief, from the non-biblical Jewish texts we discover that while the Qumrân community held worship gatherings on the sabbath, as they did on other days, the most that was required of any other observant Jews in the way of positive activity on the sabbath was blessing God and being content. As my definition of worship depends on the worshippers' awareness that they are communally addressing their worship activities to their god, this activity of blessing God could count as worship, but only if the blessing were to be given communally. However, this is domestic sabbath celebration.

In the writings of Philo and Josephus, separated either by distance or time from the practices of the Jerusalem Temple, the communal gatherings of Jews for prayers, festivals, or sabbath, were of groups called 'synagogues' and in buildings called προσευχαί and—by Josephus—συναγωγαί. These sabbath gatherings are depicted as comprising reading and listening to the law with a time for explanation and discussion thereafter.

The account Josephus gives of the prolonged three-day complex of events at the προσευχή in Tiberias includes various activities—prayers, public fast and sabbath assembly—but for the sabbath gathering he describes only a general assembly in which a heated political discussion took place and the interruption of that meeting for the regular sabbath meal at noon. There is no reference to prayers or psalms—or even, for that matter, to reading Torah—in his account of that sabbath in the προσευχή in Tiberias.

Both these cultured and educated Jewish writers describe the sabbath gatherings—and the privileges accorded them under Roman law—several times, but they refer to no worship activities whatsoever. This, of course, does not rule out the possibility that worship took place, but if we have no evidence of it we must remain at a loss about its possible ritual content.

The secular Greek and Roman writers noticed, in the main, the domestic aspects of the Jewish religion. So, for the sabbath, Persius describes a Friday evening meal of fish with wine, served after the lamps had been lit. Seneca knows of the lighting of sabbath lamps—also referred to by Josephus—and portrays it as a religious act carried out by Jews in worship of their god. Many of the writers regarded the Jews' sabbath inaction as 'idleness', but Frontinus recognised it as the fulfilment of a religious obligation. What is of greatest interest for the present study is that the writers observed nothing distinctive in the Jews' sabbath behaviour apart from their inactivity. They knew of prayer-houses as buildings obvious to passers-by when thronged with Jews, but they never connect prayer-houses with sabbath—as if they had never seen Jews congregating at prayer-houses on that day.

The gospels contain several stories about the actions or teaching of Jesus on the sabbath. But the main thrust of the argument they make is that Jesus had the power to supersede the sabbath law and could redefine suitable sabbath activity. The stories reveal little about what happened in the 'synagogues' of Jesus' day. Part of the reason for this, I believe, is that the gospel writers are writing out of their own social world and portray 'synagogues' as they knew them—synagogues later than the time of Jesus, synagogues where Jews were in opposition to Christians. What is more, the gospel stories set in the 'synagogues' are not told for the purpose of giving a description of what happened there; it is to make persuasive arguments about the value of Jesus in reforming the Jewish religion. But what the gospel accounts of synagogues do show is that the gatherings were informal and flexible in structure, allowing interactions, healings, discussions and disputes to take place—all in the normal course of the sabbath morning's activities.

The early Christian writers spend much of their literary energy in encouraging their respective flocks to be busily active on the sabbath so that they will not be mistaken for Jews. They also require them to celebrate their seventh day of rest and worship distinctively on Sunday. But they make no reference to the Jews doing anything active on the sabbath; rather they simply make ironic comments about the Jews' trust in idleness as a way of showing honour to God. They do not appear to be aware of special sabbath gatherings of Jews; they treat all gatherings of Jews indiscriminately, and in the same inimical way.

The Mishnah adds little to what has been discovered from the other texts. There the rules about the sabbath gathering make the privileging of the sabbath readings from Torah quite overt, and the prescribing of seven readers for the sabbath, who must stand and read singly from the Torah, shows that the sabbath gathering was somewhat more important than the gatherings on Mondays and Thursdays. But details about any worship activities that should be included in the sabbath gathering are entirely lacking.

The data from archaeological and epigraphic materials, representing Jewish life across the Mediterranean world, confirm what has been found in the literary texts. The 'synagogue' of the Jews was normally, at least up to the first century CE, a group of men who met together. Sometimes these 'synagogues' met in a building called a προσευχή or an οἶκος or—in one place—a συναγωγή. There is no archaeological or epigraphic evidence that points unequivocally to the existence of synagogue buildings in first-century Palestine, although there exists a photograph of one inscription that refers to a synagogue building in the North African city of Berenice during the reign of Nero. First-century 'synagogues' are—on the whole—groups of male Jews. Any architectural remains of synagogue buildings in Palestine belong to a time later than the first century CE.

The lack of convincing evidence—whether archaeological, epigraphic or literary—of the existence of 'synagogue' buildings during the first century makes the belief in sabbath worship 'services' at that time difficult to sustain. It is only in the last few years of the century that Josephus writes of synagogue buildings in Dora, Antioch and Caesarea. And while Philo and the Graeco-Roman authors are familiar with Jewish prayer-houses they do not depict them as places where sabbath worship took place. To be sure, Philo—and Josephus too—speaks of reading and study of Torah, but both these Jews depict the activity as being essentially philosophical and educational, rather than part of a ceremony of worship. Luke's depictions of the synagogue activities are closely similar to theirs—only the reading and discussing of texts are described.

Evidence that the sabbath was celebrated in a domestic setting, with lamps being lit and a meal of fish and wine, is found in the writings of Persius and Seneca and in the Mishnah. But there is no unequivocal evidence that the sabbath was a day of worship for non-priestly Jews certainly as far as the end of the second century of the Common Era. Public, collective worship was an annual, or daily, but not a weekly, activity.

BIBLIOGRAPHY

Ancient Authors

Apuleius, *Metamorphoses* (tr. J.A. Hanson; LCL; Cambridge, MA: Harvard University Press, 1989).

Artemidorus, *The Interpretation of Dreams: Oneirocritica* (tr. R.J. White; Noyes Classical Studies; Park Ridge, NJ: Noyes, 1975).

Augustine, *The City of God against the Pagans*, II (tr. W.H. Green; LCL; Cambridge, MA: Harvard University Press, 1963).

Barnabas, *Epître de Barnabé* (ed. and tr. P. Prigent and R.A. Kraft; Sources Chrétiennes; Paris: Les Editions du Cerf, 1971).

——*The Epistle of Barnabas*, in *The Apostolic Fathers* (tr. A. Roberts and J. Donaldson; *Ante-Nicene Christian Library*, 1; Edinburgh: T. & T. Clark, 1867), pp. 97-135.

Cicero, *Pro Flacco*, in *Cicero*, X (tr. C. MacDonald; LCL; Cambridge, MA: Harvard University Press, 1977).

——*Pro Fonteio* in *Cicero*, XIV (tr. N.H. Watts; LCL; Cambridge, MA: Harvard University Press, 1972).

——*Pro Scauro* in *Cicero*, XIV (tr. N.H. Watts; LCL; Cambridge, MA: Harvard University Press, 1972).

Cleomedes, in Cléomède, *Théorie élémentaire: De motu circulari corporum caelestium* (tr. R. Goulet; Librairie Philosophique; Paris: J. Vrin, 1980).

——in *Cleomedis de motu circulari corporum caelestium* (tr. H. Ziegler; Leipzig: Teubner, 1891).

Epictetus, *Discourses*, preserved by Arrianus, in *The Discourses of Epictetus* (tr. G. Long; London: George Bell and Sons, 1890).

——*Moral Discourses: Enchiridion and Fragments* (tr. E. Carter; London: J.M. Dent & Sons, 1910).

——*The Discourses of Epictetus* (tr. W.A. Oldfather; LCL; Cambridge, MA: Harvard University Press, 1980).

Frontinus, *Stratagems*, in *The Stratagems and the Aqueducts of Rome* (tr. C.E. Bennett, rev. M.B. McElwain; LCL; Cambridge, MA: Harvard University Press, 1980).

Galen, *De pulsuum differentiis*, in M. Stern, M., *Greek and Latin Authors on Jews and Judaism. II. From Tacitus to Simplicius* (Jerusalem: The Israel Academy of Sciences and Humanities, 1980), pp. 313-15.

Hippolytus, *Refutation of All Heresies*, in *Hippolytus, Bishop of Rome*, 2 (tr. J.H. MacMahon; *Ante-Nicene Christian Library*, 6; Edinburgh: T. & T. Clark, 1868).

——*Refutation of All Heresies*, in M. Marcovich, *Refutatio omnium haeresium* (Patristische Texte und Studien, 25; Berlin: de Gruyter, 1986).

Horace, *Satires* in *Satires, Epistles and Ars Poetica* (tr. H.R. Fairclough; LCL; Cambridge, MA: Harvard University Press, 1970).

Ignatius, in *Ignace d'Antioche and Polycarpe de Smyrna*, *Lettres. Martyre de Polycarpe* (tr. P.T. Camelot; Sources Chrétiennes; Paris: Les Editions du Cerf, 1969).

——*The Epistles of Ignatius (Shorter and Longer)*, in *The Apostolic Fathers* (tr. A. Roberts and J. Donaldson; *Ante-Nicene Christian Library*, 1; Edinburgh: T. & T. Clark, 1897), pp. 137-267.

Josephus, *The Life*, in *Josephus*, I (tr. H.St.J. Thackeray; LCL; Cambridge, MA: Harvard University Press, 1926).

——*Against Apion*, in *Josephus*, I (tr. H.St.J. Thackeray; LCL; Cambridge, MA: Harvard University Press, 1926).

——*Jewish War*, Books I–III, in *Josephus*, II (tr. H.St.J. Thackeray; LCL; Cambridge, MA: Harvard University Press, 1976).

——*Jewish War*, Books IV–VII, in *Josephus*, III (tr. H.St.J. Thackeray; LCL; Cambridge, MA: Harvard University Press, 1928).

——*Jewish Antiquities*, Books I–IV, in *Josephus*, IV (tr. H.St.J. Thackeray; LCL; Cambridge, MA: Harvard University Press, 1930).

——*Jewish Antiquities*, Books XII–XIV, in *Josephus*, VII (tr. R. Marcus; LCL; Cambridge, MA: Harvard University Press, 1961).

——*Jewish Antiquities*, Books XV–XVII, in *Josephus*, VIII (tr. R. Marcus; LCL; Cambridge, MA: Harvard University Press, 1963).

——*Jewish Antiquities*, Books XVIII–XX, in *Josephus*, IX (tr. L.H. Feldman; LCL; Cambridge, MA: Harvard University Press, 1965).

Justin, *The First Apology*, in *The Writings of Justin Martyr and Athenagoras* (tr. M. Dods; *Ante-Nicene Christian Library*, 2; Edinburgh: T. & T. Clark, 1897).

——*The Second Apology*, in *The Writings of Justin Martyr and Athenagoras* (tr. M. Dods; *Ante-Nicene Christian Library* 2; Edinburgh: T. & T. Clark, 1897).

——*The Dialogue with Trypho, a Jew*, in *The Writings of Justin Martyr and Athenagoras* (tr. G. Reith; *Ante-Nicene Christian Library*, 2; Edinburgh: T. & T. Clark, 1897).

Justinus, *Historiae Philippicae*, in *Justin Cornelius Nepos and Eutropius* (tr. J.S. Watson; London: George Bell and Sons, 1902).

Juvenal, *Satires*, in *Juvenal and Persius* (tr. G.G. Ramsay; LCL; Cambridge, MA: Harvard University Press, 1940).

——*Satires*, in *Sixteen Satires upon the Ancient Harlot* (tr. S. Robinson; Manchester: Carcanet, 1983).

——*Satires*, in *Juvenal: The Sixteen Satires* (tr. P. Green; Harmondsworth, Middlesex: Penguin, 1967).

Martial, *Epigrams* (tr. W.C.A. Ker; LCL; Cambridge, MA: Harvard University Press, 1919; rev. edn, 1968).

——*Epigrammes*, I–II (tr. H.J. Izaac; Paris: Les Belles Lettres, 1930).

——*The Epigrams of Martial* (London: Bohn, 1860).

——*Epigrams*, in *Martial: The Twelve Books of Epigrams* (tr. J.A. Pott and F.A. Wright; London: George Routledge & Sons, n.d., ca 1921–1936).

Meleager, *The Greek Anthology*, I (tr. W.R. Paton; LCL; Cambridge, MA: Harvard University Press, 1916).

——in P. Whigham and P. Jay, *The Poems of Meleager* (London: Anvil Press, 1975).

Ovid, *The Art of Love*, in *Ovid*, II (tr. J.H. Mozley, rev. G.P. Goold; LCL; Cambridge, MA: Harvard University Press, 1979).

Persius, *Satires*, in *Juvenal and Persius* (tr. G.G. Ramsay; LCL; Cambridge, MA: Harvard University Press, 1940).

——*Satires*, in *The Satires of A. Persius Flaccus* (tr. J. Conington; Oxford: Clarendon Press, 1893).

——*Satires*, in *Persius: The Satires* (tr. J.R. Jenkinson; Warminster: Aris & Phillips, 1980).

Petronius, *The Satyricon of Petronius* (tr. W. Arrowsmith; Ann Arbor: University of Michigan Press, 1959).

——*Petrone: Le Satyricon* (tr. A. Ernout; Paris: Les Belles Lettres, 1950).

——*The Satyricon of T. Petronius Arbiter* (tr. W. Burnaby, 1694; ed. C.K. Scott Moncrieff; The Abbey Classics: London, n.d., ca 1961).

——*Petronius* (tr. M. Heseltine; Cambridge, MA: Harvard University Press, 1975).

Philo, *Cherubim*, in *Philo*, II (tr. F.H. Colson and G.L. Whitaker; LCL; Cambridge, MA: Harvard University Press, 1929).

——*Abraham*, in *Philo*, VI (tr. F.H. Colson and G.L. Whitaker; LCL; Cambridge, MA: Harvard University Press, 1935).

——*On Dreams*, in *Philo*, V (tr. F.H. Colson and G.L. Whitaker; LCL; Cambridge, MA: Harvard University Press, 1949).

——*Moses*, in *Philo*, VI (tr. F.H. Colson; LCL; Cambridge, MA: Harvard University Press, 1935).

——*The Decalogue*, in *Philo*, VII (tr. F.H. Colson; LCL; Cambridge, MA: Harvard University Press, 1937).

——*The Special Laws*, I, in *Philo*, VII (tr. F.H. Colson; LCL; Cambridge, MA: Harvard University Press, 1937).

——*The Special Laws*, II, in *Philo*, VII (tr. F.H. Colson; LCL; Cambridge, MA: Harvard University Press, 1937).

——*Every Good Man is Free*, in *Philo*, IX (tr. F.H. Colson; LCL; Cambridge, MA: Harvard University Press, 1960).

——*On the Contemplative Life*, in *Philo*, IX (tr. F.H. Colson; LCL; Cambridge, MA: Harvard University Press, 1960).

——*Flaccus*, in *Philo*, IX (tr. F.H. Colson; LCL; Cambridge, MA: Harvard University Press, 1960).

——*Hypothetica*, in *Philo*, IX (tr. F.H. Colson; LCL; Cambridge, MA: Harvard University Press, 1960).

——*The Embassy to Gaius*, in *Philo*, X (tr. F.H. Colson; LCL; Cambridge, MA: Harvard University Press, 1962).

Pliny the Younger, *C. Plinii Caecilii secundi: Epistulae ad Traianum imperatorem cum eiusdem responsis* (tr. E.G. Hardy; London: Macmillan, 1889).

——*The Letters of Pliny the Younger* (tr. B. Radice; Harmondsworth, Middlesex: Penguin, 1963).

Pompeius Trogus, preserved in Justinus, *Historiae Philippicae*, in *Justin Cornelius Nepos and Eutropius* (tr. J.S. Watson; London: George Bell and Sons, 1902).

Plutarch, *De superstitione* in *Plutarch's Moralia*, II (tr. F.C. Babbitt; LCL; Cambridge, MA: Harvard University Press, 1928).

——*De la superstition* in *Plutarque: Oeuvres morales*, II (tr. J. Dafradas, J. Hani and R. Klaerr; Paris: Les Belles Lettres, 1985).

——*Quaestiones conviviales* (tr. H.B. Hoffleit), in *Plutarch's Moralia*, VIII (tr. P.A. Clement and H.B. Hoffleit; LCL; London: Heinemann, 1969).

——*Propos de table* in *Plutarque: Oeuvres morales*, VIII (tr. F. Fuhrmann; Paris: Les Belles Lettres, 1978).

Seneca, *Ad Lucilium epistulae morales* (tr. R.M. Gummere; LCL; Cambridge, MA: Harvard University Press, 1925).

——*On Superstition*, preserved in Augustine, *The City of God against the Pagans*, II (tr. W.H. Green; LCL; Cambridge, MA: Harvard University Press, 1963).

Suetonius, *The Lives of the Caesars*, II in *Suetonius*, I (tr. J.C. Rolfe; LCL; Cambridge, MA: Harvard University Press, 1914).

Tacitus, *Histories*, in *Tacitus in Five Volumes*, III (tr. C.H. Moore and J. Jackson; LCL; Cambridge, MA: Harvard University Press, 1969).

——*The History of Tacitus* (tr. A.J. Church and W.J. Brodribb; London: Macmillan, 1927).

Tertullian, *Tertullianus against Marcion* (tr. P. Holmes; *Ante-Nicene Christian Library*, 7; Edinburgh: T. & T. Clark, 1868).

——*Apology*, in *The Writings of Tertullian*, I (tr. A. Roberts and J. Donaldson; *Ante-Nicene Christian Library*, 11; Edinburgh: T. & T. Clark, 1869), pp. 53-140.

——*On Idolatry*, in *The Writings of Tertullian*, I (tr. S. Thelwall; *Ante-Nicene Christian Library*, 11; Edinburgh: T. & T. Clark, 1869), pp. 141-77.

——*To the Nations (To the Heathen)*, in *The Writings of Tertullian*, I (tr. P. Holmes; *Ante-Nicene Christian Library*, 11; Edinburgh: T. & T. Clark, 1869), pp. 416-506.

——*An Answer to the Jews*, in *The Writings of Tertullian*, III (tr. S. Thelwall; *Ante-Nicene Christian Library*, 18; Edinburgh: T. & T. Clark, 1897), pp. 201-58.

Tibullus, *Books I–III*, in *Catullus, Tibullus and Pervigilium Veneris* (tr. F.W. Cornish, J.P. Postgate and J.W. Mackail; LCL; Cambridge, MA: Harvard University Press, 1968).

Modern Authors

Albright, W.F. and Mann, C.S., *Matthew* (The Anchor Bible, 26; Garden City, NY: Doubleday, 1971).

Allen, W.C., *A Critical and Exegetical Commentary on the Gospel according to S. Matthew* (Edinburgh: T. & T. Clark, 1907).

Andersen, F.I, and Freedman, D.N., *Hosea: A New Translation with Introduction and Commentary* (The Anchor Bible, 24; Garden City, NY: Doubleday, 1980).

Andreasen, N.-E.A., *The Old Testament Sabbath: A Tradition-Historical Investigation* (SBLDS, 7; Missoula: SBL, 1972).

Applebaum, S., *Jews and Greeks in Ancient Cyrene* (Studies in Judaism in Late Antiquity, 28; Leiden: Brill, 1979).

——'A New Jewish Inscription from Berenice in Cyrenaica', ‫ש. אפלבאם‬ ‫כתובת יהודית חדשה מברניקי שבקירינאיקה,‬ *BIES*25 (1961), pp. 167-74.

Argyle, A.W., *The Gospel according to Matthew* (CBC; Cambridge: CUP, 1963).

Bacchiocchi, S., *From Sabbath to Sunday: A Historical Investigation of the Rise of Sunday Observance in Early Christianity* (Rome: The Pontifical Gregorian University Press, 1977).

Baillet, M., *Qumrân Grotte 4. III. 4Q482–4Q520* (DJD, 7; Oxford: OUP, 1982).

Barnard, L.W., *Justin Martyr: His Life and Thought* (Cambridge: CUP, 1967).

Barrett, C.K., *A Commentary on the First Epistle to the Corinthians* (London: A. & C. Black, 1968).

Bartlett, J.R., *The First and Second Books of the Maccabees* (CBC; Cambridge: CUP, 1973).

Batten, L.W., *The Books of Ezra and Nehemiah* (ICC; Edinburgh: T. & T. Clark, 1913).

Baumgarten, J.M., 'The Counting of the Sabbath', *Vetus Testamentum* 16 (1966), pp. 277-86.

——'Recent Discoveries and Halakhah in the Hellenistic-Roman Period', in S. Talmon, ed., *Jewish Civilization in the Hellenistic-Roman Period* (Sheffield: JSOT Press and Philadelphia: Trinity Press International, 1991), pp. 147-58.

Bell, H.I., *Jews and Christians in Egypt* (London: The Trustees of the British Museum, 1924).

Blackman, P., *Mishnayoth*. II. *Order Mo'ed* (New York: The Judaica Press, 1963).

Blenkinsopp, J., *Ezra–Nehemiah: A Commentary* (OTL; London: SCM Press, 1988).

Bowman, J., *The Gospel of Mark: The New Christian Jewish Passover Haggadah* (Studia Post-Biblica, 8; Leiden: Brill, 1965).

Branscomb, B.H., *The Gospel of Mark* (The Moffatt New Testament Commentary; London: Hodder & Stoughton, 1937).

Breccia, E., *Inscriptiones graecae Aegypti. II. Inscriptiones nunc Alexandriae in museo* (Chicago: Ares Publishers, 1978).

Brooten, B.J., *Women Leaders in the Ancient Synagogue* (Brown Judaic Studies, 36; Chico, CA: Scholars Press, 1982).

Brown, R.E., *The Gospel according to John, I–XII* (The Anchor Bible, 29; Garden City, NY: Doubleday, 1966).

Bruce, F.F., *Commentary on the Book of Acts* (The New London Commentary on the New Testament; London: Marshall, Morgan & Scott, 1954).

—— *1 and 2 Corinthians* (New Century Bible; London: Oliphants, 1971).

Camelot, P.T., tr., *Ignace d'Antioche: Lettres* (Sources Chrétiennes; Paris: Les Editions du Cerf, 1969).

Carson, D.A., 'Jesus and the Sabbath in the Four Gospels', in *From Sabbath to Lord's Day: A Biblical, Historical and Theological Investigation* (ed. D.A. Carson; Grand Rapids: Zondervan, 1982), pp. 57-97.

Charlesworth, J.H., *The Old Testament Pseudepigrapha*, II (London: Darton, Longman & Todd, 1985).

Chiat, M., 'First-Century Synagogue Architecture: Methodological Problems', in *Ancient Synagogues: The State of Research* (ed. J. Gutmann; Missoula: Scholars Press, 1981), pp. 49-60.

——*Handbook of Synagogue Architecture* (Brown Judaic Studies, 29; Chico, CA: Scholars Press, 1982).

Clements, R.E., *God and Temple* (Oxford: Blackwell, 1965).

Clermont-Ganneau, C., 'Découverte à Jérusalem d'une synagogue de l'époque hérodienne', *Syrie* 1 (1920), pp. 190-97.

Coggins, R.J., *Ezra and Nehemiah* (CBC; Cambridge: CUP, 1976).

Collins, A.Y., 'Insiders and Outsiders in the Book of Revelation', in *The Jews among Pagans and Christians* (London: Routledge, 1992), pp. 187-218.

Conington, J., tr., *The Satires of A. Persius Flaccus* (Oxford: Clarendon Press, 1893).

Conzelmann, H., *Acts of the Apostles* (Hermeneia; Philadelphia: Fortress Press, 1987).

Cooke, G.A., *The Book of Ezekiel* (ICC; Edinburgh: T. & T. Clark, 1936).

Courtney, E.B., *A Commentary on the Satires of Juvenal* (London: The Athlone Press, 1980).

Danby, H., *The Mishnah* (Oxford: OUP, 1933).

Davids, P.H., *The Epistle of James* (The New International Greek Testament Commentary; Exeter: Paternoster Press, 1982).

Davies, W.D. and Allison, D.C., *The Gospel according to Matthew*, I (ICC; Edinburgh: T. & T. Clark, 1988).

——*The Gospel according to Matthew*, II (ICC; Edinburgh: T. & T. Clark, 1991).

Derrett, J.D.M., 'Mark's Technique: The Haemorrhaging Woman and Jairus'

Daughter', in his *Studies in the New Testament*, IV (Leiden: Brill, 1986), pp. 30-61.

Dressler, H.H.P., 'The Sabbath in the Old Testament', in *From Sabbath to Lord's Day: A Biblical, Historical and Theological Investigation* (ed. D.A. Carson; Grand Rapids: Zondervan, 1982), pp. 21-41.

Edersheim, A., *The Life and Times of Jesus the Messiah*, 2 vols. (London: Longmans, 1897).

Edwards, R.A., *Matthew's Story of Jesus* (Philadelphia: Fortress Press, 1985).

Fensham, F.C., *The Books of Ezra and Nehemiah* (New International Commentary on the Old Testament; Grand Rapids: Eerdmans, 1982).

Fenton, J.C., *The Gospel of St Matthew* (Harmondsworth, Middlesex: Penguin, 1963).

Ferguson, E., *Backgrounds of Early Christianity* (Grand Rapids: Eerdmans, 1987).

Filson, F.V., *A Commentary on the Gospel according to St Matthew* (Black's New Testament Commentaries; London: A. & C. Black, 1960).

——'Ancient Greek Synagogue Inscriptions', *The Biblical Archaeologist* 32 (1969), pp. 41-46.

Fisch, S., *Ezekiel* (Soncino Books of the Bible; Hindhead, Surrey: The Soncino Press, 1950).

Fitzmyer, J.A., *The Gospel according to Luke I–IX* (The Anchor Bible, 28; Garden City, NY: Doubleday, 1981).

——*The Gospel according to Luke X–XXIV* (The Anchor Bible, 28a; Garden City, NY: Doubleday, 1985).

Frey, J.-B., *Corpus inscriptionum judaicarum. I. Europe* (rev. B. Lifshitz, ed.; New York: Ktav, 1975).

——*Corpus inscriptionum judaicarum. II. Asie–Afrique* (Città del Vaticano, Rome: Pontificio Istituto di Archeologia Cristiana, 1952).

Gager, J.G., *The Origins of Anti-Semitism* (Oxford: OUP, 1985).

Glatt, D.A., and Tigay, J.H., 'Sabbath', in *Harper's Bible Dictionary* (ed. P.J. Achtemeier; San Francisco: Harper & Row, 1985), pp. 888-89.

Goldenberg, R., 'The Jewish Sabbath in the Roman World up to the Time of Constantine the Great', in *ANRW* II.19.1 (Berlin: de Gruyter, 1979), pp. 411-47.

——'The Sabbath in Rabbinic Judaism', in *The Sabbath in Jewish and Christian Traditions* (ed. T.C. Eskenazi, D.J. Harrington and W.H. Shea; New York: Crossroad, 1991), pp. 31-44.

Goldstein, J.A., *I Maccabees: A New Translation with Introduction and Commentary* (The Anchor Bible, 41; Garden City, NY: Doubleday, 1976).

——*II Maccabees: A New Translation with Introduction and Commentary* (The Anchor Bible, 41a; Garden City, NY: Doubleday, 1983).

Goodman, M., *State and Society in Roman Galilee AD 132–212* (Oxford Centre for Postgraduate Hebrew Studies; Totowa, NJ: Rowman & Allanheld, 1983).

Goudge, H.L., *The First Epistle to the Corinthians* (Westminster Commentaries; London: Methuen, 1911).

Gould, E.P., *A Critical and Exegetical Commentary on the Gospel according to Mark* (ICC; Edinburgh: T. & T. Clark, 1896).

Goulet, R., tr., Cléomède, *Théorie élémentaire: De motu circulari corporum caelestium* (Librairie Philosophique; Paris: J. Vrin, 1980).

Grabbe, L.L., 'Synagogues in Pre-70 Palestine: A Re-Assessment', *JTS* n.s. 39 (1988), pp. 401-10.

Grant, M., *The Jews in the Roman World* (London: Weidenfeld & Nicolson, 1973).

Gray, J., *I and II Kings: A Commentary* (OTL; 3rd edn; London: SCM Press, 1977).

Green, P., tr., *Juvenal: The Sixteen Satires* (Harmondsworth, Middlesex: Penguin, 1967).

Greenberg, M., 'Sabbath', in *Encyclopaedia Judaica*, XIV (Jerusalem: Keter Publishing House, 1972), pp. 558-62.

Griffiths, J.G., 'Egypt and the Rise of the Synagogue', *JTS* n.s. 38 (1987), pp. 1-15.

Gundry, R.H., *Matthew: A Commentary on his Literary and Theological Art* (Grand Rapids: Eerdmans, 1982).

Gutmann, J., 'Synagogue Origins: Theories and Facts', in *Ancient Synagogues: The State of Research* (ed. J. Gutmann; Missoula: Scholars Press, 1981), pp. 1-6.

——ed., *Ancient Synagogues: The State of Research* (Missoula: Scholars Press, 1981).

——'The Origin of the Synagogue: The Current State of Research', in *The Synagogue: Studies in Origins, Archaeology and Architecture* (ed. J. Gutmann; The Library of Biblical Studies, ed. H.M. Orlinsky; New York: Ktav, 1975), pp. 72-76.

Guy, F., 'The Lord's Day in the Letter of Ignatius to the Magnesians', *AUSS* 2 (1964), pp. 1-17.

Haenchen, E., *The Acts of the Apostles: A Commentary* (tr. B. Noble, G. Shinn and H. Anderson, rev. R.McL. Wilson; Oxford: Blackwell, 1971).

Handelman, S.A., *The Slayers of Moses: The Emergence of Rabbinic Interpretation in Modern Literary Theory* (Albany: State University of New York Press, 1982).

Hannah, J.W., 'The Setting of the Ignatian Long Recension', *JBL* 79 (1960), pp. 221-38.

Haran, M., *Temples and Temple-Service in Ancient Israel* (Oxford: Clarendon Press, 1978).

Hare, D.R.A., *The Theme of Jewish Persecution of Christians in the Gospel according to St Matthew* (SNTS Monograph Series, 6; Cambridge: CUP, 1967).

Harrington, D.J., 'Sabbath Tensions', in *The Sabbath in Jewish and Christian Traditions* (ed. T.C. Eskenazi, D.J. Harrington and W.H. Shea; New York: Crossroad, 1991), pp. 47-56.

Harvey, R.A., *A Commentary on Persius* (Mnemosyne Supplements, 64; Leiden: Brill, 1981).

Hasel, G.F., 'The Sabbath in the Pentateuch', in *The Sabbath in Scripture and History* (ed. K.A. Strand; Washington, DC: Review and Herald Publishing Corporation, 1982), pp. 21-43.

Hauret, C., *Amos et Osée* (Paris: Beauchesne, 1969).

Hengel, M., *Judaism and Hellenism: Studies in their Encounter in Palestine during the Early Hellenistic Period*, 2 vols. (tr. J. Bowden; London: SCM Press, 1974).

——*Acts and the History of Earliest Christianity* (London: SCM Press, 1979).

Herbert, A.S., *Worship in Ancient Israel* (Ecumenical Studies in Worship, 5; London: Lutterworth, 1959).

Héring, J., *The First Epistle of Saint Paul to the Corinthians* (tr. A.W. Heathcote and P.J. Allcock; London: Epworth Press, 1962).

Highet, G., *Juvenal the Satirist: A Study* (Oxford: Clarendon Press, 1954).

Hill, D., *The Gospel of Matthew* (New Century Bible; London: Oliphants, 1972).

Hoenig, S.B., 'The Ancient City-Square: The Forerunner of the Synagogue', in *ANRW* II.19.1 (Berlin: de Gruyter, 1979), pp. 448-76.

——'Temple-Synagogue', in *The Synagogue: Studies in Origins, Archaeology and Architecture* (ed. J. Gutmann; The Library of Biblical Studies, ed. H.M. Orlinsky; New York: Ktav, 1975), pp. 55-71.

Horbury, W., 'The Benediction of the Minim' in *JTS* n.s. 33 (1982), pp. 19-61.

Jenkinson, J.R., tr., *Persius: The Satires* (Warminster: Aris & Phillips, 1980).

Juster, J., *Les Juifs dans l'empire romain: Leur condition juridique, économique et sociale*, 2 vols. (Burt Franklin Research & Source Works Series, 79; New York: Burt Franklin, reprint, n.d.; first published Paris, 1914).

Kaiser, O., *Isaiah 1–12: A Commentary* (English translation of 5th German edition; OTL; London: SCM Press, 1983).

Kee, H.C., 'The Transformation of the Synagogue after 70 CE: Its Import for Early Christianity', *NTS* 36 (1990), pp. 1-24.

Knowling, R.J., *The Epistle of St James* (Westminster Commentaries; London: Methuen, 1904).

Kraabel, A.T., 'The Diaspora Synagogue: Archaeological and Epigraphic Evidence', in *ANRW* II.19.1 (1979), pp. 477-510.

——'The Roman Diaspora: Six Questionable Assumptions', *JJS* 33 (1982), pp. 445-64.

——'Synagoga Caeca', in *'To See Ourselves as Others See Us'* (ed. J. Neusner and E.S. Frerichs; Chico, CA: Scholars Press, 1985), pp. 219-46.

Kraus, H.-J., *Worship in Israel* (tr. G. Buswell; Oxford: Blackwell, 1966).

Kubo, S., 'The Sabbath in the Intertestamental Period', in *The Sabbath in Scripture and History*, ed. K.A. Strand (Washington, DC: Review and Herald Publishing Corporation, 1982), pp. 57-69.

Latyschev, B., ed., *Inscriptiones antiquae orae septentrionalis ponti Euxini graecae et latinae. I. Inscriptiones Tyrae, Olbiae, Chersonesi Tauricae aliorum locorum a Danubio usque ad regnum Bosporanum* (2nd edn; Petersburg, 1916; r.p. Hildesheim: Georg Olms Verlagsbuchhandlung, 1965).

——*Inscriptiones antiquae orae septentrionalis ponti Euxini graecae et latinae.* II: *Inscriptiones regni Bosporani graecae et latinae* (2nd edn; Petersburg, 1916; r.p. Hildesheim: Georg Olms Verlagsbuchhandlung, 1965).

Leaney, A.R.C., *The Jewish and Christian World 200 BC to AD 200* (Cambridge Commentaries on the Writings of the Jewish and Christian World 200 BC to AD 200, 7; Cambridge: CUP, 1984).

Lee, G., *Tibullus: Elegies: Introduction Text, Translation and Notes* (2nd edn; Liverpool Latin Texts [Classical and Mediaeval], 3; Liverpool: Frances Cairns, The University of Liverpool, 1982).

Leon, H.J., *The Jews of Ancient Rome* (Philadelphia: The Jewish Publication Society of America, 1960).

Levine, L.I., *Caesarea under Roman Rule* (Studies in Judaism in Late Antiquity, 7; Leiden: Brill, 1975).

——ed., *Ancient Synagogues Revealed* (Jerusalem: The Israel Exploration Society, 1981).

Lewis, D.M., 'Appendix I: The Jewish Inscriptions of Egypt', in *Corpus papyrorum Judaicarum*, III (ed. V.A. Tcherikover, A. Fuks and M. Stern; Cambridge, MA: Harvard University Press, 1964), pp. 138-66.

Lewis, R.B., 'Ignatius and the "Lord's Day"', *AUSS* 6 (1968), pp. 46-59.

Lieu, J., 'History and Theology in Christian Views of Judaism', in *The Jews among Pagans and Christians* (London: Routledge, 1992), pp. 79-96.

Lifshitz, B., *Donateurs et fondateurs dans les synagogues juives: Répertoire des dédicaces grecques relatives à la construction et à la réfection des synagogues* (Cahiers de la Revue Biblique, 7; Paris: Gabalda, 1967).

Lightfoot, J.B., *The Apostolic Fathers*, Part 2, *S. Ignatius, S. Polycarp* (London: Macmillan, 1889).

Lincoln, A.T., 'Sabbath, Rest, and Eschatology in the New Testament', in *From Sabbath to Lord's Day: A Biblical, Historical and Theological Investigation* (ed.

D.A. Carson; Grand Rapids: Zondervan, 1982), pp. 197-220.

Lindars, B., *The Gospel of John* (New Century Bible; London: Oliphants, 1972).

Long, G., tr., *The Discourses of Epictetus* (London: George Bell and Sons, 1890).

Lüdemann, G., *Early Christianity according to the Tradition in Acts: A Commentary* (tr. J. Bowden; London: SCM Press, 1989).

McKay, H.A., 'New Moon or Sabbath?', in *The Sabbath in Jewish and Christian Tradition* (ed. T.C. Eskenazi, D.J. Harrington and W.H. Shea; New York: Crossroad, 1991), pp. 13-27.

——'From Evidence to Edifice: Four Fallacies about the Sabbath', in *Text as Pretext: Essays in Honour of Robert Davidson* (ed. R.P. Carroll; JSOT Supplement Series, 138; Sheffield: JSOT Press, 1992), pp. 179-99.

MacLennan, R.S., *Early Christian Texts on Jews and Judaism* (Brown Judaic Studies, 194; Chico, CA: Scholars Press, 1982).

Marcovich, M., ed., *Hippolytus: Refutatio omnium haeresium* (Patristische Texte und Studien, 25; Berlin: de Gruyter, 1986).

Marshall, I.H., *The Gospel of Luke: A Commentary on the Greek Text* (The New International Greek Testament Commentary; Exeter: Paternoster Press, 1978).

Mattill, A.J., 'The Value of Acts as a Source for the Study of Paul', in *Perspectives on Luke–Acts* (ed. C.H. Talbert; Edinburgh: T. & T. Clark, 1978), pp. 76-98.

Mayor, J.B., *The Epistle of St. James* (London: Macmillan, 1897).

Mays, J.L., *Hosea: A Commentary* (OTL; London: SCM Press, 1969).

Meeks, W.A., Breaking Away', in *'To See Ourselves as Others See Us'* (ed. J. Neusner and E.S. Frerichs. Chico, CA: Scholars Press, 1985), pp. 93-116.

Meeks, W.A., and R.L. Wilken, *Jews and Christians in Antioch in the First Four Centuries of the Common Era* (Missoula: Scholars Press, 1978).

Meyer, H.A.W., *Critical and Exegetical Handbook to the Epistles to the Corinthians* (tr. D.D. Bannerman and W.P. Dickson; Edinburgh: T. & T. Clark, 1877).

Meyers, E.M., and J.F. Strange, *Archaeology, the Rabbis and Early Christianity* (London: SCM Press, 1981).

Micklem, P.A., *St Matthew* (London: Methuen, 1917).

Michael, J.H., 'The Jewish Sabbath in the Latin Classical Writers', *AJSL* 40 (1924), pp. 117-24.

Montgomery, J.A., *A Critical and Exegetical Commentary on the Book of Kings* (ICC; Edinburgh: T. & T. Clark, 1951).

Moore, C.A., *Judith: A New Translation with Introduction and Commentary* (The Anchor Bible, 40; Garden City, NY: Doubleday, 1985).

Morgenstern, J., 'Sabbath', in *The Interpreter's Dictionary of the Bible*, IV (New York: Abingdon Press, 1962), pp. 137-39.

Murdoch, W.G.C., 'The Sabbath in the Prophetic and Historical Literature of the Old Testament', in *The Sabbath in Scripture and History* (ed. K.A. Strand; Washington, DC: Review and Herald Publishing Corporation, 1982), pp. 44-56.

Myers, J.M., *Ezra. Nehemiah* (The Anchor Bible, 14; Garden City, NY: Doubleday, 1965).

——*I and II Esdras: Introduction, Translation and Commentary* (The Anchor Bible, 42; Garden City, NY: Doubleday, 1974).

Nelson, R.D., *First and Second Kings* (Atlanta: John Knox Press, 1987).

Neusner, J., *Formative Judaism: Religious, Historical, and Literary Studies* (Brown Judaic Studies, 37; Chico, CA: Scholars Press, 1982).

Neusner, J. and E.S. Frerichs, ed., *'To See Ourselves as Others See Us'* (Chico, CA: Scholars Press), 1985.

Newsom, C., *Songs of the Sabbath Sacrifice: A Critical Edition* (Harvard Semitic Studies, 27; Atlanta: Scholars Press, 1985).

North, R., 'Sabbath', in *New Catholic Encyclopedia*, XII (Washington, DC: McGraw–Hill, 1967), pp. 778-82.

Oppenheimer, A., *The 'Am Ha-Aretz* (Arbeiten zur Literatur und Geschichte des hellenistischen Judentums, 8; Leiden: Brill, 1977).

Otzen, B., *Judaism in Antiquity: Political Development and Religious Currents from Alexander to Hadrian* (The Biblical Seminar, 7; Sheffield: JSOT Press, 1990).

Pesch, R., *Die Apostelgeschichte*, 2 vols. (EKK; Neukirchen–Vluyn: Benziger Verlag, 1986).

Posner, R., 'Synagogue', in *Encyclopaedia Judaica*, XV (Jerusalem: Keter Publishing House, 1972), pp. 579-95.

Pott, J.A. and F.A. Wright, *Martial: The Twelve Books of Epigrams* (London: George Routledge & Sons, n.d., ca 1921–1936).

Prigent, P., and Kraft, R.A., ed. and tr., *Epître de Barnabé* (Sources Chrétiennes; Paris: Les Editions du Cerf, 1971).

Ramsay, G.G., tr., *Juvenal and Persius* (LCL; Cambridge, MA: Harvard University Press, 1940).

Rattray, S., 'Worship', in *Harper's Bible Dictionary* (ed. P.J. Achtemeier; San Francisco: Harper & Row, 1985), pp. 1143-47.

Rawlinson, A.E.J., *St Mark* (Westminster Commentaries; London: Methuen, 1925).

Reinach, T., 'L'inscription de Théodotus' , *Revue des études juives* 71 (1920), pp. 46-56.

Richardson, C.C., *The Christianity of Ignatius of Antioch* (New York: AMS Press, 1967).

Riesner, R., *Jesus als Lehrer* (Wissenschaftliche Untersuchungen zum Neuen Testament, II/7; Tübingen: J.C.B. Mohr, 1981).

Rivkin, E., 'Ben Sira and the Nonexistence of the Synagogue: A Study in Historical Method', in *In the Time of Harvest: Essays in Honor of Abba Hillel Silver* (New York: Macmillan, 1963), pp. 320-54.

Robert, J. and L. Robert, 'Bulletin Epigraphique: 514. Berenikè', *Revue des études grecques* 72 (1959), pp. 275-76.

Robinson, S., tr., *Sixteen Satires upon the Ancient Harlot* (Manchester: Carcanet, 1983).

Ropes, J.H., *A Critical and Exegetical Commentary on Epistle of St. James* (ICC; Edinburgh: T. & T. Clark, 1916).

Rordorf, W., *Sunday: The History of the Day of Rest and Worship in the Earliest Centuries of the Christian Church* (London: SCM Press, 1968).

Roux, J. and G. Roux, 'Un décret du politeuma des juifs de Bérénikè en Cyrénaïque', *Revue des études grecques* 62 (1949), pp. 281-96.

Rowley, H.H., *Worship in Ancient Israel* (London: SPCK, 1967).

Russell, D.A., *Plutarch* (London: Duckworth, 1973).

Safrai, S., ed., *The Literature of the Sages*, I (Assen: van Gorcum, 1987).

Saldarini, A.J., 'Synagogue', in *Harper's Bible Dictionary* (ed. P.J. Achtemeier; San Francisco: Harper & Row, 1985), pp.1007-1008.

Sanders, E.P., *Jewish Law from Jesus to the Mishnah: Five Studies* (London: SCM Press, 1990).

Sanders, J.A., *The Psalms Scroll of Cave 11* (DJD, 4; Oxford: Clarendon Press, 1972).

Sanders, J.T., *The Jews in Luke–Acts* (London: SCM Press, 1987).

Sandmel, S., *The First Christian Century in Judaism and Christianity* (New York: OUP, 1969).

Schoedel, W.R., *Ignatius of Antioch: A Commentary on the Letters of Ignatius of Antioch* (ed. H. Koester; Hermeneia; Philadelphia: Fortress Press, 1985).

Schürer, E., *The History of the Jewish People in the Age of Jesus Christ*, 3 vols. (rev. and ed. G. Vermes, F. Millar and M. Goodman; Edinburgh: T. & T. Clark, 1986).

Schweizer, E., *The Good News according to Matthew* (tr. D.E. Green; London: SPCK, 1975).

——*The Letter to the Colossians: A Commentary* (tr. A. Chester; London: SPCK, 1982).

Seager, A.R., 'Ancient Synagogue Architecture: An Overview', in *Ancient Synagogues: The State of Research* (ed. J. Gutmann; Missoula: Scholars Press, 1981), pp. 39-48.

Shea, W.H., 'The Sabbath in the Epistle of Barnabas', *AUSS* 4 (1966), pp. 149-75.

Simon, M., 'Judaism: Its Faith and Worship', in *A Companion to the Bible* (2nd edn; ed. H.H. Rowley; Edinburgh: T. & T. Clark, 1963), pp. 381-417.

——*Verus Israel: A Study of the Relations between Christians and Jews in the Roman Empire 135–425* (tr. H. McKeating; Oxford: OUP, 1986).

Smallwood, E.M., *The Jews under Roman Rule: From Pompey to Diocletian* (Studies in Judaism in Late Antiquity, 20; Leiden: Brill, 1976).

Smart, J.D., *History and Theology in Second Isaiah: A Commentary on Isaiah 35, 40–66* (London: Epworth Press, 1967).

Snaith, N.H., 'Worship', in *A Companion to the Bible* (2nd edn; ed. H.H. Rowley; Edinburgh: T. & T. Clark, 1963), pp. 523-45.

Sonne, I., 'Synagogue', in *The Interpreter's Dictionary of the Bible*, III (New York: Abingdon Press, 1962), pp. 476-91.

Spier, E., *Sabbat* (Das Judentum: Abhandlungen und Entwürfe für Studium und Unterricht, 1; Berlin: Institut Kirche und Judentum, 1989).

Stern, M., ed., *Greek and Latin Authors on Jews and Judaism*. I. *From Herodotus to Plutarch* (Jerusalem: The Israel Academy of Sciences and Humanities, 1976).

——*Greek and Latin Authors on Jews and Judaism*. II. *From Tacitus to Simplicius* (Jerusalem: The Israel Academy of Sciences and Humanities, 1980).

Strand, K.A., 'Tertullian and the Sabbath', *AUSS* 9 (1971), pp. 129-46.

Strand, K.A., ed., *The Sabbath in Scripture and History* (Washington, DC: Review and Herald Publishing Corporation, 1982).

Strugnell, J., 'The Angelic Liturgy at Qumrân—4Q Serek Šîrôt 'Ôlat Haššabbāt', in *Congress Volume: Oxford 1959* (Vetus Testamentum Supplements, 7; Leiden: Brill, 1960), pp. 318-45.

Sukenik, E.L., *Ancient Synagogues in Palestine and Greece* (The Schweich Lectures of the British Academy; London: British Academy, OUP, 1934).

Sullivan, J.P., 'Synchronic and Diachronic Aspects of Some Related Poems of Martial', in *Contemporary Literary Hermeneutics and Interpretation of Classical Texts* (ed. S. Kresic; Ottawa: Ottawa University Press, 1981), pp. 215-25.

Talmon, S., 'The Emergence of Institutionalized Prayer in Israel in the Light of the Qumrân Literature', in *Qumrân: Sa piété, sa théologie et son milieu* (Bibliotheca ephemeridum theologicarum lovaniensum, 46; Gembloux: Duculot; Leuven: Leuven University Press, 1978), pp. 265-84.

Tcherikover, V.A. and A. Fuks, *Corpus papyrorum judaicarum*, I (Cambridge, MA: Harvard University Press, 1957).

——*Corpus papyrorum judaicarum*, II (Cambridge, MA: Harvard University Press, 1960).

Tcherikover, V.A., A. Fuks and M. Stern, eds., with an Epigraphical Contribution by

D.M. Lewis, *Corpus papyrorum judaicarum*, III (Cambridge, MA: Harvard University Press, 1964).

Torrey, C.C., *The Second Isaiah: A New Interpretation* (Edinburgh: T. & T. Clark, 1928).

Trebilco, P.R., *Jewish Communities in Asia Minor* (SNTS Monograph Series, 69; Cambridge: CUP, 1991).

Trocmé, E., 'The Jews as Seen by Paul and Luke', in *'To See Ourselves as Others See Us'* (ed. J. Neusner and E.S. Frerichs; Chico, CA: Scholars Press, 1985), pp. 145-62.

Turner, M.M.B., 'Sabbath', in *From Sabbath to Lord's Day: A Biblical, Historical and Theological Investigation* (ed. D.A. Carson; Grand Rapids: Zondervan, 1982), pp. 99-157.

Turro, J.C., 'Synagogue', in *New Catholic Encyclopedia*, XII (Washington, DC: McGraw–Hill, 1967), pp. 879-80.

VanderKam, J.C., 'The Book of Jubilees', in *Outside the Old Testament* (ed. M. de Jonge; Cambridge Commentaries on the Writings of the Jewish and Christian World 200 BC to AD 200, 4; Cambridge: CUP, 1985), pp. 111-44.

Vermes, G., *The Dead Sea Scrolls in English* (3rd edn; Sheffield: JSOT Press, 1987).

Vermes, G., and M.D. Goodman, *The Essenes: According to the Classical Sources* (Oxford Centre Text-Books, 1; Sheffield: JSOT Press, 1989).

Vincent, L.L., 'Découverte de la "Synagogue des affranchis" à Jérusalem', RB 30 (1921), pp. 247-77.

Volz, P., *Jesaia II: übersetzt und erklärt* (KAT, 9; Leipzig: A. Deichert, 1932).

Vouga, F., *L'Epître de Saint Jacques* (Commentaire du Nouveau Testament, II/13a; Genève: Editions Labor et Fides, 1984).

Watts, J.D.W., *Isaiah 1–33* (WBC, 24; Waco, TX: Word Books, 1972).

Whigham, P. and P. Jay, *The Poems of Meleager* (London: Anvil Press, 1975).

Whittaker, M., *Jews and Christians: Graeco-Roman Views* (Cambridge Commentaries on the Writings of the Jewish and Christian World 200 BC to AD 200, 6; Cambridge: CUP, 1984).

Wildberger, H., *Jesaja*, I (BKAT, X/I; Neukirchen–Vluyn: Neukirchener Verlag, 1972).

Williamson, H.G.M., *Ezra, Nehemiah* (WBC, 16; Waco, TX: Word Books, 1985).

Wintermute, O.S., tr., 'Jubilees' in *The Old Testament Pseudepigrapha*, II (J.H. Charlesworth, ed.; London: Darton, Longman & Todd, 1985), pp. 35-142.

Wolff, H.W., *Hosea: A Commentary on the Book of the Prophet Hosea* (Hermeneia; tr. G. Stansell; Philadelphia: Fortress Press, 1965).

Woodhead, A.G., *The Study of Greek Inscriptions* (Cambridge: CUP, 1981).

Yadin, Y., *The Scroll of the War of the Sons of Light against the Sons of Darkness* (tr. B. and C. Rabin; Oxford: OUP, 1962).

Zeitlin, S., 'The Origin of the Synagogue', *PAAJR* 1 (1930–31), pp. 69-81.

Zimmerli, W., *A Commentary on the Book of the Prophet Ezekiel*, II (Hermeneia; tr. J.D. Martin; Philadelphia: Fortress Press, 1983).

Books of Reference

The Anchor Bible Dictionary, 6 vols. (ed. D.N. Freedman, G.A. Herion, D.F. Graf, J.D. Pleins; New York: Doubleday, 1992).

A Companion to the Bible (2nd edn; ed. H.H. Rowley; Edinburgh: T. & T. Clark, 1963).

Concise Dictionary of the Bible (ed. S. Neill, J. Goodwin, A. Dowle; London:

Lutterworth, 1967).

A Concordance to the Apocrypha/Deuterocanonical Books of the Revised Standard Version (Centre Informatique et Bible, Abbaye de Maredsous, Belgium; Grand Rapids: Eerdmans, 1983).

A Dictionary of the Bible (ed. J. Hastings; rev. F.C. Grant and H.H. Rowley; Edinburgh: T. & T. Clark, 1963).

Encyclopaedia Judaica (Jerusalem: Keter Publishing House, 1972).

A Greek–English Lexicon (ed. G. Liddell and R. Scott; rev. H.S. Jones; Oxford: Clarendon Press, 1940).

A Greek–English Lexicon of the New Testament (rev. W.F. Arndt and F.W. Gingrich; Cambridge: CUP and Chicago: University of Chicago Press, 1957).

Harper's Bible Dictionary (ed. P.J. Achtemeier; San Francisco: Harper & Row, 1985).

The Interpreter's Dictionary of the Bible (Nashville: Abingdon Press, 1962).

A Latin Dictionary (ed. C.T. Lewis and C. Short; Oxford: Clarendon Press, 1962).

New Catholic Encyclopedia (Washington, DC: McGraw–Hill, 1967).

The Oxford Dictionary of the Christian Church (ed. F.L. Cross; London: OUP, 1957).

Oxford Latin Dictionary (ed. P.G.W. Glare; Oxford: Clarendon Press, 1982).

A Patristic Greek Lexicon (ed. G.W.H. Lampe; Oxford: Clarendon Press, 1961).

A Smaller English–Latin Dictionary (ed. W. Smith, London: John Murray, 1970).

Theological Dictionary of the New Testament, II (ed. G. Kittel and H. Greeven; Grand Rapids: Eerdmans, 1964).

Indices to Ancient Authors and Texts

Josephus: *A Complete Concordance to Flavius Josephus* (ed. K.H. Rengstorf; Leiden: Brill, 1983).

Justin: Goodspeed, E.J., *Index apologeticus sive clavis Iustini Martyris operum* (Leipzig: J.C. Hinrich'sche Buchhandlung, 1912).

Kuhn, H.G., *Konkordanz zu den Qumrantexten* (Göttingen: Vandenhoeck & Ruprecht, 1960).

Philo: *Index Philoneus* (ed. G. Mayer; Berlin: de Gruyter, 1974).

INDEX OF BIBLICAL AND RELATED TEXTS

INDEX OF ANCIENT AUTHORS

INDEX OF MODERN AUTHORS

INDEX OF SUBJECTS

RELIGIONS IN
THE GRAECO-ROMAN WORLD

Recent publications:

114. GREEN, T.M., *The City of the Moon God.* Religious Traditions of Harran. 1992. ISBN 90 04 09513 6

115/1. TROMBLEY, F.R., *Hellenic Religion and Christianization c. 370-529.* 1993. ISBN 90 04 09691 4

115/2. TROMBLEY, F.R., *Hellenic Religion and Christianization c. 370-529.* 1993. ISBN 90 04 09691 4

116. FRIESEN, S.J., *Twice Neokros.* Ephesus, Asia and the Cult of the Flavian Imperial Family. 1993. ISBN 90 04 09689 2

117. HORNUM, M.B., *Nemesis, the Roman State, and the Games.* 1993. ISBN 90 04 09745 7

118. LIEU, S.N.C., *Manichaeism in Mesopotamia and the Roman East.* 1994. ISBN 90 04 09742 2

119. PIETERSMA, A., *The Apocryphon of Jannes and Jambres the Magicians.* P. Chester Beatty XVI (with New Editions of Papyrus Vindobonensis Greek inv. 29456 + 29828 verso and British Library Cotton Tiberius B. v f. 87). Edited with Introduction, Translation and Commentary. With full facsimile of all three texts. 1994. ISBN 90 04 09938 7

120. BLOK, J.H. *The Early Amazons.* Modern and Ancient Perspectives. on a Persistent Myth. 1994. ISBN 90 04 10077 6

121. MEYBOOM, P.G.P. *The Nile Mosaic of Palestrina.* Earle Evidence of Egyptian Religion in Italy. 1994. ISBN 90 04 10137 3

122. McKAY, H.A. *Sabbath and Synagogue.* The Question of Sabbath Worship in Ancient Judaism. 1994. ISBN 90 04 10060 1